PROJECT FINANCE, SUBORDINATED DEBT AND STATE LOANS

QUICK REFERENCE GUIDE

LAW AND PRACTICE OF INTERNATIONAL FINANCE

PROJECT FINANCE, SUBORDINATED DEBT AND STATE LOANS

AUSTRALIA
The Law Book Company
Brisbane * Sydney * Melbourne * Perth

CANADA
Carswell
Ottawa * Toronto * Calgary * Montreal * Vancouver

AGENTS:
Steimatzky's Agency Ltd., Tel Aviv;
N.M. Tripathi (Private) Ltd., Bombay;
Eastern Law House (Private) Ltd., Calcutta;
M.P.P. House, Bangalore;
Universal Book Traders, Delhi;
Aditya Books, Delhi;
MacMillan Shuppan KK, Tokyo;
Pakistan Law House, Karachi, Lahore.

LAW AND PRACTICE OF INTERNATIONAL FINANCE

PROJECT FINANCE, SUBORDINATED DEBT AND STATE LOANS

By

Philip R Wood

BA (Cape Town), MA (Oxon)

Solicitor of the Supreme Court

Visiting Professor, Queen Mary
& Westfield College,
University of London

LONDON
SWEET & MAXWELL
1995

Published in 1995 by
Sweet and Maxwell Limited of
100 Avenue Road, London NW3 3PF
Computerset by Interactive Sciences, Gloucester
Printed and bound in Great Britain by
Butler & Tanner Ltd, Frome and London

Reprinted 1995
Reprinted 1996

No natural forests were destroyed to make this product:
only farmed timber was used and re-planted

**A CIP catalogue record for this book is
available from the British Library**

ISBN 0 421 54300 0

To my wife Marie-elisabeth, my twin sons
John Barnaby and Richard,
my daughter Sophie and my son Timothy

PREFACE

This book is one in a series of six works on international financial law which, taken together, are the successor to my *Law & Practice of International Finance* which was published in 1980 and which was reprinted eight times.

The works now cover a much broader range of subjects, with substantial additions in the fields of comparative law, insolvency, security, set-off, netting payments, and title finance, as well as specialist subjects like securitisations and swaps and derivatives. But the works have the same objectives as the original book. However great a gap there may be between the aim and the actuality, the objectives I have sought to achieve are to be practical as well as academic, to provide both a theoretical guide and legal sourcebook as well as a practitioner's manual, to be international, to provide serious comparative law information, to get to the point as quickly as possible, to simplify the difficulties, to find the principles underlying the particularity, to inform, and, most of all, to be useful.

The six works are separate but they are nevertheless related. Together the books are intended to form a complete library for the international banking and financial lawyer, as well as for specialists in related areas such as insolvency, leasing, and ship and aircraft finance. The topics covered by each volume are summarised on the inside of the front cover.

These books offer what I hope is a fundamentally new approach to comparative law in this area and, for the first time perhaps, provide the essential keys to an understanding of the world's jurisdictions, the keys to unlock the dark cupboard of financial law so that the light may shine in. These keys are not merely functional; they are also ethical and they are driven by history. The ideas are really quite simple, once discovered, but this should not obscure the difficulty of their application to the variety of circumstances. The core of the first book, entitled *Comparative Financial Law*, is a classification and snap-shot of virtually all the jurisdictions in the world – more than 300 of them – according to various financial law criteria. These criteria are developed in succeeding books in the series and applied to particular transactions. I believe that this is also the first time that a classification of this type has been done in this detail; but it has to be done because comparative law is no longer an academic luxury: it is a practical necessity if we are to have an orderly international legal regime.

My hope is that my voyage of discovery into what is really going on in world financial law will help to mitigate international legal surprises and legal risks and, in the wider context, that jurisdictions will be better equipped to make essential choices as to what their legal systems should achieve. This is particularly important in view of the fact that at least 30 per cent of the world's population live under legal systems which are still emerging and that the remainder live in jurisdictions divided into camps which often do not agree on basic policies. There is no reason why we should not agree on the basic policies: we do not have to have a muddle. The law is our servant, not our master. It must set us free, not tie us down. It must satisfy our sense of justice.

This book concludes the series with discussions of topics which are not particularly related but which are nevertheless of considerable importance in international finance. The chapter on project finance really has to be read with chapters in other works in this series – on international loans, on syndication, on security, on guarantees, on insolvency – and I did not think it right to try and duplicate the material. The Appendix contains outlines of typical project finance documents. The chapter on subordinated debt builds on my work *The Law of Subordinated Debt* (1990), also published by Sweet & Maxwell. The chapter on state loans offers what is, I hope, a reasonably comprehensive treatment of an area of international finance which has been of major significance over the last century and more.

The books also contain lists of about 250 research topics in total which might be appropriate for further research and which I hope will be useful to prospective writers.

I am acutely conscious of the fact that, in writing about legal systems other than my own (which is England), I will often have committed some real howlers and I hope that my foreign colleagues will be tolerant of my ignorance. Obviously one must always confirm the position with competent local lawyers.

As regards style, I have endeavoured to be as economical as possible in these works. The citation is selective: there are now millions of cases and it is hopeless to try and list even a proportion of them. I am easily terrorised by footnotes and therefore, if material is good enough to go in the footnotes, it is good enough to go in the text: as a result there are no footnotes in these works. At least one does not have to read the text in two places at once. Tables of cases and statutes seemed less sensible in a work endeavouring to cover hundreds of jurisdictions where there is an avalanche of names and numbers and dates and acts and statutes and decrees, and, in view of this, I decided to omit them.

I have endeavoured to reflect the law round about the middle of 1994 based on the international materials then available to me, although some subsequent changes were introduced in the course of publication.

Philip R Wood
One New Change
London

Request for Information

Works on the law in the jurisdictions of the world must rely heavily on information from private sources. With a view to improving the information in any subsequent editions there may be, I would be very pleased to receive papers of all kinds on subjects covered by this and other works in this series – seminar papers, essays, articles, client briefings by law firms, memoranda, notices of book publications, and the like. Material should be sent to me at the following address:

Philip R Wood
Allen & Overy
One New Change
London EC4 9QQ

Fax: 0171 330 9999

ACKNOWLEDGEMENTS

I owe to many a debt of gratitude in the help they gave me in preparing this work.

I am grateful to many partners and colleagues at Allen & Overy and to secondees from foreign offices for their advice and assistance. Graham Vinter and Jane Templeton Knight made helpful suggestions on aspects of project finance and David Sedgley helped with project finance materials. I owe a particular debt to the authors of the works listed in the bibliography and of a very large number of articles and books not listed in this book or in the bibliography without which it would not have been possible to write this book: if I have used their words, as I believe I often have, this is because they said it much better than I ever could. There are many others – practitioners, students, academics, bankers and others – who have contributed to this work in one way or another: it would be impossible for me to thank them all individually.

None of the above is of course responsible for the defects in this work.

I am most grateful to my secretary Sue Wisbey and to the Allen & Overy word processing department and checkers who laboured so magnificently to produce this work.

I am thankful to my publishers for their hard work and patience in bringing this work – and the other books in this series to fruition and also for their support through all the years.

My brother John, my sister Melanie and my mother all encouraged me and were tolerant of my efforts.

My late father Leslie Wood, who was also a lawyer, first inculcated in me a fascination for the law while I was a boy in Northern Rhodesia, now Zambia.

Finally, I owe an enormous debt to my wife and children and can only express my affection for them by the token of dedicating this book to them.

CONTENTS

PART III: STATE LOANS

APPENDIX: OUTLINES AND PRECEDENTS

ABBREVIATIONS

ABGB	Austrian General Civil Code
Art	Article
BA	Bankruptcy Act
BC	Bankruptcy Code
BGB	German Civil Code
BL	Bankruptcy Law
c	chapter (of laws)
CC	Civil Code
CCP	Code of Civil Procedure
CO	Code of Obligations
ComC	Commercial Code
Conflicts Restatement	Restatement of the Law, Conflict of Laws 2d, by the American Law Institute
Dicey	Lawrence Collins (general editor), *Dicey and Morris on the Conflict of Laws* (12th ed 1993) Sweet & Maxwell
EISO	Philip Wood, *English and International Set-off* (1989) Sweet & Maxwell
IA	Insolvency Act
ICSID	International Centre for the Settlement of Investment Disputes
IR	Insolvency Rules (England)
Mann, Money	FA Mann, *The Legal Aspect of Money* (5th ed 1992) Clarendon Press, Oxford
Ord	Order
PILA	Private International Law Act 1987 (Switzerland)
Restatement	Restatement of the Law by the American Law Institute
RSC	Rules of the Supreme Court (England)
s	section
Sched	Schedule
UCC	Uniform Commercial Code (United States)
ZPO	Code of Civil Procedure (*Zivilprozessordnung*)
Zweigert/Kötz	K Zweigert and H Kötz, *An Introduction to Comparative Law* (2nd ed 1987)

PART I

PROJECT FINANCE

CHAPTER 1

PROJECT FINANCE: GENERAL PRINCIPLES

Introduction

Meaning of project finance

Under project finance, banks provide finance for a single project and take a   1–1
large part of the risk of the success or failure of that project. The project
may be an oil and gas field; a mine; a mobile telephone or cable network; a
toll tunnel, bridge or highway; a refinery, power station or pipeline; or
offices or shops, or any other venture involving construction or engineering.
The amount of finance required for large projects may run to several billion
US dollars.

Project finance is applied banking and many of the topics covered elsewhere in this series of works, of which this book is a member, on international financial law will be relevant, e.g. term loans and syndication,
guarantees, security, insolvency and conflict of laws. These chapters on
project finance will not repeat these subjects, but only allude to them, and
will concern itself rather with those areas which are idiosyncratic to project
finance. Outlines of typical project finance documents are set out in the
Appendix.

Basic structure

To give an initial bird's eye view, the typical basic structure is as set out   1–2
below.

1. A single-purpose **project company** is formed to build and operate the
   project. The shares in the project company are owned by the project
   sponsors who enter into a shareholders or joint venture agreement
   between themselves governing their rights and duties as shareholders.

2. A syndicate of banks enter into a **credit agreement** to finance the construction of the project. The banks are paid out of the proceeds of the

---

project product after completion. There may be several classes of lending banks, e.g. international banks lending foreign currency; local banks lending domestic currency for local costs; export credit agencies lending or guaranteeing credits to finance suppliers to the project of their national equipment; and international agencies lending or guaranteeing development credits (World Bank, Asian Development Bank, African Development Bank, European Bank for Reconstruction and Development). The latter are confidence-building. The agency may lend on a conduit basis so that the banks are sub-participants with the result that, although the banks take the risk, the lender of record is the agency. Project sponsors (and governments) may be more reluctant to countenance default on a credit from an international agency than commercial banks because of increased opprobrium in diplomatic corridors.

XD to other Agency debt

The project company grants the financiers the maximum **security** available locally over the assets. There may be an **intercreditor agreement** between the creditors.

3.   The balance of the finance needed is provided by the project sponsors, either by way of **equity subscriptions** or subordinated debt or both.

4.   The project sponsors may **guarantee** the loans under full or limited guarantees during the high-risk pre-completion period.

1–3   5.   The **main commercial contracts** are as follows:

   –   A **construction contract** whereby a contractor agrees to construct the project. The contractor's obligations may be bonded by surety companies or banks. The project sponsors or others may give a completion guarantee to the project company guaranteeing that completion will take place by a long-stop date.
   –   There may be **equipment supply** contracts whereby manufacturers agree to supply the equipment for the project. These contracts may also be bonded.
   –   **Suppliers** agree to supply to the project once it is operational, e.g. fuel for a power project, unrefined oil for refining, or raw materials for processing.
   –   **Purchasers** (or off-takers) – who are often also project sponsors – agree to buy the project product when the project is completed. The proceeds of sale are used to pay operating expenses, the loans and profits to the sponsor shareholders. But in many projects there are no initial long-term purchase contracts for the project product and pay-out depends on market prices, e.g. oil prices or traffic through a tunnel or over a bridge.
   –   An operator (often also a project sponsor) enters into an **operating**

and maintenance agreement with the project company to operate the project in return for a fee.

6. Often the government grants a **concession** to the project company to build and operate the concession, e.g. an oil or gas production licence, a mining concession, or a permit to build and operate a power plant or pipeline. These concessions vary from one-off mining concessions to routine permits, e.g. planning and environmental permissions from local authorities. The concession may be of the build-operate-transfer type whereby the government transfers the land to the project company on terms that it is to be re-transferred after a period sufficiently long to repay the finance and to give the project sponsors a reasonable profit margin.   1–4

7. Other typical ancillary contracts are: 1–5

   — **Interest hedge agreements** whereby a bank agrees with the project company to pay amounts equal to interest on the loans over a specific rate so as to protect the project from increases in the interest rate during the life of the project. Less commonly, there may also be a **currency hedge** agreement to protect the project from depreciation of the local currency receipts from the project product (e.g. power supplies) against the foreign currency loan.
   — **Insurance policies** (damage, third party liability, and sometimes environmental, delay in start-up, business interruption and, unusually, political risk).
   — **Direct agreements** whereby the project contractors agree with the lenders not to cancel their project contracts on a default by the project company if the lenders perform the contracts.
   — Appointments of **independent experts** to advise the lenders, e.g. engineers and insurance brokers.
   — Special contracts applicable to the project, e.g. in power projects, electricity grid connection agreements, and steam supply agreements in cogeneration projects producing both electricity and steam. In mobile telephone or cable projects, there will be interconnect agreements with the main telecommunications operator.

8. **Feasibility studies and information memorandum** In order to be bankable, projects require an initial feasibility study prepared by experts, e.g. engineering, construction, and technical consultants instructed by the sponsors.   1–6

   The sponsors also prepare an information memorandum with the help of the banks in order to solicit banks interested in participating in the credit. This contains a description of the project, the terms of the financing, and cash-flow forecasts showing the financial feasibility of the project on the basis of certain assumptions e.g. as to completion date, construction costs, productivity, market price, interest rates and exchange rates. These assumptions are adjusted to show the impact of the worst case, e.g. high interest rates plus low market prices – usually known as a sensitivity analysis.

Aspects of information memoranda and managing bank liabilities are reviewed elsewhere in this series of works. Inevitably because of the project risks, this information memorandum is a key document and its accuracy is warranted by the borrower in the credit agreement.

Project risks outlined

1–7 By way of an overview, it is helpful to outline the main project risks and to give examples of how they are met in the documentation. The essence of project finance is identifying the risks and determining who should bear them.

— **Completion risk** This is the risk that the project will not be completed on time or at all, e.g. because of technology failures, costs overruns, force majeure or necessary variations. If the project is late, interest will run up and perhaps not be covered by the projected cash flows. Project lenders are often not prepared to take non-recourse completion risk and require either a completion guarantee or a guarantee of the loans until completion provided by the project sponsors.

— **Permitting risk** This is the risk that official licences and consents for the project will not be forthcoming or be subject to costly conditions, e.g. construction, environmental or extractive consents from the host government. Lenders are reluctant to lend so long as the project may be blocked or delayed by the absence of a necessary permit. Hence, the important permits cannot be left to later, but must be settled – or completely assured – before non-recourse money is lent. Some minor consents might be dealt with by drawdown milestones, but usually the absence of a critical consent is fatal to early drawdown, i.e. the obtaining of all necessary consents is a condition precedent to borrowings under the credit agreement.

1–8 — **Price risk** This is, for example, the risk of volatile markets or government price controls. The risk covers both supplies to the project and sales by the project. The risk is sought to be dealt with by the matching of contracts and the pass-through of risks to the purchasers of the project product or the services. Matching might include a detailed pass-through to the purchasers of fuel/raw material costs, operating costs, tax costs, debt service costs and any dividend cost. The ideal is that a credit-worthy purchaser should agree to pay a price for the project product which covers the project costs and the loans, whether or not the project produces.

- **Resource risk** This is, for example, the risk of the adequacy of reserves of gas, minerals, people who want to transport themselves through the tunnel, and the like. This is assessed by initial expert evaluations and an engineers' report. The lenders may keep a cushion retention account financed out of proceeds, and monitor continued viability by cover ratios (discussed below).

- **Operating risks** This covers, for example, manpower costs, maintenance costs, technology, operating supply costs and the like. These risks are sometimes met by pass-throughs of extra costs to the purchaser of the product, sometimes by proceeds retention accounts, and are monitored by cover ratios.

- **Casualty risk** This is the risk of damage to the project and is usually met as far as possible by insurance in which the deductibles and exclusions are important. These may also be delay in start-up and business interruption insurance. The latter is often expensive and available for short periods only.

- **Technology risk** Does the project involve sophisticated unproven technology? Is there a risk of latent defects? This is assessed by expert evaluations, and sometimes by retention accounts to cover the projected cost of maintaining the project.

- **Political risk** This used to be a very considerable risk in the lesser developed countries but may be less so now in view of the decreasing popularity of the corporatist state and the ending of the wave of redistributive newly-independent regimes. But history tends to repeat itself, albeit in different guises.   1–9

  Political risk relates to such matters as increased taxes and royalties, employment controls (work permits, local management), compulsory monopoly sales, sales in local currency only, revocations or changes to the concession, export prohibitions, exchange controls on proceeds, excessive environmental clean-ups, forced governmental or local participation in shares, planning or construction controls and the refusal of import licences for essential foreign equipment. The expropriation may be creeping or constructive as opposed to an outright nationalisation. Government price controls within a utility sector fall within this area.

  The protections are various and may include:

  - externalisation of the project company by forming it abroad (often not practicable or particularly helpful);

- external law and jurisdiction for the main documents so as to insulate the contracts from local changes of law – a topic which is reviewed elsewhere in this series of works – but the licence or concession is invariably governed by local law or sometimes public international law – see para 2–8;

- external accounts for proceeds (there are limits to this because if the local tap is turned off, then all that is left in the foreign bucket is what is in it plus the dregs in the pipeline);
- political risk insurance (expensive);
- export credit guarantees from foreign government export credit agencies;
- contractual sharing of political risk between the lenders and external project sponsors (e.g. by providing that the sponsors will guarantee the loan to the extent that a loss is caused by a specified political risk, such as expropriation without compensation, although more commonly the banks take political risk and the sponsors commercial risk);
- government or regulatory agency undertakings to cover (a) policies on taxes, royalties, prices, monopolies etc., (b) non-termination of the concession if the banks agree to take over, and (c) the grant of a new concession to a bank vehicle if necessary pursuant to rights of the banks to step-in and take over the project – see para 5–6;
- the involvement of a supra-national agency with diplomatic clout; and
- ideally, external guarantees or quasi-guarantees such as take-or-pay contracts, investment undertakings or completion guarantees from foreign credit-worthy parties.

- **Environmental risk** This contemplates such matters as pollution and clean-up costs on abandonment. These are difficult to meet completely but may be mitigated to some extent by an initial environmental audit and by insurance. But one cannot cover potential future legal changes in advance.

1–10 – **Exchange rate risk** This is the risk that, for example, the currency of the price paid for the project product depreciates in relation to the currency of the loan, so that the loan is uncovered by sale proceeds. This may be met by currency swaps or options, but it would be unusual for currency swaps or options to be available for the whole period of the loan (e.g. anything from seven to 12 years or more), even if there is a market for the currency in question.

- **Interest rate risk** This is the risk of higher interest rates than expected. It may be met by interest cap or interest swap agreements: these are explained elsewhere in this series of works. Again, it may be difficult to purchase interest contracts in the market for whole life of the project for all of the revenue streams. The credit risk of the counterparty is an additional factor.

— **Insolvency risk** This is the risk of the insolvency of contractors, project 1–11 sponsors, suppliers, purchasers, even insurers or a syndicate bank. This is inherent in project risk and is a bank credit risk which they are used to evaluating. This is their metier. Ultimately the credit strength of the sponsors, whether or not there is recourse to sponsors, is crucial. Banks often take the credit risk of the purchasers of the product or users of the project: construction contractor risk usually has to be bonded.

Local project company or joint venture consortium?

An initial question is whether the project sponsors hold shares in a local 1–12 project company or hold the project assets directly according to their participating interests, i.e. is the borrower a project company or do the project sponsors borrow themselves?

The advantages of local project company, from the varying point of view of the parties, include: a project company isolates the sponsor's risk (except to the extent of sponsor guarantees); it isolates the project from the risk of the bankruptcy of a sponsor; it facilitates the vesting of project assets, the introduction of new sponsors, and the divestment of a non-performing sponsor (liens on shares in favour of the other sponsors and share disenfranchisement are legally more acceptable on the bankruptcy of a sponsor than a lien on a sponsor's interest and a cancellation of its direct participating interest – the "withering interest"); the sponsors are not directly subject to the risk of jurisdiction of the local courts; it is easier to grant security to the banks without becoming involved in the security laws of the various jurisdictions of the sponsors; there are often local taxation holidays to encourage foreign investment; non-consolidation of the project liabilities in the sponsor's accounts (unless the project company is a subsidiary or "subsidiary undertaking" – see the broader "dominant influence" test in Seventh EC Company Law Directive implemented by the UK Companies Act 1989); a project company may avoid the inclusion of the project in covenants in the sponsor's credit agreements (e.g. negative pledge, cross-default, financial ratios – unless the project company is a subsidiary or "material subsidiary" and these are included in the relevant clause); the sponsors are not subject to local regulation governing "doing business" locally (but the local company must comply with the local regulatory regime); and finally a project company facilitates administration by a board of directors instead of a committee of joint venturers.

The disadvantages of a local project company might include: limited recourse contracts for the finance are often technically unsatisfactory from the point of view of the sponsors (para 4–1 *et seq*); the tax position may be less advantageous (consider use by the sponsors of local capital allowances and project losses as a set-off against home profits); the political risk is increased because the company's shares are local and foreign courts will not generally question an expropriation of property within the jurisdiction of the expropriating state.

A local company may be a requirement of the host government in which event that is the end of the matter.

CHAPTER 2

PROJECT FINANCE: CONCESSIONS AND CONTRACTS

Concessions and BOT projects

Generally

A concession is a lease or licence which is usually issued by a government or **2–1** governmental agency. Governments have utilised the concession in the context of BOT projects as a means of developing the host country's infrastructure without having to invest public money whilst ensuring that the relevant assets ultimately remain in the public sector. BOT stands for "build, operate transfer". A host government grants the concession on terms that the project company (normally a special purpose vehicle company) is obliged to design and construct the relevant facilities by a certain date, operate the facilities for a period and at the end of that period transfer the ownership of the relevant facilities to the host government.

The concession will run for a finite period which will ensure that any financial institutions lending to the project company are repaid and the equity investors in the project company receive a reasonable profit on their initial investment. The period of the concession will either be a fixed period, the length of which will be determined prior to its commencement on the basis of certain key economic assumptions (e.g. if the project is to build and operate a bridge the economic assumptions might include estimated traffic flows and the impact of inflation on toll rates) or will be a variable period which will determine once a target cumulative revenue has been received by the project company.

The concession agreement imposes primary responsibility for the construction and operation of the project on the project company but the performance of the works comprised in the concession will be sub-contracted to third parties which very often have taken an equity stake in the project company. Banks lending to a BOT project will be concerned to ensure that both the performance and financial obligations of the project company to the grantor are matched by corresponding obligations on the part of sub-contractors owed to the project company and that the relevant sub-contracts impose no greater liability on the project company to the sub-contractor than that owed by the grantor to the project company under the concession agreement.

Terms of concessions

2–2   The standard terms of the concession between host government or government agency and the project company will usually include:

— An obligation on the project company to construct the relevant facilities or infrastructure to a stated specification by a stated date (often with liquidated damages being payable if this date is not met)

— Provisions entitling the grantor to impose variations to the specification

— Performance bonds/guarantees from the project company's sponsors

— Warranties from the project company relating to its design and construction work, and an agreement to comply with safety and environmental standards. Any design warranties, completion dates and liquidated damages clauses in the concession should be matched by the construction contract.

— An obligation on the project company to operate the facilities or infrastructure properly in accordance with local law and to maintain them to stated levels for a stated period

— (Sometimes) an agreement regarding product prices (e.g. power supplied to local consumers) although the level of control reserved by the grantor will vary. Clearly, if the grantor reserves absolute control on price increases the risk of cost overruns is left with the project company if the grantor cannot be persuaded of the need for an increase – this area is of major concern to the lenders to a project.

— Events of default entitling the grantor to terminate the concession in certain circumstances, e.g. breach by the project company of a provision of the concession agreement and insolvency of the project company. This may be coupled with provisions detailing the compensation payable to the project company in those circumstances. The lenders will be concerned to see a detailed compensation formula set out in the concession agreement or a side agreement with the grantor so that, notwithstanding the project company default, lenders can be sure that they will be repaid (at least in part). Grantors often maintain that because the concession holder is in breach it is not entitled to compensation, but since the events of default tend to be fairly wide ranging and may include relatively minor breaches there is a strong case for insisting on compensation in these circumstances.

— The payment of a concession fee although this is more usual where the   2–3
   concession is granted by a government or agency to exploit certain natural
   resources for a period of time rather than in the context of a BOT project

— (Sometimes) undertakings from the government as to taxes, exchange
   controls and the regulatory environment. The exclusivity of the fran-
   chise can be crucial.

— Provisions dealing with the transfer of assets and personnel at the end of
   the concession period (or early termination)

— A prohibition on the project company assigning its rights under the
   concession agreement. The concession should be assignable to the
   lenders by way of security and re-assignable on an enforcement.

— A clause which provides for restoration of the financial balance of the
   concession if certain risks, which have been assumed by the grantor,
   occur and result in material prejudice to the finances of the project. The
   type of risks typically assumed by a host government include changes in
   legislation which specifically apply to the project and have a material
   adverse effect, the occurrence of uninsurable force majeure events
   (although this will generally be coupled with fairly onerous insurance
   obligations on the project company) and unilateral changes to the terms
   of the concession by the grantor.

— A clause allowing the grantor to step-in and run the concession either
   temporarily or permanently if the project company is failing to do so to
   the required standard. This type of provision needs to interface with any
   step-in rights required by the lenders following an event of default under
   the financing documents or where the grantor wishes to terminate the
   concession for a project company default. This will normally be
   addressed in a side agreement between the grantor and the lenders.

— Detailed procedures for resolution of disputes.

Project contracts

Contract is king

In project finance, contract is king. The project contracts involve a sharing   2–4
of risk: is the risk borne by a project sponsor, a project contractor or the
project (the lenders)?

One of the main tasks of the lawyers is to conduct a "due diligence" survey of the project contracts and to report on them to the banks.

Typical general points will usually include: mismatches (pricing, delays, force majeure, performance, currency, liquidated damages) i.e. a risk not assumed by one contractor should be assumed by another and the contracts should hence be back-to-back; the levels of take-or-pay protection; and assignability (*which should allow both the grant of security and its enforcement*). Note the difference between an assignment of rights, a transfer of rights and obligations by novation, and delegation (or sub-contracting). Assignment clauses in commercial contracts often do not make these distinctions.

Construction and equipment contracts

2–5   These are contracts for the construction of the project and for the supply of the necessary equipment. They mainly involve completion risks which may be covered by a sponsor completion guarantee: para 3–4.
     Points of interest include:

(a) The responsibility for cost overruns. The contract should ideally be a turnkey fixed price lump sum contract, subject only to regulatory and permitting costs (a host government risk); possibly latent ground conditions; employer variations; employer-ordered equipment; customs/import duties and licences (political risk); and labour requirements (political risk). Extra costs from these contingencies may be passed through to the project purchasers (with an upper limit?) or passed through to the project sponsors in the form of a completion and overrun guarantee. They are not usually a bank risk.

(b) There may be a foreign currency risk if costs are incurred in a different currency to the loan.

(c) Responsibilities for delays in completion and commissioning are important. There may be a permitted force majeure period with a long-stop. For example, in power projects, the fuel supply may be on time, but the project is uncompleted. The construction, fuel supply and power purchase force majeure clauses should be matched so that the project company is not obliged to take deliveries of fuel (or pay for them) if the construction is delayed by force majeure, and the project company should not be obliged to deliver power to the purchasers if there is a delay. Extra gap costs might be passed through to the power purchaser with a long-stop. An alternative is delay in start-up insurance.
     In the case of non-permitted delays, the extra costs may be covered by the contractor's liquidated damages, and any excess of costs over liquidated damages passed through to the power purchaser or project sponsor, perhaps with an upper limit.

(d) The risk of a contractor insolvency may be covered by bonding.

Purchase agreements

These are the agreements for the purchase of the project product once the 2–6
project is completed. The proceeds are used to pay the project costs, to
repay the banks, with, hopefully, a profit for the sponsors. Hence their
terms are of pre-eminent importance. Key issues are:

(a) Pricing, e.g. in power purchase agreements, the price may include a
fixed capacity charge to cover fixed costs, e.g. station availability and
debt service; and an energy charge to cover generating costs, mainly
fuel. Under contracts for differences the power purchaser pays the
generator if the cost is more than the market price; the generator pays
the purchaser if the cost is less than market.

(b) Take-or-pay aspects: see below

(c) Does the contract term have a tail long enough to cover a slowed pay-
back?

(d) Purchaser insolvency risk

(e) Regulatory risks, environmental impositions, foreign currency incon-
vertibility, price controls, and tax (political risk)

(f) Market risk, e.g. competing (cheaper or subsidised) projects, market
demand. These factors are naturally of greater significance if there are
no fixed purchase contracts with a fixed price as in telecommunications
projects.

Supply agreements

These are agreements for the supply of raw materials, fuel or other product 2–7
to the project company for its operations. Key issues are: the resource risk,
e.g. the proven reserves of fuel in the chosen field; transportation and infrastructure completion risk to get the supplies to the project company; whether
there is a minimum supply obligation and liquidated damages cap (does the
project or the purchaser carry the risk of the excess cost of alternative supplies (e.g. fuel) over the cap?); minimum take obligations and stock-piling;
force majeure risk; and risk of the insolvency of the supplier.

Take or pay contracts

2–8   The ideal object is for the project sponsors to "guarantee" the bank loans but so that the guarantee is not a guarantee for certain purposes. For example, the sponsor's hope that it will not be a liability which must be recognised on the sponsor's balance sheet as if it were a guarantee of a loan, but rather as a trading obligation. But accounting conventions are now tending to look to commercial substance rather than legal form and may see through the clothing of a financial transaction as a trading transaction by virtue of the "true and fair view" requirement.

They also hope that it will not count as a guarantee for the purposes of financial limits and ratios in their credit agreements or constitutional documents. This depends on construing the covenants concerned.

Under the typical form, the project sponsor enters into a purchase agreement with the project company under which the sponsor agrees to buy the project product, e.g. minerals or oil, and to pay for it, even if not delivered for any reason, up to an amount equal to scheduled payments on the bank loans. Or alternatively the sponsor agrees to pay for the use of the pipeline, road or tunnel or use of the refinery, ship or aircraft. These contracts are variously called throughput, tolling or hell-or-high-water contracts. The sponsor pays for the expectation of goods and services, not for the goods or services themselves.

The project company assigns the benefit of the contract to the banks by way of security and the project sponsor agrees to pay the proceeds into a blocked external account with the lead bank.

2–9   The main points on these contracts include:

– A breach may sound in damages (not an obligation to pay a fixed debt) so that there are quantification problems and the usual rules applicable to damages for contract breach, e.g. mitigation.

– The contract must exclude force majeure preventing the purchaser from performance.

– It is more difficult (but not impossible) in trading contracts to exclude contract terms which might allow the sponsor to reduce the price or cancel the contract for breaches by the project company, e.g. warranties as to title, fitness for purpose, merchantability, misrepresentation, fundamental breach, negligence. Consider statutes and rules of law which avoid or limit exclusion clauses.

In *Resources Investment Corp v Enron Corp*, 669 F Supp 1035 (D Colo 1987) Enron had entered into take-or-pay contracts to purchase gas from RIC and to pay for any gas not taken. *Held*: the take-or-pay provisions were not unenforceable penalty clauses or liquidated damages provisions; they were not unconscionable; frustration or impossibility arising from changes in the natural gas market did not relieve Enron from performing since the parties clearly contemplated changing economic conditions. The contracts were upheld as binding. The case followed a number of other cases to the same effect.

— Should the price be accelerated if the loan is accelerated? This may be problematic if the acceleration of the loan results from the project sponsor's bankruptcy which is an event of default in the loan agreement: the sponsor's liability is increased on insolvency and this may conflict with the principle that a debtor's liability may not by contract be enlarged merely by reason of his insolvency.

— There may be timing mismatches. For example, when the obligation of the project company to sell under the purchase agreement starts, the project may be uncompleted.

— There may be a construction cost overrun. Must the purchaser inflate the purchase price or is this covered by a completion guarantee or sponsor's equity or is it project (lender) risk?

— Are there escalators in the purchase price for increased raw material, fuel and other costs, operating costs, regulatory costs?

— Are there escalators in the price to cover foreign currency mismatches between the loan and the purchase price currency and to cover interest rate increases?

Forward purchase agreements

Under the forward purchase structure, the banks' vehicle (a specially-   2–10
formed company owned by the banks) enters into a purchase agreement with the project company under which the vehicle agrees to pay in advance for product (instead of advancing loans). The project company uses the advance purchase price to pay for project construction. The project company agrees to deliver the project product to the vehicle when the project is completed. The bank vehicle sells the product under a contract of sale with a project sponsor and the project company is obliged to repay any shortfall in sale proceeds below the advance purchase price plus interest. The banks take comprehensive security over the vehicle's assets.

The main points here are: some breaches may sound in damages so that there are quantification problems; the banks may not be permitted to hold shares in a trading company (consider an "orphan company" owned by friendly charitable trustees); and the banks' vehicle may incur risks on the product (ownership and seller liabilities).

The object of these contracts is primarily to dress up the project company's "borrowings" as a trading liability and they are used more usually when the project sponsor is a direct "borrower" and wishes to obtain a favourable balance sheet treatment. Because of the "true and fair view" requirement and the superiority of substance over form in accounting conventions, it is now less likely that this structure will achieve its accounting objectives.

CHAPTER 3

PROJECT FINANCE: SPONSOR SUPPORT

It is rare for project lenders to provide 100 per cent finance or to take the 3–1 entire risk of the project. Almost invariably the project sponsors must provide some of the finance and take some of the risk.

Equity or subordinated debt

The project sponsors will generally provide their share of the capital either by way of equity or subordinated debt. (See the outline form in the Appendix.) Ideally the sponsor capital should be subscribed before the bank loans are advanced, or at least should be subscribed proportionately. Sometimes however it is subscribed on completion (with a long-stop date) – this involves an interim credit risk on the sponsors.

The usual mechanics are for the project sponsors to enter into an equity agreement with the banks whereby they agree to subscribe capital in the project company and which sets out amounts, timing and procedures. The project company agrees to issue the necessary shares or to borrow the junior loans. If a project sponsor defaults, the remedies of the banks are usually for damages, not specific performance, and these damages will be subject to the usual remoteness, quantification and mitigation rules applicable to contract breaches. For example, the damages will often not be the full amount agreed to be subscribed, but rather any losses to the banks caused by any extra costs incurred by the project company in procuring alternative finance. This could be difficult to quantify and the subject of dispute. The damages will be reduced if it can be shown that the finance would not have been repaid, even if the sponsors had subscribed their capital. A further problem is that, once the project company is in liquidation, it may be legally unable to borrow or issue shares.

One technique of circumventing these risks is for the equity support to be expressed as a financial guarantee of the loan to the extent of the agreed equity support, but on the basis that the guarantee diminishes pro tanto as

---

the equity support is actually provided. One would have to be satisfied that the guarantee is not a disguised penalty exceeding a reasonable pre-estimate of liquidated damages and therefore void. In any event the agreement should contain surety clauses along the usual lines.

Sometimes the equity agreement is solely between the project sponsors and the project company. The project company then assigns the benefit of this to the banks by way of security as part of the security package. This is an inconvenient structure from the point of view of banks because, first, the breach damages recoverable by the banks as assignees cannot exceed the damages recoverable by the project company – which may be less or nil, and which may be qualified by contributory fault of the project company. Second, the enforcement of the banks' claims against the project sponsors requires the intermediate step of security enforcement and hence whatever obstacles and depredations are encountered in applicable security law.

3–2 **Subordinated debt** Often the sponsor's capital is provided as subordinated debt, e.g. because it can be secured (subject to the banks' priority) and hence rank ahead of unsecured creditors; interest may be tax deductible, but not dividends; debt is easier to repay than share capital.

The subordination agreement should: disallow payment of the junior debt (other than reasonable interest after payment of project costs with a complete freeze on a default or if a cover ratio is not met); prevent acceleration and enforcement of the junior debt and its security; allow the banks to advance prior-ranking new money; contain no covenants (which could hamper a restructuring); subordinate the debt as well as the security (in case the senior security fails or is inadequate); permit the banks to change their credit agreement; compel the junior creditors to cooperate in a private sale and in the arrangements envisaged by the direct agreements (para 5–6); and prevent the junior creditors from instituting insolvency proceedings. In other words, the junior debt should be approximated to equity.

The disadvantage of subordinated debt compared to equity is that the project company may be obliged to stop trading sooner than if the debt were equity – because of fraudulent or wrongful trading rules.

Subordinated debt is reviewed in more detail in subsequent chapters.

Restrictions on share transfers

3–3 Sponsor shareholdings may be confidence-building, even though the sponsors are not legally liable for the project company's debts. An equity agreement with the lenders may accordingly restrict transfers of shares in the project company, especially during the pre-completion period. Less risky projects may contemplate the ultimate possibility of public participation, especially if the host government is pursuing privatisation policies.

Completion guarantees

Project sponsors typically agree with the banks to procure that project will   **3–4**
be completed by specified long-stop date, come what may. The pre-completion period is the time of highest risk because the project is sucking in money, not earning it. This guarantee is different from a full financial guarantee of the loans up to the completion date. See the form in the Appendix.

Breach usually results in damages in English-based jurisdictions (not specific performance because the courts cannot supervise compliance with the order). The damages are generally the difference between the loss if the project is uncompleted and if it had been completed on time – hence not necessarily the full amount of the loan, e.g. if the project would not pay in any event. Damages could be difficult to quantify and may involve proving a cash-flow forecast.

The project **completion test** (when the completion guarantee falls away)   **3–5**
should be as specific as possible. For example, the physical assets should be certified by an independent engineer; the project should be shown to produce at a minimum rate for a specified period; a cover ratio test should be satisfied; all legal matters should be in order under specified representations and warranties and there should be no default.

The completion guarantee should be an **indemnity**, i.e. to pay losses if completion is not actually achieved by the specified long-stop date regardless of fault, and should exclude force majeure defences. Naturally one should include standard suretyship clauses.

The completion guarantee may be accompanied by an agreement to provide **overrun finance**. As with the equity agreement, this may provide for any shortfall to be paid direct to the banks if it cannot legally be paid to the company, e.g. because the company is in liquidation (or preferably state that the sponsors guarantee the loan to extent of the overrun finance, except to the extent the overrun is validly paid to company). The remedy for breach is generally damages, not specific performance – hence quantification problems, e.g. would the loan have been repaid even if the overrun finance had been provided?

Again, if the guarantee is given initially to the project company which assigns it to the banks, the loss of the banks as assignees can be no greater than the loss to the company (which may be less). The sponsors should give performance undertakings directly to the banks.

Investment or purchase agreements

3–6   Instead of formal guarantees, the project sponsors may agree to invest cash in the project company to the extent necessary to repay the bank loans. Or they may agree to purchase the bank loan if there is a default.

     These ruses are unlikely to meet the off-balance sheet objectives of the project sponsors under the best accounting standards. Further there is the same problem concerning damages, the legal inability of the sponsors to perform on the company's liquidation, and assignees being in no better position than assignors (if the undertaking is initially given to the project company).

Interest guarantee

3–7   The project sponsors may agree to guarantee interest only, not principal. Apart from ordinary suretyship law, consider: whether the guarantee remains payable even if interest is not recoverable from the project company, e.g. because post-insolvency interest is not provable; the expiry date; a right of the banks to appropriate recoveries to unpaid principal before interest so as to preserve the guarantee (this would significantly increase the guarantor's risk); and whether the guarantee extends to rolled-up interest which is added to capital in the pre-completion period. It then ceases to be interest and so should be specifically covered, if appropriate.

Management guarantee

3–8   The project sponsors may agree to ensure that borrower's warranties (especially title to project assets, validity of project security, and availability of planning and exchange control consents) and non-financial covenants in the credit agreement are complied with by the borrower. The rationale may be that these are within their control or alternatively are basic premises of the finance, whether or not within their control.

Guarantee of environmental risks

3–9   The project sponsors may agree to indemnify the banks against liabilities for environmental hazards, e.g. pollution or clean-up costs. Again, consider the remedies for contract breach.

CHAPTER 4

PROJECT FINANCE: FINANCIAL AGREEMENTS

Limited recourse loans

The essence of project finance is that recourse by the banks to the project **4–1** sponsors is limited, albeit not absent altogether.

If the **project is owned by a company**, the banks have no recourse to the project sponsors because of the veil of incorporation. Any guarantees by project sponsors will of course override this. If there are guarantees, the recourse of the banks to the "guarantors" may be limited by express contract, for example, the guarantor may not be liable in the event a loss is caused by a political risk. Hence the guarantee might exclude the guarantor's liability if, for example, the loss is caused by exchange controls, expropriation, labour troubles, or civil disorder and if, e.g. the sponsor did not provoke the government's act and endeavoured to mitigate and if the event is not temporary; or the guarantor may not be liable if the loss is caused by the absence of recoverable reserves (subject to a floor, leading to extension of the loan?) or a fall in market prices (subject to a floor?). These are examples of risk-sharing by passing some of the risks on to the banks.

If the **project is owned directly by the project sponsors**, the recourse to **4–2** them can be limited by contract. Under a limited recourse contract, the banks agree to look only to the security (and hence take the risk of the comprehensiveness and validity of the security), and the banks exclude their rights to sue or liquidate the sponsors, to levy execution over non-project assets, or to prove in the sponsor's liquidation. These contracts are practicable only in jurisdictions which permit comprehensive business security over the project assets so that the banks can effectively look to those assets by virtue of their security and if the remedy of possessory management through a receiver is available, as in the English-based floating charge.

These limited recourse contracts are often technically unsatisfactory.

Financial agreements

Syndication

4–3   Project finance commonly involves a conventional syndicated credit agreement on usual (but modified) syndication principles, e.g. severality of lender commitments and rights, syndicate democracy, pro rata sharing between banks, and the appointment of an agent bank. (See the outline form in the Appendix.) The principles of syndicated credits are discussed in another work in this series on international financial law.

Financial terms

4–4   The financial terms differ from ordinary term loan practice:

(a) **Loans may be borrowed** only to pay specific project costs, e.g. approved capital expenditure and construction costs, together with pre-completion interest. Loan proceeds may sometimes be used to pay limited operating costs during the pre-commissioning period, and other costs, e.g. fees and permitting costs. The proceeds of the loans are sometimes payable into a disbursements account with a permitted float to avoid small or unrounded amounts. In cable or telecommunications projects, the loans may not be drawable until a commercially viable part of the network has been completed.

(b) The **conditions precedent** to the loan include the usual legal documentation, accuracy of warranties, and no default, but also the obtaining of all necessary permits for the project. Each loan is usually subject to an additional condition precedent that there is sufficient finance to meet projected costs (including overruns). Often there is no individual bank veto on drawdowns if the conditions precedent are not satisfied – contrary to normal syndication practice. This is subject to majority bank control to ensure finance availability: the banks stand or fall together.

(c) The **interest** is usually floating (but fixed rate funds may be supplied by multilateral or regional agencies or by suppliers). Interest is usually rolled-up prior to completion, ie added to principal, because the project company at that stage has no revenues. The tax and mortgage law implications are relevant (interest on interest).

(d) **Repayment** is usually by minimum instalments keyed to projected cash flows by dedicating a minimum percentage of actual project net cash flows to repayment. Hence if the proceeds are high, the loan will be repaid more quickly, but, if the proceeds are less than expected, or operating costs increase, the loan pay-back will be slower. Typically there will be a minimum repayment. An uplift in the dedicated percentage if a cover ratio is not met is a possibility.

(e) **Partial prepayments and cancellations** by the borrower are usually allowed only if sufficient finance remains available. The usual inverse order of maturity rule applies. Sometimes there is a premium to compensate for the extensive pre-project work by the banks. Also prepayments of affected banks under grossing-up, increased cost and illegality clauses may be restricted to prevent destabilisation of the project, e.g. an affected bank ranks for prepayment out of the proceeds account only if all other payments are first covered, plus a retention cushion.

Project accounts

The credit documentation will set up a number of accounts maintained by   4–5
the borrower with a bank. These accounts typically include:

— A disbursements account to receive loan proceeds. Withdrawals are subject to borrower certification.

— A proceeds account, to receive the proceeds of sale of the project product: see below

— A maintenance retention account, to receive a proportion of cashflows to cover future maintenance expenditure

— A compensation account, to receive proceeds of insurance, and requisition, nationalisation and compulsory acquisition proceeds. These may be applied towards a mandatory compulsory prepayment.

The borrower is usually permitted to invest excess sums in the accounts in safe authorised investments as scheduled, e.g. government bonds in acceptable currencies. The bank which holds the project accounts enters into an agreement with the lenders under which it agrees to supply statements, stop withdrawals on notice (e.g. on default), and not to set off.

Proceeds account

Ideally, all proceeds from the sale of the project product are paid into an   4–6
external proceeds account (to insulate them from local rationing or diversion by the local central bank).

It is usually provided that payments out prior to default are paid in a prescribed order under a "cascade" or "waterfall" clause, e.g.:

- first to pre-agreed operating costs (as certified);

- then to debt service in an agreed order (e.g. agent's costs, interest, etc., principal, other creditors);

- then (sometimes) a payment to a retention or buffer account to cover potential future shortfalls;

- then the surplus to the company for distribution to the shareholders as dividends on their equity or as payment of interest on their subordinated loans. These distributions are usually allowed only in a short "window" period after each repayment date for the loans to ensure that the above order is observed.

There is a freeze on withdrawals on a pending default, and, after a default, all proceeds are payable to the creditors.

Cover ratios

4–7 A cover ratio is a forecast of the financial viability of the project re-determined on a running basis, e.g. every six months. The main cover ratio is a financial test which compares the estimated net present value of future proceeds of the project to the (projected maximum) principal of the loan to check that the loan will be covered by the revenues and hence be paid. One arrives at the net figure by taking each projection of gross proceeds for each future six-month period and then deducting operating costs, capital expenditure, royalties, taxes, etc. Each amount is then discounted back for each six-month period at a fixed rate of discount.

The main negotiating point is – who controls the forecast assumptions if not agreed – the banks, the borrower, or independent experts? There are various solutions. The banks seek to control financial variants, e.g. interest and exchange rates, discount rates and inflation. They regard these macro-economic factors as within their special expertise and within the special competence of their econometricians. Objective tests may be used, such as retail price indexes and yields on government securities. Forecasting is highly speculative, but it is better than nothing. It is often the central plank in the documentation.

The credit agreement provides that, if a cover ratio is not met, then the sanctions are: no new drawdowns may be made; there is a default (sometimes only if a lower cover ratio is not met); there is no release of distributions to sponsors; and there is no release of the sponsors' completion or other guarantees (i.e. the completion test is not met).

Other ratios may include net cash flow tests for each six-month period, both forward-looking and backward-looking – to test the current performance of the project.

The cover ratios are usually calculated by the use of complex computer programmes developed by specialists.

For various possibilities, see Clause 12 of outline form no 1 in the Appendix.

Covenants

The covenants in project finance documentation are very extensive. The   4–8
credit agreements bristle with covenants. They are designed to give a contractual "vote" to creditors in relation to the basic management of the project since in commercial substance the banks take equity risks and so they say that they should have an "equity" vote where their interests are concerned.

Examples are covenants to: supply information, reports, inspection, notification of defaults, compliance certificates; obtain and maintain consents; achieve completion as soon as practicable; operate in accordance with good practice; maintain the concession and other contracts; promptly exercise rights under the contracts; pay royalties, taxes and debts; comply with project contracts and local laws; insure (normally very detailed requirements); repair and maintain; not to abandon unless the project is non-economic, as defined, e.g. there will be no net proceeds (the project sponsors lose interest before the banks because equity ranks after debt); not alter the project plan or material project contracts or the concession; not change the operator or major contractors; maximise production; maximise sales of product; not create other security (negative pledge); not dispose of project assets; a prohibition on other investments, borrowings, business activities, loans, guarantees, subsidiaries, capital commitments and major contracts; and not pay dividends, except out of agreed surpluses in accordance with the cascade clause described above. See clause 15 in outline form no 1 in the Appendix.

Four of the key covenants are: 4–9

(a) No changes to the **project plan** without consent. "Not to be unreasonably withheld" is usually rejected as too vague and restrictive of the banking discretion.

(b) Absolute control of the **project contracts**, e.g. the construction, supply, purchase, and operation and maintenance contracts. These controls tend to be tight and limit waivers, consents, relaxations and the variations without consent. If one thread in the contract web is to be cut, the banks often wish to be involved, even at the risk of administrative constipation.

(c) Controls on **capital expenditure**, partly because of the risk of underfunding and of a change in the project (disturbing the agreed economics) and the need to control technology and to prevent odd bolt-ons.

(d) Controls on **other debt** because other creditors may have harassment potential. The covenant limits hire purchase, leasing, borrowings and guarantees, and inhibits future funding without bank consent to finance additional works or variations. Frequently other debt is permitted if subordinated in a way which strips the other creditor of all his rights so that the senior creditors may act as if there were no junior creditor at all, i.e. the junior debt is in substance equity, not debt.

Covenants generally are discussed in detail elsewhere in this series of works.

Events of default

4–10   The view of banks is that events of default are not to be regarded as an opportunity to get one's money back or as an opportunity to pounce, but rather as the ability to be heard in the management of the project if things should go wrong, i.e. they confer management control in the specified cases. Enforcement is an absolute last resort which no one views as a sensible way to protect his capital. The argument is that banks do not call a halt to a project once their money is already in unless the position is totally irredeemable. The events of default are rather monitoring devices conferring opportunities to renegotiate.

The sanctions to confer negotiating strength on the occurrence of a default – or usually an impending unmatured default – include (apart from the ultimate nuclear bomb which nobody can use): draw-stop, i.e. no further drawings until the problem is cured (this applies only during the pre-completion period); freeze on distributions to the sponsors from the proceeds account; and (possibly) a compulsory build-up of retentions in the proceeds accounts.

4–11   Apart from usual defaults (non-payment, non-compliance, breach of warranty, cross-default, insolvency, creditor's processes, and a sweep-up material adverse change), there will usually be events of default relating to: non-completion of the project by a long-stop date, or if completion by the long-stop date appears unlikely; abandonment of the project (actual or constructive or creeping); breach of a (lower) cover ratio; destruction of the project or a material part of the project – material often being quite low, e.g. 10 per cent (because 10 per cent on the financial projections can be crucial); revocation or prejudicial variation of the concession; specified creeping expropriations or regulatory changes; insurance cover not available at commercial rates (note that defaults often do not connote moral blame or fault – these are irrelevant to the fact); defaults under major project contracts; defaults relating to the key project sponsors, thereby accentuating the mutual interdependence and cross-reliance between all the parties. The loyalty bred of interdependence is of course a banking objective.

The fine-trigger nature of the events of default may seem to increase the instability and vulnerability of the project to adverse changes. For better or for worse, the banking view tends to be that they are necessary to confer power if the project should take a downturn. See clause 16 in outline form no. 1 in the Appendix.

The essence of events of default is early warning – when has the red light gone on and is a weak flickering amber light enough? One of the most important anticipatory events of default in ordinary unsecured lending is the cross-default, but this is of limited importance in project finance because there is, or should be, no other financial debt. But if it extends to project sponsors, it assumes significance. Events of default generally are reviewed elsewhere in this series of works.

Syndicate democracy

The objectives of syndicate democracy are two-fold: to allow decision-making, since projects are commonly subject to rapid change; and to control the maverick "want-out" bank which might threaten the stability and integrity of the project. From the sponsors' point of view, syndicate democracy is an alleviation of the tight covenant and default controls.   **4–12**

Sometimes there are three tiers: (a) administrative or technical or expert matters may be decided by a small management group; (b) majority control (e.g. 50 to 75 per cent by participation) of waivers and consents under the covenants and events of default; and (c) unanimous control of changes to the financial terms (this controls overrun finance), and the introduction of new lenders.

There may also be a no-action clause, contrary to normal syndication practice, preventing syndicate members from suing, liquidating, attaching, enforcing the security and the like without a majority vote. This enhances consensus and stability.

CHAPTER 5

PROJECT FINANCE: SECURITY AND INSURANCES

Security

Objects of project security

5–1   The main objects of project security are to prime unsecured creditors; to act as a defence against unsecured creditors, and to confer control of the project on a default.

Defensive security Project security is often primarily defensive, a shield not a sword, because normal enforcement realisation may be unrealistic. Thus project assets (pipelines, mines, cables) are often non-marketable. There may be potential political interference on an attempted sale. One must also bear in mind the other potential weaknesses of security – see below.

Security is defensive against an unsecured creditor who might, e.g. harass the banks by attaching a crucial asset – the key to the project door.

5–2   **Control** Another motive of project security is to confer control of the project on the banks if there is a default. Complete control is available only if the comprehensive floating charge is possible – this charge allows the appointment of a receiver who can manage the business. If this is not available, various alternatives must be considered. One possibility is ring-fencing covenants, restricting other liabilities. These cannot prevent liabilities which spring from contract damages, tort liabilities, environmental liabilities, government impositions and inevitable commitments, and there is a breach risk. The banks could take a mortgage of the project company shares, so that the banks can appoint directors on default – assuming that applicable security law confers a right of possession as opposed to sale. There may be a special golden share issued to the banks entitling the banks to appoint a governing director of the project company on a default. But here there is a risk of director's liability for fraudulent trading and shadow director liability. Also directors owe duties to the company as a whole not just its creditors. There may be regulatory problems, e.g. banks which cannot invest in unlisted equities. Finally the special share or its exercise may make the company a subsidiary or associate of a bank.

Scope of security

Security is discussed generally in another work (on the comparative law of   5—3 security) in this series of works.

Ideally the security should cover all the project assets, but this is not usually possible outside the common law group. These assets mainly comprise: the project land and fixtures; project plant, equipment and other moveable goods; project product in course of production; the project construction contract; contracts for the supply of raw materials, fuel or the like to the project; project sale contracts; the proceeds account and authorised investments; the project company's claims against third parties; the host government concession; the operating agreement; insurances; requisition and nationalisation proceeds; and industrial proprietary rights.

General problems of security

Examples of the type of problems commonly found are: the floating charge   5—4 is not available; enforcement is limited to judicial public sale, not private sale; there is no right to possessory management (through a floating charge receiver), only sale (so the banks cannot manage the project assets); burdensome formalities, especially for debts; prior preferential creditors; no sale to aliens; cancellation of the concession and of construction and other contracts on default by project company (see below); no sale for foreign currency and exchange controls; non-possessory security over tangible movables is invalid or cumbersome; and environmental liabilities on enforcement.

One may parenthetically note the weakness of financing a minority participant in, say, a gas field because under the joint venture agreement his interest is generally removed by the other joint venturers if he defaults, so there is nothing left, and because he cannot procure performance of project covenants by minority vote. The assets which may be charged in telecommunications projects are often very limited.

One may also note the **production payment** as an alternative to security. This is a US oil and gas financing technique whereby the project company grants the financier ownership of a proprietary slice of the oil-field and assets until the financier is paid. It had tax advantages. The structure is not available in the United Kingdom for hydrocarbon fields because the state owns the petroleum and mineral reserves, but a production payment of sale proceeds could be structured. Whether the interest is recharacterised as a mortgage would depend upon local law.

Common trustee for designated debt

5–5   In common law countries a trustee may be appointed to hold the debt and the security for the benefit of all creditors. The advantages include: there is no need for separate security for separate creditors; the security for all creditors has common terms (covenants, insurance, enforcement); novations by existing banks of their debt and commitments to new banks are possible without discharging the security (so that the banks can transfer undrawn commitments to lend, as well as assign loans already made); and new creditors can be introduced as future beneficiaries by a pre-agreed deed of accession without re-creating the security in their favour. The introduction of new creditors is usually subject to financial tests so that the existing creditors are not diluted.

The main obstacle is that a trustee may not be recognised locally, in which event the security must be granted to the actual creditors. The international reception of the trust is discussed elsewhere in this series.

Direct agreements

5–6   "Direct agreements" between (1) the project contractors (construction, purchase, supply, operation) and the host government (concession, licence), and (2) the banks are often entered into. These freeze the rights of cancellation of the project contractors on a default by the project company under their default clauses (typically non-compliance, non-payment, insolvency, security enforcement). If the contracts could be cancelled, the project company would be left with nothing and the project company would become a useless shell.

Under usual terms, the contractor agrees to notify defaults to the lenders; there is a freeze on contractor cancellation during an observation period; the contractors agree not to cancel if the lenders agree to remedy past defaults and to perform the project company's payment obligations (often for a short initial step-in period pending a final decision to take over); and the lenders have a right to compel novation of the contract to another company, e.g. on a hive-down of the project assets via a lender sale as mortgagee.

The main problem is that the assumption of the contract involves extra exposure for the lenders. There can be difficulties in designating an acceptable alternative project company. The structure is mechanically difficult to apply in the absence of the remedy of possessory management through a floating charge receiver: in that event the lenders as mortgagees cannot take control of the assets.

See the outline form in the Appendix and accompanying note.

Collateral warranties

Collateral warranties are most frequently found in property development 5–7 financings. Under a collateral warranty a party contracting with a project company (e.g. a contractor or a professional adviser such as an architect or electrical and mechanical engineer) gives certain undertakings and acknow-ledgements direct to the project company's lenders. They typically include an acknowledgement that the third party owes a duty of care to the lenders; (in the case of a contractor) a warranty that its work will be fit for the pur-pose for which it was carried out and will comply with all relevant statutory requirements; an undertaking not to use certain "deleterious materials" in the construction work; provisions entitling the lenders to have access to any relevant plans and specifications on an enforcement; and a representation as to the level of the third party's insurance and an undertaking to continue a minimum amount of cover for a specified period (usually the relevant limi-tation period).

Intercreditor agreements

If there are many creditors of the project company, e.g. commercial banks, 5–8 subordinated sponsors, lessors, an international agency and export credit agencies, the main creditors may enter into an intercreditor agreement to regulate their relationships.

These agreements typically contain: common terms applying to all credi-tors (warranties, covenants, events of default, currency indemnity, assign-ments, set-off, notices, confidentiality, jurisdiction, governing law and other boiler-plate); provision for pro rata drawdowns; provision for disbursement of payments pro rata or in an agreed hierarchy out of the proceeds account; provision for management and monitoring by a single agent (conduit pipe for payments, voting, administration); limitations on creditor powers to vary their credit agreements (e.g. changes in financial terms); voting powers for waivers, consents, default acceleration and security enforcement; notifi-cation of defaults known to agents of groups of creditors; no action by creditors without specified creditor approvals (suit, execution, insolvency petitions, but not set-offs or judicial declarations); and the sharing of recov-eries pro rata or in a prescribed hierarchy.

If the project finance is partially guaranteed by independent guarantors, e.g. export credit agencies, the agreement will deal with their rights of subrogation. Subrogation of a partial guarantor results in dilution of the lender's security – the guarantor gives with one hand by paying under the guarantee but takes with the other hand by being subrogated. The agreement should deal with the management of voting rights of subrogated creditors.

See the outline form in the Appendix for a range of terms.

Insurance

5–9   Insurance attracts much lender attention in project finance and the credit agreement will contain elaborate and detailed insurance requirements. The main types of cover are insurance against physical damage or loss; third party liability; pollution; delay in start-up; business interruption; and (unusually) political risk.

There may also be a mortgagee interest insurance policy which insures the lenders against the risk that the main policies are avoided by the insurers, e.g. for non-disclosure or for breach of condition or warranty by the insured. As assignees of the main policies, the lenders can be in no better position than the assignor-insured.

The parties will be interested in the amounts of cover, the exclusions and the deductibles. Security over the insurances include notices of assignment, loss payable clauses and brokers' undertakings to the lenders agreeing to notify non-payment of premiums, cancellations and amendments and agreeing to waive their lien on the policies. There is a detailed review of insurances elsewhere in this series of works in relation to the archetypal project finance: shipping loans. The overall law and approach have much in common. See clauses 13.4 and 15.33 in outline form no 1 in the Appendix.

If the project is damaged, the credit agreement usually contains an obligation on the borrower to use the proceeds either to reinstate or (if the damage is over an agreed threshold which would delay the project, so that it is substantially a different project) to repay the loan. To achieve this, the occurrence of substantial damage to the project should be an event of default. The law or the policy may require reinstatement.

PART II

SUBORDINATED DEBT

CHAPTER 6

SUBORDINATED DEBT: GENERAL PRINCIPLES

Meaning and purposes of subordination

Definitions

Subordination is a transaction whereby one creditor (the subordinated or 6–1
junior creditor) agrees not to be paid by a borrower or other debtor until
another creditor of the common debtor (the senior creditor) has been paid.

Like security, subordination is relevant only if the debtor is insolvent
because until then both junior and senior creditors can be paid in full. Hence
the fundamental object of a subordination is that it should be successful on
insolvency.

Turnover and contractual subordination A subordination on insolvency
may be achieved by:

— a **turnover agreement** by the junior creditor to hold dividends and distri- 6–2
   butions receivable by him on trust for the senior creditor for application
   towards the senior debt, or (less commonly) an agreement by him to pay
   to the senior creditor an amount equal to recoveries on the junior debt;
   or

— a **contractual subordination** which is an agreement between the debtor
   and the junior creditor, with or without the senior creditor, that the
   junior debt is entitled to be paid only after the senior debt has been paid
   in full.

These two techniques of a turnover subordination and a contractual subordination are studied later: para 6–15 *et seq.*

Complete and springing subordinations A subordination may be a complete 6–3
subordination or a springing subordination. Under a **complete subordination,** the junior debt is postponed from the time of the subordination contract and may not be paid so long as the senior debt is outstanding.

6–4   Under a **springing (or inchoate) subordination,** the junior debt may be paid (or interest and like sums may be paid) until a specified event happens, such as the insolvency of the debtor, the occurrence of an event of default under the senior credit agreement, or the breach by the debtor of a financial ratio.

      In any event, all subordinations spring into effect on the debtor's liquidation or insolvency proceedings because it is then that the subordination is essential so far as the senior creditor is concerned.

6–5   **Other hierarchies of claims** Apart from subordination contracts between creditors, there are other methods whereby one claim may rank junior to another. Thus share capital may be divided into preferred, ordinary and deferred shares ranking down the ladder of priority on the liquidation of the company concerned. Shares rank for payment after debt. Unsecured debt ranks after secured debt. Both claims may be secured on the same assets of the debtor but the junior debt has second-ranking priority.

Purposes of subordination

6–6   Some usual objectives of subordination are:

(a) **Insiders** A senior creditor, such as a bank, may wish to subordinate insiders of the debtor, such as a parent company or major shareholder (especially in project finance). The insider's debt is treated as proprietors' capital which must remain locked in until the outside creditors are paid. The senior creditor relies on the cushion of the subordinated capital and the junior debt is postponed to ensure that the senior loans are used for the business and not to repay the insider's debt.

6–7   (b) **Capital adequacy** The debtor wishes to increase its capital base for regulatory purposes. Thus subordinated debt may rank as primary locked-in capital or as near primary capital for the purposes of central bank supervision of the capital adequacy of banks. Supervision of the capital adequacy of business is common in the banking, insurance and securities sectors. This type of debt is often intended to rank as more or less permanent capital and is sometimes perpetual debt. Typical requirements for subordinated debt might include requirements that (a) the debt be subordinated to all other debt, (b) events of default and onerous covenants be excluded subject to limited exceptions, (c) the debt is not repayable without the consent of the regulator, (d) the issuer has the option to defer interest payments, and (e) the debt is not treated as debt for the purposes of solvency rules so that the debtor can continue trading.

See especially, the Basle Committee Report of July 1988 on Banking Regulations and Supervisory Practices on International Convergence of Capital Measurement and Capital Standards; the Basle Convergence Agreement was implemented in the United Kingdom by the Bank of England's Notice No BSD/1988/3 of October 1988. Details of the qualifying attributes of primary perpetual subordinated debt and of term subordinated debt are set out in the Bank of England's Notice No BSD/1986/2 of March 1986, as amended, in particular by Notice No BSD/1994/3. See also EC Council Directive of April 17, 1989, on the own funds of credit institutions (89/299/EEC)]; Building Societies (Supplementary Capital) Order 1988 (SI 1988 No 777) for UK building societies; Financial Services (Financial Resources) Rules 1987 made by the Securities and Investments Board pursuant to s 49 of the Financial Services Act 1986 for UK investment businesses.

(c) **Change of control financings: mezzanine debt** Where the loans are to   6–8
finance a takeover or a management buy-out on highly leveraged terms, lenders may be prepared to lend on a subordinated basis. This increases the money available. The senior creditors benefit from the cushion of the junior debt and therefore may lend more. The junior creditors benefit from a high interest rate to compensate them for the larger risk and may be further sweetened by warrants for shares in the debtor or the ability to convert their debt into shares. The junior creditors may be institutional investors or a shareholder who agrees to take a portion of his purchase price as subordinated debt and who is thereby able to squeeze out extra price. The terms of this type of subordination are the most complex, partly because the junior creditors expect to have some control over their investment, partly because the junior debt is intended merely to support a transaction and may therefore be interim short-term finance as opposed to a permanent fixed component of the debtor's capital, and partly because the finance is often very risky. The market jargon for this type of financing located midway between debt and equity is mezzanine debt – a term which, one must admit, hits the target. In the US mezzanine bonds have been dubbed junk bonds – which also hits the target.

(d) **Improved credit** The debtor may wish to improve its balance sheet by enlarging the capital base ranking after senior creditors and thereby encouraging fresh senior credit.

(e) **Borrowing limits** The debtor may wish to raise money without eroding   6–9
the room available under borrowing restrictions in the debtor's loan agreements or constitutional documents. This may be achieved if the borrowing limit – which provides that borrowings must not exceed a prescribed multiple of equity capital and reserves – defines equity capital as including subordinated debt.

(f) **Work-outs** By subordinating debt, a borrower may seek to survive without going through a formal insolvency rehabilitation proceeding or going into liquidation. Typically, insiders or major suppliers might be persuaded to agree to subordinate their claims to induce bank creditors not to enforce their loans in the hope that the borrower will live to see better days. If the junior creditor is also a major shareholder as well as a creditor, subordination may be the only way of protecting his investment from total loss.

Comparison of subordinated debt and equity

6–10   **Advantages of subordinated debt** A simple way to subordinate an investor is for him to take shares, not debt. But subordinated debt may be preferable to equity for the following reasons:

—   A debtor is usually entitled to deduct interest payable by it from gross profits in calculating its net profits on which the debtor pays tax. Dividends invariably are not deductible. But interest may be treated as a dividend if the interest varies with the profits or the subordinated debt is treated as quasi-equity.

—   Interest may not be subject to a withholding tax but dividends may be.

—   The debtor may be liable to pay capital duty on the issue of shares, but not on the issue of loan capital. UK capital duty on the issue of shares has been abolished.

—   The liability of a debtor to pay interest on debt is not dependent on the debtor's profits and is therefore mandatorily payable in full. The payment of dividends is usually dependent on profits. But even here junior debt can be very similar to preferred shares in economic substance if, e.g. the debt is perpetual and non-payment of interest is not a default if the borrower is also not able to pay dividends.

—   Some institutions cannot invest in equities (particularly unlisted shares) but may be able to invest in debt. This may be true of pension funds and insurance companies.

—   A corporate debtor can repay debt without complying with legal restrictions on the ability of the company to reduce its share capital.

—   The interest rate on debt is usually less than preferred share dividends because debt is higher in the pecking order and therefore less risky. Hence the debtor's cost of capital is reduced.

—   If the subordination is achieved by a turnover by the junior creditor to the senior creditor of dividends on the junior debt, the senior creditor receives a double dividend and is hence in a better position than if the junior creditor were instead a holder of preferred shares: para 6–20.

— The double dividend resulting from a turnover subordination is a way of giving the senior creditor some security in a case where the debtor is prevented by a negative pledge in its credit agreements from granting security or where the debtor does not wish to grant security on the ground that it might inhibit future trade or bank credit.

— Debt can be secured but equity cannot be. Hence a secured junior creditor can rank himself ahead of trade creditors.

— The debtor's shareholders may wish to exclude the subordinated investor from benefiting from an expected appreciation in the debtor's business and hence watering their equity. A similar result could of course be achieved by preference shares.

— Subordinated debt can be issued without disturbing shareholder class rights and without any need to satisfy pre-emption rights in favour of shareholders or to obtain the consent of shareholders to the issue of new shares.

Disadvantages of subordinated debt On the other hand, debt may have the   6–11
following disadvantages compared to equity. Creditors have no right to vote and can control management only through covenants in the debt instrument. Creditors do not share in profits. A right to share in profits may result in the debt being treated as equity on insolvency: see, e.g. the English Partnership Act 1890 s 3. Debt does not benefit from appreciations in the capital value of the debtor's business. Trade creditors who do not benefit from the subordination as senior creditors may be less inclined to continue credit than if the junior debt were equity. Some classes of subordinated debt are treated as a liability in determining whether a debtor is insolvent and for the purposes of wrongful trading by the directors, but equity never is: para 6–23 *et seq.*

Senior and junior debt

The senior debt may, for example, be all other debt except subordinated   6–12
debt (typical of subordinated bond issues); or debt of a particular creditor or class of creditors such as banks; or debt arising under a specific credit agreement (typical of insider subordinations); or a class of debt, such as borrowings or listed borrowings. Thus the definition of senior debt may be defined so as to exclude trade debt and hence apply only to borrowings,

purchase price credits maturing more than 90 days after incurrence, liabilities under finance leases, and guarantees of these obligations. The object of the debtor would be to benefit financial creditors but not ordinary suppliers and hence improve access to financial credit.

The wider the definition, then the more deeply subordinated is the junior debt. Under a turnover subordination, the senior creditor's double dividend is diluted by inclusion of other creditors because the proceeds of the junior debt have to spread over a larger amount of senior debt. Hence a senior creditor will seek to narrow the scope of senior debt. But borrowers will wish to widen the definition of senior debt so as to enhance their ability to raise additional money on the strength of the subordinated cushion. In financings of leveraged bids, the senior debt may include not only debt under the senior credit agreement but also ancillary working capital loans under separate financings.

6–13   The junior debt owed by the debtor to the junior creditor may be all debt; or all debt incurred under a specific junior credit agreement; or debt incurred to particular creditors prior to a specified date (typical in workouts – thus a supplier agreeing to subordinate existing credits should be permitted to rank senior for future credits as an inducement to continued trading with the debtor); or debt to a particular creditor up to a specified amount; or debt constituted by specific issue of debt securities, as in the case of a subordinated bond issue (to maintain a maximum cushion of subordinated capital).

If a junior creditor is entitled to rescind the junior debt, the junior creditor's claim for damages or restitution should also be subordinated, lest the subordination be defeated. For example, a junior creditor may be entitled to rescind the subordinated claim if it is evidenced by a bond and the prospectus for the bond issue contained fraudulent or negligent misstatements. Attempts by a junior creditor to de-subordinate himself in this way have not been unheard of.

6–14   In the United States some cases held that the damages claim is also subordinated or alternatively that the junior creditor is not entitled to rescind; see, e.g. *Re Holiday Mart, Inc*, 715 F 2d 430 (9th Cir 1983); *Re Weis Securities, Inc*, 605 F 2d 590 (2d Cir 1978).

The US position is now covered by s 510(b) of the Bankruptcy Code of 1978 which provides as follows:

> "For the purpose of distribution under this title, a claim arising from rescission of a purchase or sale of a security of the debtor or of an affiliate of the debtor, for damages arising from the purchase or sale of such a security, or for reimbursement or contribution allowed under s 502 on account of such a claim, shall be subordinated to all claims or interests that are senior to or equal the claim or

interest represented by such security, except that if such security is common stock, such claim has the same priority as common stock."

The term "security" as used in this section includes both debt securities and equity securities: see s 101(35)(A).

Methods of subordination

Generally

There are two basic methods of subordination – turnover subordinations   6–15
and contractual subordinations. The technique used has a major impact on the efficiency of the subordination, the recoveries by the senior creditor and the risks run by the senior creditor. These techniques are primarily directed to subordinating the junior debt or the insolvency of the debtor: prior to a forced distribution of assets the subordination can largely be achieved by simple contractual prohibitions on the payment of the junior debt.

Turnover subordinations

In the case of a turnover subordination, on the insolvency of the debtor the   6–16
junior creditor agrees to turn over to the senior creditor all recoveries received by the junior creditor in respect of the junior debt. This is the classic traditional form and the method which is most widely used. Indeed, it is apparently the only available method if the junior creditor is to be subordinated only to a single senior debt, or class of senior debt, but wishes to rank pari passu with other debt. There are two basic forms.

1. Under a subordination trust, the junior creditor agrees to hold dividends, proceeds and other payments on the junior debt received by the junior creditor on trust for the senior creditor as property of the senior creditor, for application towards the senior debt until the senior debt is paid in full. This is the most satisfactory method and confers on the senior creditor a proprietary claim against the junior creditor for recoveries on the junior debt.

    Under English law, there is no objection to a trust for future persons provided that the beneficiaries of the trust can be ascertained with certainty when the trust property vests.

    The junior creditor could go one step further and assign the junior debt to the senior creditor as collateral security for the senior debt. For the differences between a security assignment and a subordination trust, see para 9–1 *et seq.*

2.   Under the (somewhat unusual) debtor-creditor turnover subordination the junior creditor agrees to claim or prove for the junior debt on the insolvency of the debtor and to pay an amount equal to dividends or other payments received by him to the senior creditor. The main disadvantage is that the junior creditor is merely a debtor to the senior creditor to the extent of those recoveries and the senior creditor relies on the continued solvency of the junior creditor. The senior creditor does not have a proprietary claim for those recoveries since the junior creditor does not transfer them to or hold them on trust for the senior creditor. Hence this method is suitable only where the junior creditor can be relied on not to become insolvent. But the technique has been used where there have been fears that a contractual subordination conflicts with a mandatory insolvency rule providing for pari passu payment of the insolvent's debts and that the conventional subordination trust may create a security interest.

6–17   In practice, even if the subordination is achieved by a trust of proceeds of the junior debt, this will usually also be accompanied by a back-stop debtor-creditor turnover obligation imposed on the junior creditor. Thus the junior creditor is obliged to pay to the senior creditor amounts equal to recoveries (instead of holding the recoveries on trust) in order to cover situations where the junior debt is discharged by a set-off (there is no recovery of an asset to turn over) or the subordination trust is invalid, e.g. because it is an unregistered security interest, or because the trust is an assignment requiring to be perfected by formalities which have not been complied with.

Potential inhibitions on subordinations by a junior creditor should be considered. For example, if the subordination is constituted by a subordination trust, the transfer of proceeds might conflict with a restriction in the junior creditor's loan agreements on disposals of assets of the junior creditor. If the subordination is a debtor-creditor turnover subordination (whereby the junior creditor agrees to pay the senior creditor amounts equal to recoveries on the junior debt until the senior debt is paid), the contingent debt liability may be counted towards indebtedness of the junior creditor under financial ratios or restrictions on liabilities in its credit agreements or constitutional documents or for the purposes of supervision by regulatory authorities of the financial condition of the junior creditor. The junior debt may be non-assignable, e.g. because there is an express restriction on assignments. A prohibition on assignments may not however restrict a trust of proceeds since the law construes limitations on free dispositions narrowly: see, e.g. *Re Turcan* (1888) 40 Ch D 5.

Contractual or "contingent debt" subordinations

The junior creditor agrees with the debtor that, so long as the senior debt is   6–18
outstanding, the junior debt is not payable unless and until the senior debt
has been paid in full. If the debtor becomes subject to insolvency or dissolution proceedings, the junior debt will rank in right of payment subordinate
to and after the prior payment of the senior debt and the liquidator is
directed to pay the senior debt first.

Because this formulation or others like it may (unusually) conflict with a
mandatory insolvency rule that unsecured debts are to be paid pari passu
(para 8–1 *et seq*), a contractual subordination is sometimes framed as a
contingent debt subordination. This states that if the debtor goes into liquidation or becomes subject to a rehabilitation proceeding or any other insolvency proceedings, the junior debt is contingent or conditional on the
debtor being able to pay the senior debt in full. If the debtor is insolvent, the
senior creditor will not be paid in full and in that event the junior creditor in
effect renounces his junior debt. If the debtor would be solvent if the junior
debt were shaved down but not wholly wiped out, then the junior debt is
diminished accordingly.

A provision that, on solvent liquidation, the junior creditor must convert
into preferred shares is undesirable since a company may not be able to issue
shares once it is in liquidation: see, e.g. s 88 of the British Insolvency Act
1986. It is preferable to state that in that event the junior creditor is deemed
to have converted immediately prior to the liquidation.

A sample clause might provide: 6–19

> "(1) If the debtor becomes subject to any liquidation, dissolution or similar
> insolvency proceedings or to any assignment for the benefit of its credi-
> tors or any other distribution of its assets, the junior debt will be payable
> only on condition that the senior debt has been or is capable of being
> paid in full. Accordingly in any such event the junior debt will be
> reduced to such amount down to zero as is necessary to ensure that the
> debtor is able to pay the senior debt in full.
> (2) The reduction of the junior debt will be applied first to costs and
> expenses, second to interest, and third to principal of the junior debt."

The main feature of contractual or "contingent debt" subordinations is
that the junior debtor is in effect subordinated to all creditors and not just to
a particular senior loan or class of senior debt.

This method is unsuitable if the junior debt is secured, because the contingency may prevent recovery by the junior creditor even though the security is sufficient. Hence the contingency should not apply to the extent that
the junior debt is recoverable out of the security.

Comparison of recoveries

6–20   The chief distinction between a contractual subordination and a turnover subordination is that the senior debt benefits from the turnover of dividends on the junior debt and hence receives a double dividend. The economic effect is as if the senior creditor had a charge over the junior debt. The value of this "collateral" or double dip is unpredictable because it depends upon the amount of the distribution in the bankruptcy of the debtor. The turnover will also be affected by the validity of the junior debt and whether it is convertible into shares.

In the case of a contractual subordination, other non-senior debt benefits even though the other debt is not intended to rank as senior debt in relation to the junior debt. This is because, if the junior debt is not payable until the senior debt is paid, by reason of the pari passu payment of all ordinary debt on insolvency, the senior debt will not be paid until other debt is paid. Hence contractual subordinations are suitable only where the junior debt is to be subordinated to all other debt.

The effect is that, in the case of a turnover subordination, both junior debt and senior debt achieve a better recovery, at the expense of other debt, than with a contractual subordination of the junior debt to all creditors.

Other subordinations

6–21   Other effective subordinations may be noted:

(a) **Preference shares** In some jurisdictions, a subordination can be achieved by the issue of preference shares by a parent company to a finance subsidiary which the finance subsidiary charges in favour of bondholders to secure an issue of bonds by the finance subsidiary matching the preference shares as to income and maturity. The preference shares are similar to a subordinated guarantee by the parent but in the meantime rank as share capital of the parent company, e.g. for the purposes of capital adequacy. Consideration should be given to any prohibitions on a subsidiary holding shares of its parent, even if they are preference shares only.

(b) **Spanish escritura publica** Under Spanish law and the law of some Spanish-based jurisdictions (such as Panama) a unsecured creditor whose debt instrument is formalised as an *escritura publica* ranks ahead of unperfected creditors. The procedure generally involves the execution of the senior debt instrument before a notary and the payment of a significant documentary tax.

(c) **Structural subordinations** A lender to a holding company is generally in   6–22
a worse position than a lender to the operating subsidiaries since the
lender to the holding company looks only to the value of the shares in
the subsidiaries, i.e. what is left after the creditors of the subsidiaries
have been paid. Many practical "subordinations" are achieved in this
way. But this structural subordination will be weakened if the holding
company on-lends the proceeds of the "junior" loan to the subsidiary or
is a creditor of the subsidiary since the holding company and its creditors will then effectively rank equally with the "senior" lenders to the
subsidiaries – exactly in economic substance as if the junior creditor
were ranking equally.

If the junior creditor makes a loan to a subsidiary under the guarantee of the parent and the guarantee is subordinated, the loan itself
should also be subordinated. Otherwise the liquidator of the subsidiary
might be able to claim from the parent-guarantor any on-lending of the
loan by the subsidiary to the parent; the subsidiary pays dividends out
of the proceeds to the junior creditor as a creditor of the subsidiary so
that the junior creditor thereby side-steps the subordinated guarantee.

(d) **Compulsory subordinations on insolvency** Some claims are compulsorily subordinated on insolvency as a matter of law. Depending on the
jurisdiction, these may include (a) subordination to depositors of banks
or insurancy policy-holders, (b) equitable subordination under the US
Deep Rock doctrine, (c) certain profit-sharing loans (e.g. under s 3 of
the Partnership Act 1890, reflected in other English-based countries)
and (d) subordination of shareholder loans in Germany: GmbH Law
s 32(a).

If a senior creditor is relying on a turnover of dividends from a junior
creditor whose claim is subordinated by law, the senior creditor will get
no turnover if the junior creditor's claim is effectively treated as equity.

Subordination, insolvency tests and wrongful trading

An important question is whether subordinated debt counts as a liability for   6–23
the purposes of determining the insolvency of the debtor. Insolvency is normally a ground for a petition for winding-up or rehabilitation proceedings
and attracts the liability of directors for wrongful or fraudulent trading in
many English-based jurisdictions and a mandatory duty on the debtor's
management to apply for insolvency proceedings in numerous other jurisi-
dictions. It marks the beginning of the suspect period for the purposes of
preferences and transactions at an undervalue capable of being set aside on
insolvency.

In this context, many jurisdictions adopt one of two definitions of insolvency, or both of them, namely, inability to pay debts as they fall due and excess of liabilities over assets. Thus s 123 of the British Insolvency Act 1986 adopts both the cash-flow and the balance sheet test in the alternative: "a company is also deemed to be unable to pay its debts as they fall due if it is proved to the satisfaction of the court that the value of the company's assets is less than the amount of its liabilities, taking into account its contingent and prospective liabilities".

If the junior debt can be ignored for the purposes of solvency tests, then in this respect it is like equity. If it cannot, then it is like debt.

6–24   Where the maturity of payment of the junior debt is postponed, then plainly the junior debt is not relevant to the cash-flow test of inability to pay debts as they fall due: the junior debt is not payable.

Where the test is excess of liabilities over assets, the junior debt will count as a liability in the case of a turnover subordination because, as between the debtor and the junior creditor, the junior debt is unconditionally payable and the turnover is purely an arrangement between the junior and the senior creditor. Hence turnover subordinations never approximate the junior debt to equity for the purposes of these solvency tests.

6–25   The application of the balance sheet solvency test in the case of contractual or contingent debt subordinations, where the payment of the junior debt is conditional upon payment of the senior debt or upon the solvency of the debtor, depends upon whether, at the time the solvency test must be made, the junior debt is renounced or shaved down by contract to the extent necessary to ensure solvency. If it has been, then the junior debt is like equity.

For example, s 214 of the British Insolvency Act 1986 provides that a director is potentially liable to contribute to the assets of the company if the company has gone into insolvent liquidation (meaning "goes into liquidation at a time when its assets are insufficient for the payment of its debts and other liabilities and the expenses of the winding up") and the director "knew or ought to have concluded that there was no reasonable prospect that the company would avoid going into insolvent liquidation", subject to a "best efforts to minimise losses" defence. If the effect of the subordination contract is that the junior creditor has renounced his claim at the time that the winding up order is made or resolution passed to the extent necessary to ensure solvency, the directors ought to be entitled to disregard the junior debt as a liability in determining whether the company would avoid going into insolvent liquidation. The directors could therefore trade longer than would be the case with ordinary debt and in this respect the junior debt has the cushion function of equity.

But there is also fraudulent trading. Section 213 of the Insolvency Act   6–26
1986 provides that, if in the course of a winding up it appears that any business of the company has been carried on with intent to defraud creditors of
the company, the court may order that persons knowingly parties to the
fraud are to be liable to contribute to the company's assets. One effect of
this is that, if the directors incur debts when they know that there is little
prospect of those debts being paid, the directors are potentially liable to
contribute to the company's assets.

In determining whether a new creditor will be paid, the directors ought to
be able to take into account the fact that junior debt will be subordinated to
the creditor and therefore the directors again ought to be able to ignore the
junior debt for this purpose when they incur new senior debt. This was the
reasoning adopted in the South African case of *Re Carbon Development
(Property) Ltd*, 1992 (2) SA 95.

Director liability for wrongful or fraudulent trading is not known to US
or Canadian corporate insolvency law.

Where the suspect period for preferences and the like commences on
insolvency defined as negative net assets, the question of whether the junior
debt is to be counted as a liability ought again to depend upon whether or
not the junior debt at that point has validly been renounced. Often the
renunciation takes effect only in the case of insolvency proceedings in which
event the junior debt will count as a liability prior to that time. Similar principles should apply to insolvency petitions. But rules that the management
must take action when half or some other proportion of "capital" is lost will
often not be affected by subordinations. The rules are summarised in
another work (on the comparative law of insolvency) in this series on international financial law.

CHAPTER 7

SUBORDINATED DEBT: ASPECTS OF TURNOVER SUBORDINATIONS

Introduction

7–1   If the junior creditor is willing to be subordinated to one senior creditor (or group of senior creditors) but to rank equally with other creditors, this can effectively be achieved only by an arrangement whereby the junior creditor transfers the dividends on his claim to the senior creditor or otherwise gives the benefit of the junior debt to the senior creditor until the latter is paid. If he agrees not to be paid so long as the senior creditor is unpaid, then, as shown in the previous chapter, the junior creditor is inevitably also subordinated to other creditors on the insolvency of the debtor since, by reason of the pari passu payment of ordinary debts on insolvency, the payment of the senior creditor will normally also involve the payment of other creditors.

Turnover of proceeds

7–2   Most Anglo-American turnover subordinations are trusts of proceeds of the junior debt which occur upon a future contingency, notably the insolvency of the debtor.

The "trust" language is used to create a proprietary in rem claim, but civilian lawyers should not be perplexed: this is in substance a transfer of future proceeds.

A transfer or trust or assignment of the *proceeds* of a debt, as opposed to the debt itself, is a curious half-way house. The debt is not transferred, only its fruits. Interesting questions may arise as to: whether it is possible under local law to assign proceeds; whether the assignment destroys set-off mutuality between the junior creditor and the debtor (para 9–11); whether a priority notice can be given to the debtor before the proceeds come into existence (para 10–19); whether the proceeds are a future asset which falls into the pool of the junior creditor's estate if he should become insolvent before the debtor (para 8–10); whether the senior creditor is owner of the junior debt for the purposes of insolvency proof and voting (para 8–8 *et seq*); and whether the trust of proceeds is a gift of a future asset which is revocable by the junior creditor before the asset comes into existence (para 10–15 *et seq*). The common sense solution is to treat the assignment of proceeds as an assignment of the debt itself for these purposes since economically this is the effect.

In any event, English law allows an assignment of proceeds. Most of the cases have concerned the question of whether a prohibition on assignments prohibits assignments of proceeds, to which the answer has generally been "no".

> See: *Re Turcan* (1888) 40 Ch D 5 (non-assignable insurance policy); *Glegg v Bromley* [1912] 3 KB 474; *Russell & Co Ltd v Austin Fryers* (1909) 25 TLR 414 (non-assignable contract of personal service). See also *The Litison Pride* [1985] 1 Lloyds Rep 437 (assignee of insurance proceeds loses claim if policy is avoided for a fraudulent claim).

Assignments of proceeds are common in other contexts, e.g. security assignments of insurance proceeds and of the proceeds of letters of credit: see Art 59 of the Uniform Customs and Practice for Documentary Credits (1994 Revision).

> In *Re Irving, ex p Brett* (1877) 7 Ch D 419, a Mr Bushby wrote to his bank as follows: "I hereby undertake that I will, when and as received, pay over to you all dividends coming to me in respect of my proof upon the Estate of Mr John Irving." Mr Bushby became bankrupt and the bank gave notice of its claim to the trustees in the bankruptcy of Mr Irving. *Held*: this was a good equitable assignment of the dividend and that the bank was entitled as against Mr Bushby's trustee in bankruptcy.

Similarly, under US law, there is no objection to a transfer of proceeds   7–3
and indeed in numerous cases the courts have held that the effect of a subordination is to transfer proceeds.

Prior to the enactment of s 510(a) of the Bankruptcy Code of 1978 (see para 8–3), US courts generally gave effect to subordination agreements, with only limited exceptions. This outline is based mainly upon the useful summary by Dobbs in Ruda (ed) *Asset-Based Financing* (1988) Matthew Bender.

> In some cases the US courts treated the senior creditor's right to the proceeds of the junior debt as an equitable lien (as opposed to a full security assignment): *Searle v Mechanics' Loan & Trust Co*, 249 Fed 942 (9th Cir 1918); *Re George P Schinzel & Son*, 16 F 2d 289 (SDNY 1926); *Bank of America v Engleman*, 101 Ca App 2d 390, 225 P2d 597 (1950). Or they treated it as an equitable

assignment which the junior creditor agreed to effect in the event of the bankruptcy of the debtor: *Re Handy-Andy Community Stores*, 2 F Supp 97(WD La 1932); *Re Itemlab, Inc*, 197 F Supp 194 (EDNY 1961). Or the courts found that the junior creditor held the benefit of the subordination agreement for the senior creditor as a third party beneficiary: *Re National Discount Corp*, 212 F Supp 929 (WDSC), affirmed sub nom *Austin v National Discount Corp*, 322 F 2d 928 (4th Cir 1963). Or it was held that the junior debtor was a constructive trustee of his claim against the creditor for the benefit of the senior creditor.

In *Re Dodge-Freedman Poultry Company*, 148 F Supp 647 (DNH 1956) affirmed sub nom *Dodge-Freedman Poultry Co v Delaware Mills Inc*, 244 F 2d 314 (1st Cir 1957), the junior creditor, who was the president and principal shareholder of the borrower, sought to defeat the senior creditor's right to receive distributions allowable on the junior debt in the borrower's chapter IX case by waiving his claim against the borrower. *Held*: the waiver was tantamount to the junior creditor returning to the borrower money to which the senior creditor was equitably entitled. The junior creditor could not give effect to the waiver since he was constructive trustee of the money for the senior creditor.

Or if it could be shown that the senior creditor incurred his debt in reliance upon the junior debt, the junior creditor was equitably estopped from claiming parity with the senior creditor in a distribution from the insolvent debtor's assets: see *Lodner v Pearlman*, 129 App Div 93, 113 NYS 420 (1908). However if the senior debt is incurred prior to the subordination or after but without knowledge of the subordination, then the senior creditor cannot show reliance and hence cannot rely on the estoppel: *Re Joe Newcomer Fin Co*, 226 F Supp 387 (D Colo 1964); *Re Temple of Music, Inc*, 114 F Supp 759 (EDNY 1953) affirmed 220 F2d 749 (2d Cir 1955).

Subsequently the US courts abandoned the above theories of enforcing subordination agreements and instead simply gave effect to them as ordinary contracts: see, e.g. *First National Bank v Am Foam Rubber Corp*, 530 F 2d 450 (2d Cir 1976), cert denied sub nom *Buchman v Am Foam Rubber Corp*, 429 US 858 (1976); *Re Credit Indust Corp*, 366 F 2d 402 (2d Cir 1966); *Re Bird & Sons Sales Corp*, 78 F 2d 371 (8th Cir 1935); *Re Eaton Factors Co, Inc*, 3 BR 20 (BC, SDNY 1980); *New York Stock Exch v Pickard & Co, Inc*, 296 A2d 143 (Del 1972).

7–4   There seems to be no objection in **Germany** to an agreement to turn over dividends received on bankruptcy: Scholz Lwowski, *Das Recht der Kreditsicherung* (6th ed) p 591. Similarly no special formalities are required in the **Netherlands** and the transaction is probably possible in **Sweden**.

In **Denmark**, a subordination in favour of one creditor or a specific group of creditors is regarded as a transaction whereby the junior creditor assigns only his right to dividend until the senior creditor has been paid in full, and not as an assignment of his full claim. The validity of the agreement is not affected according to whether or not the debtor is a party.

In *Ingeniør T Dahl's Shipservice A/S in bankruptcy v Eksportkreditradet* (Ugeskrift for Retsvaesen 1964, p 253), the Ministry of Commerce issued a guarantee for a loan advanced to the company by its bank. As a condition to the issue of the guarantee to the company's bank, the Ministry required that the company's subsidiaries in Sweden and Norway subordinate their claims against the Danish company to the Ministry's eventual claim arising out of the guarantee. The subsidiaries subordinated in favour of the Ministry. *Held*: the Ministry was entitled to claim dividends on the subsidiaries' claims against the Danish company, even though the subsidiaries at a later stage had subordinated their debts in favour of all other creditors of the Danish company. The contractual subordination in favour of the other creditors of the Danish company was regarded as null and void and they could not rely on a third party promise in their favour.

In *Aktieselskabet Københavns Handelsbank v Schou-Danlon A/S in liquidation* (Ugeskrift for Retsvaesen 1983, pp 1141–1147), a bank made a loan to company A in a group on terms that debts owing by company A to company B in the group were subordinated to the bank. Some 14 years later the bank made new loans to company A. Both the bank and the management of the group of companies had forgotten about the old subordination. *Held*: the subordination agreement applied to the later bank credit. Consequently, dividends on claims owing by company A to company B had to be paid to the bank.

In a number of civil code countries, such as France and probably Belgium, 7–5 Luxembourg, Greece and possibly Japan, the benefit of the subordination could be achieved by the *stipulation pour autrui* (or equivalent) which is the civil code analogue of a third party beneficiary contract. The junior creditor agrees that the benefit of his subordination is available to the senior creditors as third party beneficiaries who can take the benefit of the contract by declaring their acceptance of it. In France this procedure is widely used in the case of assignments of the proceeds of insurance policies and has the advantage that it does not require special formalities to render it valid on the insolvency of the "assignor". An example of this third party promise is Art 537 of the Japanese Civil Code, although it is evidently not possible in Japan to dispense with the requirement of an affirmative declaration of acceptance by the senior creditor: Supreme Court decision of July 5, 1916, *Min-roku* vol 22, pp 1336 *et seq*. This decision has been doubted by commentators. Whether the third party beneficiary contract can give the senior creditor a proprietary claim to the proceeds of the junior debt, as opposed to mere contract claims against the junior creditor for payment, is a matter for investigation. Third party beneficiary contracts are widely available in civil code countries, e.g. France CC Art 1121, Germany BGB s 328, Switzerland CO Art 112.

Security assignment of junior debt

7–6   Alternatively, the junior creditor could assign his entire claim to the senior creditor by way of collateral security. This has the obvious disadvantages of real security, e.g. registration or filing, violation of negative pledges and the like.

In countries such as France, Belgium, Luxembourg, Japan and South Korea, an assignment is void against creditors of the assignor (the junior creditor) and on his insolvency unless the assignment is either consented to by the debtor or notified to the debtor in a formal manner prescribed by law. Thus in France, Arts 1690 and 2075 of the Civil Code require the formal service of a translation of the assignment on the debtor by a *huissier* (bailiff) or the debtor's acceptance or acknowledgement of the transfer by an *acte authentique*. Article 467 of the Japanese Civil Code is to similar effect: the notice or consent must be in writing as a notarial act (*kakuteihizuke*). Ditto South Korea. The Italian position is also similar: CC Art 2800.

These formalities are not required in England to validate the transfer as against creditors of the junior creditor as transferor. In England an assignment of a specific debt without notice to the debtor is effective against judgment creditors of the assignor who attempt to garnish the assigned debt (see, e.g. *Pickering v Ilfracombe Ry* (1868) LR 3 CP 235) and is also effective on the assignor's subsequent insolvency. Notice to the debtor merely affects such matters as priority between successive assignees, who the debtor pays, and set-off.

Distribution by liquidator to senior creditor

7–7   Turnover subordinations commonly direct the liquidator, trustee in bankruptcy or other insolvency representative to pay dividends on the junior debt direct to the senior creditor until the senior debt is paid. The advantage of this is that it short-circuits the double procedure of payment to the junior creditor who then hands over the payment to the senior creditor. It also avoids the necessity for the senior creditor to seek out the junior creditor (difficult or impracticable in the case of issues of junior debt securities not constituted by a trust deed) and it avoids the risk that the junior creditor might divert the proceeds.

Other forms appoint a trustee for the junior debt and direct the trustee to pay dividends on the junior debt back to the liquidator on trust to pay them to the senior creditor first, e.g. the liquidator is constituted a sub-trustee. It is thought that a liquidator should normally accept a trusteeship which is beneficial to creditors: if not, equity does not want for a trustee.

The direction to pay the senior creditor is pure mechanics of channelling the payment through a nominee for convenience and does not obscure the fact that the junior creditor transfers beneficial ownership of the junior debt or its proceeds to the senior creditor.

Under the US Bankruptcy Code 1978 there appears to be no objection to   **7–8** imposing this duty on the trustee in bankruptcy: see s 510(a).

Under English insolvency law, it also seems that a liquidator can be required to pay dividends to the assignee of those dividends under a turnover subordination trust: consider IR 1986, r 11.11(1). The court can enable an assignee of a dividend to file a proof in substitution for the assignor's proof: *Re Frost* [1899] 2 QB 50; *Re Iliff* (1902) 51 WR 80; *Re Hills* (1913) 107 LT 95.

Scope of turnover obligation: recoveries from all sources

Under a turnover subordination, the turnover obligation should ideally   **7–9** apply to all recoveries on the junior debt from whatever source, even if not from the debtor. Examples are: payments under guarantees of the junior debt; proceeds of security given by a third party for the junior debt; turnover from creditors who are themselves subordinated to the junior debt, as where there are multiple layers of subordinated debt; receipts by the junior creditor from other syndicate members under a pro rata sharing clause in a syndicated credit agreement; and evasive payments by a third party to the junior creditor out of money provided by the debtor.

If the junior debt is guaranteed and it is not intended that payments on the guarantee should be turned over, the intercreditor agreement between the junior and senior creditor should so provide. From the point of view of the junior creditor, the guarantor should remain liable to pay the junior creditor until the junior creditor has recovered the full junior debt for its own benefit and all its turnover obligations have been satisfied. But this results in the unhappy guarantor guaranteeing both junior and senior debt.

Turnover of recoveries in kind

The turnover obligation should also apply to distributions in kind on the   **7–10** junior debt as well as payments in cash and provide for the conversion of the distribution into cash. Thus the junior debt may be "paid" by an issue of debt or equity securities in a bankruptcy rehabilitation proceeding.

However, as an exception, it is sometimes provided under the so-called "X clause" that the turnover will not apply to securities issued to the junior creditor on a reorganisation of the debtor if those securities are subordinated to the senior debt or if securities are issued to the senior creditors on terms no less protective of the senior creditors than the original subordination.

The agreement may provide that, if turnover proceeds are received by the senior creditor in a currency different to the senior debt, the senior debt is discharged only when the proceeds, converted by the senior creditor at a market rate of exchange, are applied to the senior debt. Liquidation dividends are usually payable in local currency since most commercial jurisdictions convert foreign currency debts into local currency for the purposes of an insolvency proof.

Circular subordinations

7–11 If C subordinates to B who subordinates to A who subordinates to C, the subordination is circular. A, who should be the most senior creditor, has subordinated himself to C who is the most junior creditor. The turnover would go round and round infinitely.

This puzzle usually arises because of drafting error. For example, A may be senior to B and C and then subordinate his debt to all other creditors, forgetting that he should have added "all other creditors except B and C".

Many solutions to this conundrum have been attempted but the solution is likely to be determined largely by the terms of each subordination (which may be very different) and whether one subordination is to a specific creditor and another to all creditors. A useful approach is an elegant solution proposed by Gilmore in *Security Interests in Personal Property* (1965) at p 1021 which unhappily only resolves one particular situation. In the end, it may be necessary to breach the circle, e.g. by not compelling a junior creditor to turn over dividends received from a turnover to him, but only dividends received from the debtor on his own claim.

Rule against perpetuities

7–12 The rule against perpetuities limits the time by which trust property must vest: see, e.g. the English Perpetuities and Accumulations Act 1964 which will usually result in a maximum period of 21 years. This period will not generally present a problem except in the case of perpetual subordinated loans.

CHAPTER 8

SUBORDINATED DEBT: BANKRUPTCY OF DEBTOR OF JUNIOR CREDITOR

Subordination and the debtor's bankruptcy

Mandatory pari passu rules

In most developed jurisdictions insolvency law prescribes that the liabilities   8–1
of the insolvent must be paid pari passu.

The provision for pari passu payment is almost invariably expressed to be mandatory: **Britain**: IA 1986 s 107 and IR 1986, r 4.181(1) as amended; **Belgium**: Art 8 of the Law on Preferences and Mortgages of December 16, 1851; **Canada**: s 141 of the Bankruptcy Act 1985; **Denmark**: Art 97 of the Bankruptcy Act; **France**: Arts 2092 and 2093 of the Civil Code, Art 166–1 of the Bankruptcy Act of January 25, 1985; **Greece**: Art 660 of the Commercial Code; **Italy**: Art 52 of the Bankruptcy Act 1942; **Japan**: Art 40 of the Bankruptcy Law; the **Netherlands**: Art 1178 of the Civil Code; **Luxembourg**: Art 561 of the Commercial Code; **Sweden**: s 18 of the Priority Act.

But in these jurisdictions the policy of mandatory pari passu provisions is not infringed where one creditor agrees to be paid after another creditor since the object of the pari passu rule is to ensure that a creditor is not paid ahead of the general body of creditors rather than that one creditor agrees to be deferred. No policy of the insolvency laws is offended if one creditor voluntarily agrees to postpone himself to the others, but only if he seeks to put himself ahead of other unsecured creditors.

In any event, the rule will not be infringed by a subordination trust or a   8–2
debtor-creditor turnover subordination because in both cases the junior creditor claims the full amount of the junior debt on the insolvency of the debtor pari passu with all other general creditors, including the senior creditor. The turnover obligation, which achieves the subordination, is purely a relationship between the junior creditor and the senior creditor.

If there is a question under the statute, a contingent debt subordination (whereby the junior debt is contingent on the debtor's solvency) should save the day because the junior debt is inherently contingent and is hence prov-

---

able only in its contingent amount. If the debtor is insolvent and the junior debt is conditional on solvency, the provable amount will usually be nil. Bankruptcy statutes usually contemplate the proof of contingent claims, e.g. the British IR 1986, r 4.86; Art 95 of the Italian Bankruptcy Act; Arts 271 and 275 and of the Japanese Bankruptcy Law; and Arts 130 and 131 of the Netherlands Bankruptcy Code.

Country survey

8–3 Subordinations are permitted under US insolvency law. The Bankruptcy Code of 1978 codifies previous law by providing in s 510(a) as follows:

> "A subordination agreement is enforceable in a case under this title to the same extent that such agreement is enforceable under applicable nonbankruptcy law."

In **England** subordination contracts do not infringe the mandatory pari passu rule.

> In *Re Maxwell Communications Corpn plc (No 3)* [1993] BCC 369, a Swiss law guarantee, granted by an English company in insolvent administration, of bonds issued by its subsidiary was contractually subordinated without a turn-over provision. The guarantee merely stated that on liquidation or bankruptcy the claims of unsubordinated creditors would be paid before the claims of the bondholders under the guarantee. *Held*: the subordination was valid and did not conflict with the mandatory pari passu section. A creditor could waive his claim and so there should be no reason why he should not agree to subordinate it.

A similar result has been reached in South Africa: *Re Carbon Development (Property) Ltd*, 1992 (2) SA 95.

8–4 In **Australia** and **New Zealand** it has been held that a deferment of debt which does not prejudice the equal ranking of other creditors is not prohibited by the terms of equivalent provisions in Australian insolvency legislation: *Horne v Chester & Fein Property Developments Pty Ltd* [1987] ACLR 245. See also *Re Walker Construction Co Ltd* [1960] NZLR 523; *Re Marlborough Construction Co* [1978] ACLC 29, 487 (Australia) – although this case involved a scheme of arrangement sanctioned by the court; *Re Industrial Welding Co Pty Ltd* (1977–1978) ACLR 30, 168 (Australia) obiter; *Re NBT Builders Pty Ltd* [1984] 8 ACLR 724, 727–8 (obiter). *Anfrank Nominees Pty Ltd v Connell* [1990] 1 ACSR 365 (W Australia S Ct). Contrary dicta in *Re Orion Sound Ltd* [1979] 2 NZLR 574 are considered incorrect. As to Canada, consider *Re Orzy* (1923) 53 OLR 323; [1924] 1 DLR 250; 3 CBR 737 (Ont CA).

In *Horne v Chester & Fein Property Developments Pty Ltd* [1987] ACLR 245, an agreement provided that "all moneys advanced to [G] shall be accepted by it as loans" and "shall rank equally in order of priority as to repayment by [G]". There was a proviso that if any creditor made an "additional loan" to G, such amounts should be repaid before any other repayments of loans to other creditors. Two creditors had made "additional loans" to G. *Held*: notwithstanding mandatory pari passu payment of creditors under s 440 of the Companies (Vic) Code, the liquidator may distribute in accordance with an agreement between the parties where to do so could not adversely affect any creditor not a party to the agreement.

In *Re United States Trust Co of New York* (1993) 11 ACLC 707 (New South Wales S Ct), a company's debentures provided that they were to be subordinated to all senior creditors of the company. The company went into liquidation. *Held*: the subordination provision was valid and did not offend the pari passu provisions of the Companies Code.

In *Re Walker Construction Co Ltd* [1960] NZLR 523, a company called a meeting of creditors, at which it was resolved that liabilities for goods supplied after a certain date be treated as preferred, and prior liabilities should be deferred. Later a deed of arrangement was executed by most creditors and a scheme of arrangement was submitted to meetings of creditors. The New Zealand Companies Act 1955 provided that a company's debts shall be paid pari passu. *Held*: the deferment should be upheld. The court said that it would be unconscionable to permit any deferred creditor who assented to the arrangement, and whose assent was acted on, to prove in competition with the current creditors. The statutory right of a creditor may be qualified or renounced as the creditor thinks fit: and, to the extent to which he has waived or qualified his right to pari passu payment, the liquidator's duty to him would be affected accordingly.

Although New Zealand case law has approved the transaction, subordination was statutorily permitted in New Zealand in 1994 and has also been introduced into Australian corporate law.

In **Germany** pursuant to s 64 of the German GmbH Law the management   8–5
of a company with limited liability is obliged to apply for bankruptcy if the company is insolvent or if its liabilities are in excess of its assets ("overindebtedness"). In order to avoid this, a creditor may agree to subordinate his claim to the claims of all other creditors. Subordination clauses of this type have been recognised by court decisions and in the legal literature as being legally valid under civil law and bankruptcy law: BGH, judgment of February 9, 1987, Betriebsberater 1987, 728. If, in spite of subordination, the debtor corporation becomes bankrupt, the subordinated creditor has no claim against the bankrupt estate, as he has waived his claim by virtue of the subordination. An agreement whereby an employee waives his priority claim on bankruptcy for unpaid wages has been upheld: Bremen Labour

Court, September 6, 1983 ZIP 1983 1360–ZIP 1984. 623. Profit-sharing rights may be given to a creditor of a company in the form of *Genussrechte* (participation rights). The company and the relevant creditor are free to agree on the terms of these rights and hence these instruments enable the company to raise funds without granting membership or voting rights. *Genussrechte* may be issued as subordinated debt having a similar function to equity capital.

There appears to be no case law on contractual subordinations in **Belgium**, **Finland**, **Greece**, **Luxembourg**, the **Netherlands** or **Sweden**.

8–6   **France** is one of the few countries which has expressly regulated the rules applicable to subordinated debt by statute. Three laws have validated subordinations.

> *Prêts participatifs* Act no 78–741 of July 13, 1978, constituted *prêts participatifs* as subordinated securities. The *prêts participatifs* need not carry a right to share in profits and are primarily a subordinated loan which is only paid on liquidation of the company after payment in full of all other creditors: Art 26.
>
> The disadvantages of *prêts participatifs* are: (a) they are loans, and as such, they cannot be assigned as easily as securities would be; and (b) *prêts participatifs* can be redeemed and are therefore not as good as equity capital. They merely cheapen the cost of capital without achieving the benefit to creditors of equity which is fully locked-in. As a result, the use of *prêts participatifs* has declined.
>
> *Titres participatifs* Act no 83–1 of the January 3, 1983, included in the Companies Act of 1966, created participating securities, *titres participatifs*, the issue of which is reserved to government-owned companies or cooperative companies, to permit a strengthening of the capital base of companies. The *titres participatifs* were a method of introducing securities in government-owned companies which would have the same money rights as shares for their holders, but without diluting the capital. Articles 283–6 of the Companies Act of 1966 provides that these securities can be paid only at the expiration of the life of the company or at least not before seven years. The securities rank after the *prêts participatifs* and they participate in profits.
>
> **Subordinated bonds** The last and most important Act sanctioning subordinated debt is Act no 85–1321 of December 14, 1985, adding new Arts 339–7 to the Companies Act of 1966 and allowing various composite bonds to be issued. Article 339–7 states:
>
> > "In the issue of securities representing debts of the issuer company . . . , it can

be provided that these securities will be redeemed only after payment of all other creditors, although before creditors of *prêts* or *titres participatifs*".

Subordinated bonds have the advantage over *prêts participatifs* that, as securities, they can easily be transferred.

Accordingly creditors may rank in the following ladder on the liquidation of the company:

— secured creditors;
— all ordinary creditors;
— subordinated bondholders (Art 339–7, 1.66);
— lenders under *prêts participatifs* (Art 26, 1.78);
— lenders under *titres participatifs* (Art 283–6, 1.66).

Insolvency reorganisation plans

Insolvency rehabilitation proceedings or schemes of arrangement involving   8–7
a plan for the survival of the debtor as a going concern should reflect the subordination. Examples are the US Chapter 11 proceedings and the British administration order or voluntary arrangement under the Insolvency Act 1986. The British provisions do not require that creditors be grouped in classes, but s 1122(a) of the US Bankruptcy Code of 1978 provides that a "plan may place a claim or an interest in a particular class only if such claim or interest is substantially similar to the other claims or interests of such class". There is an unfair discrimination test in s 1129(b)(i) of the US Bankruptcy Code of 1978 and an "unfair prejudice" test in s 27 of the British Insolvency Act 1986 in relation to administrations.

If the plan provides for a degree of debt forgiveness or conversion into equity, junior debt should be reduced or converted before senior debt in order to reflect the subordination.

Turnover subordinations are primarily contracts between junior and senior creditors and should ideally contemplate turnovers of junior dividends under the composition. This is more ticklish if both classes of debt are converted into equity.

Proof and voting on junior debt

In turnover subordinations, on the insolvency of the debtor the senior credi-   8–8
tor should have the ability either to prove for the junior debt himself or to compel the junior creditor to prove for the junior debt (so as to produce turnovers to the senior creditor) and the senior creditor should control the vote on the junior debt.

Turnover subordination contracts commonly contain express provisions to cover these situations. In the case of subordination trusts it may be uncertain whether the senior creditor, as transferee of the proceeds of the junior debt, is the "creditor" for the purposes of proof and voting and hence entitled to prove for and vote on the junior debt. This is because his rights do not spring up until the proceeds come into existence. Further, the whole of the junior debt may not have to be turned over to cover the senior debt, but only part of it: the entitlement of the senior creditor and the balance left to the junior creditor will only be known when the insolvent estate is fully realised.

As to claiming the junior debt, it is often provided that the junior creditor must file a proof of claim and, if he fails to do so within good time, e.g. 14 days before the expiry date for proofs, the senior creditor has power of attorney to do so on his behalf. If the junior creditor did not claim the junior debt, the junior debt would of course not compete with the senior debt, but the senior creditor would lose the advantage of the double dividend.

As to voting, the agreement may provide that the senior creditor may vote on the junior creditor's claim in insolvency proceedings and has power of attorney to do so or that the junior creditor will vote as the senior creditor directs. Creditors can usually vote in relation to such matters as the appointment of an insolvency representative, the approval of transactions by the insolvency representative and, more importantly, the approval of a reorganisation plan. A vote protecting junior creditors may not protect senior creditors.

Since control of voting may confer too much power on the senior creditor, the provision may allow the junior creditor to vote but state (vaguely) that the junior creditor will not vote the junior debt so as to impair the subordination. The degree of freedom which the senior creditor has to vote, e.g. to deplete the junior creditor's claim, will depend on the contract.

Usually it is the "creditor" or "holder" of the claim who votes. Whether the junior creditor may grant a power of attorney or proxy to a senior creditor to vote his claim (assuming that the senior creditor is not a transferee of the full junior debt) depends upon applicable bankruptcy law.

8–9   US cases are divided on whether the senior creditor may vote the junior debt if not expressly authorised to do so. These cases illustrate the equivocal approach of the law to transfers of proceeds.

> In *Re Alda Commercial Corp*, 300 F Supp 294 (SDNY 1969), the subordination agreement did not expressly authorise the senior creditor to vote on the junior debt. *Held*: the senior creditor was not entitled to vote the claim of the junior creditor on the election of a trustee in a straight bankruptcy case. The reason was that the bankruptcy laws entitle all creditors to vote on the election of a trustee, regardless of whether their claims may be subordinated as to eventual payment.

On the other hand in *Re Itemland Inc*, 197 F Supp 194 (EDNY 1961), a senior creditor challenged the acceptance of a Chapter IX plan of arrangement by the junior creditor on the ground that the senior creditor, by virtue of the subordination, had the exclusive right to vote the junior debt. The subordination agreement did not expressly authorise the senior creditor to vote on the junior debt. *Held*: the senior creditor was entitled to vote on this issue. The reason was that the vote attached to the claim was the only means of determining how and when the claim was to be enforced and the terms of its payment. If the senior creditor was not entitled to vote, then the junior creditor had the power to use his vote to determine how the senior creditor should collect a claim in which the junior creditor no longer had any interest. The effective transfer of the claim carried control of the claim via voting.

In the Danish case of *Phoenix Materials Corporation v Topsil af 1981 A/S* (Ugeskrift for Retsvaesen 1983, p 1116), it was held that a declaration of subordination, although it was silent on the subject of voting rights, gave the senior creditor the right to vote on behalf of the junior debt for the election of a bankruptcy trustee.

The junior creditors may not be entitled to vote at all on a plan if the assets are insufficient to pay them.

In *Re British & Commonwealth Holdings PLC No 3* [1992] 1 WLR 672, a company was subject to an administration which is a type of insolvency rescue proceeding. The administrators wished to put forward a scheme for the distribution of cash to creditors. The company had issued debentures which were subordinated to all other creditors on the winding-up of the company. *Held*: on a winding-up the junior creditors would receive nothing. Although a winding-up had not taken place, the junior creditors had no interest in the assets of the company and hence were not entitled to vote on the scheme.

Subordination and the junior creditor's insolvency

The efficacy of the subordination should be tested in the event of the junior   8–10
creditor's bankruptcy as well as that of the debtor. This question is likely to be more important in relation to insider subordinations and issues of subordinated notes to small investors than to mezzanine debt held by major institutions. Nevertheless bankruptcy is blind and strikes down the big as well as the small.

Assets of the junior creditor's estate

Where a subordination trust springs up to grasp payments on the junior debt paid by the debtor after the junior creditor's insolvency, under English insolvency law the proceeds of the junior debt would not fall into the junior creditor's insolvent estate. The trust would bite on to the proceeds as soon as they come into existence even though this is after the insolvency. The junior creditor has transferred them prior to his insolvency. Even if the proceeds were a future asset, the same reasoning would apply.

> See *Re Irving, ex p Brett* (1877) 7 Ch D 419; *Re Lind* [1915] 2 Ch 345; *Re Davis & Co, ex p Rawlings* (1889) 22 QBD 193, CA (future instalments of hire); *Re Tout & Finch Ltd* [1954] 1 All ER 127 (building employer's retention moneys for work done pre-insolvency but payable after insolvency). The contrary case of *Collyer v Isaacs* (1881) 19 Ch D 347, CA, is considered to be wrong. The proceeds belong to the assignor's estate only if the liquidator of the assignor has to earn those proceeds after the insolvency, e.g. by completing works: *Re Jones, ex p Nichols* (1883) 22 Ch D 782, CA; *Wilmot v Alton* [1897] 1 QB 17, CA.

Preference of senior creditor by junior creditor

8–11   If a junior creditor agrees during the junior creditor's suspect period to subordinate his debt to a specified senior creditor, this may constitute a voidable preference of that senior creditor or a voidable transaction at an undervalue on the junior creditor's bankruptcy. The effect of the subordination is to improve the senior creditor's position and potentially to diminish the assets of the insolvent junior creditor to the detriment of his other creditors. This is most likely to affect subsequent subordinations by a junior creditor of debt which was previously unsubordinated, e.g. on a work-out.

By reason of tougher rules for connected persons, such as related companies and directors, the rules are particularly important for insider subordinations where the debtor is in financial difficulties.

CHAPTER 9

SUBORDINATION TRUSTS AS SECURITY INTERESTS; SET-OFF

Subordination trusts as security interests

Introduction

A turnover subordination trust is in economic substance a collateral charge   9–1
by the junior creditor over the junior creditor's debt or the proceeds of that
debt to secure the senior debt, but without imposing any personal liability
on the junior creditor to pay the senior debt himself. The question is
whether the transfer of proceeds is in law to be recharacterised as a security
interest. A purchaser of subordinated debt securities would be very surprised to be told he is buying a debt security which is subject to a charge
created by the initial holder over the proceeds of the debt security in favour
of senior creditors.

In the **United States,** a revised s 1–209 was recommended for inclusion in
the Uniform Commercial Code in 1966 as follows:

> "An obligation may be issued as subordinated to payment of another obli-
> gation of the person obligated, or a creditor may subordinate his right to pay-
> ment of an obligation by agreement with either the person obligated or another
> creditor of the person obligated. Such a subordination does not create a secur-
> ity interest as against either the common debtor or a subordinated creditor."

This stemmed from the doubts provoked by s 9–102(1)(a) of the Uniform
Commercial Code which provides that Art 9 applies to any transaction
"which is *intended* to create a security interest in personal property"
(emphasis added). The Official Comment to the revised section states that
Art 9 was never intended to cover debt subordination agreements although
nothing in the section prevents the creation of a security interest in a case
where the parties to the agreement so intend. Hence the problem has gone
away in those US states that have adopted s 1–209 – including financially
important states such as New York, California and Illinois. The relevant Art
9 does not apply in Louisiana.

9–2   In **England** the better view is that a properly drafted subordination trust of proceeds should not create a security interest under English law, but the matter is undecided.

One of the main tests of a security interest is whether the grantor has an equity of redemption, i.e. a right to the return of the asset over which the security is granted when the secured debt is paid. A trust of receipts by the junior creditor in favour of the senior creditor *up to an amount equal to* the senior debt leaves no equity of redemption since the junior creditor never transfers more than is required to pay the senior debt: there is no surplus to swing back. The beneficial ownership in the proceeds is split. By contrast, a security assignment of the junior debt by the junior creditor to the senior creditor is a security assignment of the *whole* of the junior debt or its proceeds to secure the junior debt. The junior creditor has an equity of redemption for the surplus if recoveries on the junior debt exceed the unpaid amount of the senior debt. The English courts are very ready to erect form over substance.

> The leading cases include *Re George Inglefield Ltd* [1933] 1 Ch 1; *Ashby Warner & Co Ltd v Simmons* [1936] 2 All ER 697; *Siebe Gorman & Co Ltd v Barclays Bank Ltd* [1979] 2 Lloyds LR 142. Consider the building contract retention money cases of *Re Tout & Finch Ltd* [1954] 1 All ER 127; *Re Arthur Sanders Ltd* (1981) 17 Build LR 125; *Gericevich & Contracting Pty Ltd v Sabemo (WA) Pty Ltd* (1984) 9 ACLR 452 (W Australia S Ct). See also the retention of title case *Clough Mill Ltd v Martin* [1984] 3 All ER 982, 988, CA.

It follows that the junior creditor's liability should be to pay over amounts up to the senior debt, and not all proceeds received on terms that any surplus is handed back.

Consequences of security

9–3   If the turnover does in law constitute security then the consequences listed below may ensue.

Registration Registration or filing requirements may be attracted. If the security is not duly perfected, then it is usually void on the insolvency of the junior creditor or void against attaching creditors. Because of doubts, sometimes the senior creditor registers in English-based jurisdictions as a precautionary measure. But in a particular case, a senior creditor may be prepared to take a view that the junior creditor is unlikely to become insolvent.

As mentioned, US law under the UCC does not recharacterise in Article 9 States.

English-based corporate registration systems commonly require registration of charges treated by a company over its "book debts": see s 396 of the Companies Act 1985 as amended by the Companies Act 1989 (amending sections not yet in force). If the trust is only over recoveries on liquidation of the debtor, the better view is that this contingent right to the proceeds of a liquidation dividend is not a "book debt" within these registration requirements but this is undecided. Book debts have been judicially defined as "debts arising in a business ... which ought to be entered in the company's books": per Lord Esher MR in *Official Receiver v Tailby* (1886) 18 QBD 25, 29, affirmed (1888) 13 AC 523. See also *Paul & Frank v Discount Bank (Overseas) Ltd* [1967] Ch. 348; *Watson v Parapara Coal Co Ltd* (1915) 17 CLR 791; *Re Stevens* (1883) WN 110; *Re Brightlife Ltd* [1986] 3 All ER 673. Consider whether an alternative registration head applies, e.g. a charge to secure an issue of debentures which may apply if the senior debt is evidenced by an issue of debt securities.

In **Ontario** an agreement to pay over proceeds received from the debtor would constitute a "transfer of an account" which would be subject to the Personal Property Security Act, 1989 (Ontario) and similar legislation in certain other provinces. Such a transfer would not be effective against a trustee in bankruptcy or assignee for the benefit of creditors of the junior creditor unless it had been perfected pursuant to the Act, usually by filing. The Act applies both to absolute assignments and to assignments as security.

Negative pledges The charge may conflict with negative pledges granted 9–4 by the junior creditor.

Regulatory prohibitions Creditors which are banks or other institutions (such as insurance companies) may be inhibited by law, official guidelines or internal policy from creating charges.

Secured creditor on insolvency The senior creditor would be a secured creditor on the *junior creditor's* insolvency and might therefore be excluded from proof or voting to the extent he is secured: see, e.g. r 488 of the British Insolvency Rules 1986. The same may apply on rehabilitation proceedings. Thus a secured creditor cannot vote in relation to a voluntary arrangement or an administration under the British Insolvency Act 1986: see rr 1.19(3)(b) and 2.24 of the Insolvency Rules 1986. But the senior creditor should not be excluded from voting and proof where the insolvency proceedings relate to the debtor, as opposed to the junior creditor, since the security is not given by the debtor.

9–5   **Bankruptcy freezes** The security may be subject to bankruptcy freezes on the enforcement of security in the event of the junior creditor's insolvency.

Other mortgage rules The security may be subject to other special restrictive mortgage laws protecting debtors, e.g. onerous enforcement remedies, formalties, limitations on the debt secured and so on.

Subordinations and set-off

Set-off defeats subordination

9–6   If a junior creditor can set off the junior debt against a debt owed by the junior creditor to the debtor, this will defeat the subordination: the junior creditor gets paid by his set-off. The same would apply where the debtor exercises the set-off. The question may arise (a) prior to insolvency, or (b) when either the debtor or the junior creditor becomes an insolvent.

Questions of set-off will often arise. For example, in the case of mezzanine finance for a leveraged bid, the junior creditors may be banks owing deposits to the borrower potentially eligible for set-off against the junior debt. In the case of insider subordinations a junior parent company may have trading relationships with its subsidiary giving rise to claims by the subsidiary against the parent. A junior creditor may attempt to evade the subordination by taking a deposit from the debtor eligible for set-off. Set-off is discussed elsewhere in this series on international financial law.

Contracts against solvent set-off

9–7   Under English law (and in most developed systems, it seems) an agreement by the debtor or the junior creditor not to exercise a set-off is effective as between themselves prior to the insolvency of either and overrides the policies of judicial economy requiring cross-claims to be litigated in the same proceedings. See, e.g. *Hong Kong and Shanghai Banking Corpn v Kloeckner & Co AG* [1990] 2 QB 514; *First National Bank of Chicago v Moorgate Properties Ltd, The Times*, October 25, 1975, CA; *Mottram Consultants v Bernard Sunley Ltd*, [1975] 2 Lloyds LR 197, HL. In other words sanctity of contract overtops the policy of the avoidance of multiplicity of proceedings. Accordingly both the debtor and the junior creditor should agree with the senior creditor not to raise set-offs which operate as a discharge of the junior debt except to the extent that the terms of the subordination permit the junior debt to be paid. Note that both parties should agree not to set off, since both may be debtor-creditors and generally each debtor-creditor has a reciprocal right of set-off.

In the case of a subordination trust, the common debtor could not set off, against the senior creditor's claim for the proceeds, a cross-claim owed by the junior creditor to the debtor if the debtor has agreed in the junior debt instrument not to raise set-offs against transferees. This has been established in numerous cases involving transferable debentures.

A solvent set-off may in any event be prevented by the terms of the subordination. Thus: **9–8**

(a) If the subordination postpones payment of the junior debt, a solvent set-off may be defeated by the fact that set-off requires both cross-claims to have matured due and payable: see Wood, *English & International Set-off* (1989) ("EISO") para 2–131 *et seq.*

(b) A solvent set-off may be prevented if the junior debt and the claim owed by the junior creditor to the debtor are not mutual as in the case of certain subordination trusts: see below.

(c) Usually a debtor on a negotiable instrument cannot set off, against the first payee of the instrument, a cross-claim owed by the payee to the debtor: see EISO (1989) para 12–68.

In an Alberta case a holder of subordinated notes was held disentitled to use the notes as a cross-claim for set-off on the ground that only the trustee of the notes could sue for them. This reasoning seems doubtful since the availability of set-off depends on beneficial ownership, not procedural ability to sue: EISO para 14–40. But the result of the decision was correct.

> In *Atlantic Acceptance Corpn Ltd v Burns & Dutton Construction (1962) Ltd* (1971) 1 WWR 84 (Alberta S Ct), a company as assignee of a debt owed by a debtor sued for the assigned debt. The debtor held subordinated notes of the assignee. By the terms of these notes, once an event of default had occurred (which it had), only the trustee for the noteholders could sue and there was a turnover of receipts to the holders of senior debt. *Held*: no set-off. The debtor did not have an enforceable claim which he could sue for. A better explanation would have been that the subordination, by establishing a subordination trust of the junior claim in favour of the senior creditors, destroyed mutuality between the debtor and the company.

A solvent set-off may impliedly be prohibited by the terms of the ranking of security if the junior creditor has agreed not to accept payment before the senior creditor. **9–9**

In *H Wilkins & Elkington Ltd v Milton* (1916) 32 TLR, H the holder of second mortgage debentures agreed with the issuing company that the second debentures would not be entitled to payment until the first debentures were redeemed. H appointed a receiver of the second debentures which accordingly became due. A debt from H to the company on a bill of exchange became due the following day. On that day a receiver (apparently at the request of the first debenture-holders) was appointed by the court. *Held*: H could not set off the second debenture debt against the bill of exchange debt. H had agreed that the second debentures were to be postponed to the first debenture and the effect of allowing the set-off would be to give the second debentureholder H preference to the first debentures contrary to the agreement.

But the mere fact that a junior creditor's security is expressed to rank after the senior security (as opposed to the debt itself) may not amount to an agreement not to set off.

In *Nelson & Co Ltd v Faber & Co* [1903] 2 KB 367, Joyce J said at 377:

"In my view, it is immaterial that the debentures held by the defendants are expressed to be subsequent to the existing issue of prior debentures. This only had reference to the order of priority of the debentures considered as charges, and does not preclude the defendants from obtaining payment of their debentures in cash or by setting off the amount."

Insolvency set-off

9–10   Many developed commercial jurisdictions allow insolvency set-off, including British Commonwealth countries, the United States, Scandinavia, Germany, Switzerland, the Netherlands, Italy, Japan, South Korea, Thailand and many others. Exceptions are many Franco-Latin states such as France, Belgium, Luxembourg, Spain, Greece and many Latin American countries. In the refusing states, there is normally no risk of a desubordination on insolvency because insolvency set-off is disallowed.

In England and many other common law jurisdictions basing their insolvency law on the English model (such as Australia, New Zealand, Bermuda, Hong Kong and Singapore), insolvency set-off is mandatory and it is not possible to contract out. Insolvency set-off is probably not mandatory in Canada or under s 553 of the US Bankruptcy Code of 1978 – although there are likely to be variations in state law – or in Germany, Italy, the Netherlands or Sweden.

9–11   Whether or not the set-off is mandatory, a subordination trust of the entire junior claim should destroy the mutuality necessary for insolvency set-off between the junior debt and another debt owed by the junior creditor to the debtor. Under the doctrine of set-off mutuality, one person's money must not be used to pay another's debt. In the result, there must be only two debtor-creditors, each of whom is beneficial owner of the claim owed to him (regardless of who is the titular or nominal owner and regardless of who has the procedural right to sue) and each must be personally liable for the debt owed by him.

This ought to be the position even if the trust is over liquidation dividends only or proceeds only, as opposed to the junior debt itself. The set-off would lead to the junior creditor using the senior creditor's ultimate asset (the proceeds of the junior debt) to pay the junior creditor's debt (his liability to the debtor) contrary to the principle on which mutuality is based.

If the junior debt is treated as a contingent debt and the debtor is insol- **9–12** vent, the amount of the junior debt eligible for insolvency set-off will be the valued amount of the contingent junior debt: EISO para 7–71 *et seq.* Hence if the debtor is hopelessly insolvent and there would be no dividend on the junior debt, the junior creditor has no provable claim and hence nothing to set off. Similar principles should apply if the junior creditor is insolvent.

As to the set-off of contingencies owing to, rather than by, a debtor, see EISO para 10–56 *et seq.*

Junior creditor to pay amounts equal to set-offs

Although set-off is usually either contractually stopped or unavailable, it is **9–13** desirable (to cover the odd case) that the junior creditor should agree to pay the senior creditor amounts equal to any discharge of the junior debt by reason of a set-off. The weaknesses of the claim are: (a) the junior creditor's liability will be a debt claim and hence irrecoverable in full if the junior creditor is insolvent; and (b) if there are numerous or anonymous junior creditors, as in the case of subordinated bond issues, the senior creditors may face practical difficulties in claiming from the junior creditors.

CHAPTER 10

TERMS OF SUBORDINATION AGREEMENTS

Documents

10–1 The terms of the subordination may be contained in:

- the junior debt instrument between the debtor and the junior creditor, such as a bearer bond and trust deed;

- an intercreditor agreement between the debtor, the junior creditor and the senior creditor.

It is usually useful for a trustee to be appointed in the case of junior debt issues and in the case of secured debt: para 11–12 *et seq.*

For a summary of the usual undertakings of junior debtor and creditor, see the forms in the Appendix.

Springing subordinations and payment freezes

10–2 As mentioned, a subordination may be a complete subordination in the sense that the junior creditor may not receive or retain any payments on the junior debt so long as the senior debt is outstanding, or it may be a springing (or inchoate) subordination in which event the junior creditor may receive payments until certain events happen. The object is to block payments on the junior debt when an event occurs which indicates that the senior debt is at risk because insolvency is looming.

In the case of turnover subordinations, the block on payments of the junior debt only applies prior to insolvency proceedings against the debtor. However once the debtor becomes subject to insolvency proceedings, payments on the junior debt are not merely liberated but must compulsorily be claimed so that they can be turned over to the senior creditor who thereby has the benefit of the double dividend. In summary, therefore, prior to insolvency proceedings payments of the junior debt are blocked on the prescribed events. After insolvency proceedings, payments are unblocked, must be claimed and must be turned over.

Default interest may be expressed to run on junior debt which is frozen but overdue.

Payment freezes: insider subordinations Where an insider of the debtor, such as a parent, affiliate, shareholder or officer, is subordinated to bank loans, the subordination is often complete and the junior creditor has no rights to any payment so long as the senior debt is outstanding. 10–3

The objects are (a) to ensure that the senior creditor's loans are used in the borrower's business and not to repay the insider's debt, (b) to ensure that undue strain is not put on the borrower's resources in having to repay both junior and senior debt, and to control the possible temptation of insiders to engineer a payment before the springing event: insiders who also manage the borrower are likely to have advance knowledge of the borrower's financial deterioration and of a looming springing event. In effect, the junior debt is treated as equity and payments are allowed only to the extent dividends could be paid or equity redeemed.

Thus, the junior creditor may be permitted to recover if, say, a specified financial test is met by the debtor indicating a margin of solvency, or if at the time of payment an auditor's certificate shows that the debtor is solvent and would be solvent after the payment, or if the debtor could pay dividends up to that amount.

Salaries and fringe benefits, reasonable arms-length payment for services or supplies provided by the junior creditor or rent payable to the junior creditor may be liberated until an event of default on the ground that they are proper payments for services or supplies, and not the subordinated "equity".

Payment freezes: junior bond issues At the other extreme are subordinations which spring only on bankruptcy of the debtor. These springing subordinations are typical of subordinated bond issues intended to qualify as capital for capital adequacy purposes. The bondholders may receive principal and interest until the commencement of insolvency proceedings. Their remedies for default are limited to petitioning for insolvency. 10–4

Payment freezes: mezzanine debt The above extremes are not usually appropriate in leveraged finance for acquisitions, management buy-outs and other change of control financings comprising layers of senior and junior debt: in the first place the junior lenders commonly lend short-term in order to finance the transaction and the junior debt is not intended as part of the borrower's long-term capital structure; secondly, the junior creditors are often institutional investors or banks who wish to be paid current principal and interest so long as the debtor is in good financial health: they are prepared only to invest in performing assets. 10–5

It is usually agreed that the junior creditor may be paid scheduled payments (not voluntary prepayments, and usually staggered so as to fall due after payments on the senior debt) until a prescribed event occurs which unleashes the catch on the spring. The senior creditor must aim to freeze the junior debt before it is too late. The junior creditor will wish to ensure that payment of the junior debt is not frozen for trivial defaults.

10–6   Commonly payments on the junior debt are frozen on (a) a payment default on the senior debt which blocks payments on the junior debt (because the junior creditors should never be paid while the senior debt is due but unpaid); (b) insolvency events, such as liquidation, which always block payments since subordinations always bite on insolvency; (c) an acceleration by the junior or senior creditors; and (d) sometimes any other event of default or pending event of default in relation to senior or junior debt (which are usually both cross-defaulted so that an event of default in one is an event of default in the other).

Some, mainly US issues, sought to limit the period of the payment freeze on the junior debt to, say 90 to 360 days – the "fish-or-cut-bait" period – after the freezing event. The object was to exclude freezes for trivial defaults and to prevent the suspension from going on indefinitely. In that period the senior creditors must either waive the default (e.g. a restructuring) or accelerate and enforce, thereby crystallizing the freeze once and for all, or negotiate an extension of the freeze period with the junior creditors.

Restrictions on rights of junior creditor

10–7   **Generally** An important question from the point of view of the senior creditor is the extent to which he has freedom of action in the management of the senior debt, particularly if the debtor gets into financial difficulties, and the extent of the junior creditor's ability to rock the boat, e.g. by precipitating a liquidation of the debtor at an inopportune time. If the junior creditor has too much power to veto a work-out of the debtor sponsored by the senior creditor or can force the senior creditor into springing the subordination by liquidating the debtor, the junior creditor might harass the senior creditor into paying out the junior creditor and thereby, commercially, to turn the subordination upside down. In change of control financings, sharks or spoilers might buy up the junior debt specifically with a view to extracting more money from the company debtor or senior creditors under threat of exploding the transaction, liquidating the debtor or vetoing routine changes to the financing agreements to accommodate sensible changes of plan.

The main points to be considered are :

– the advance of new money by the senior creditor;

– variations of the senior debt;

– the borrower's covenants in the junior credit agreement;

– events of default and acceleration rights in the junior credit agreement and other remedies of the junior creditor.

The scope of the restrictions on the rights of the junior creditor depend fundamentally on the particular transaction, e.g. whether the junior debt is insider debt equivalent to equity, or is a junior bond issue or is mezzanine finance provided by an institution.

The scope of the protections is also influenced by the ability of the senior creditors to negotiate with the junior creditors if there is a downturn in the debtor's business. It is, for example, easier to negotiate with junior institutional lenders than multitudinous bondholders.

Advance of prior-ranking new money by senior creditor If the debtor gets   10–8
into financial difficulties, new money for working capital will almost invariably be required and the question will be whether new money lent by the senior creditor will rank ahead of the junior debt. The senior creditors ought to be able to tide the debtor over a difficult patch or to finance unexpected cash-flow deficits without a veto from the junior creditors.

In insider subordinations, the senior creditor should have freedom to add on as much senior debt as he wishes. If the insider controls the debtor, he can in any event control whether the debtor will increase senior borrowings from the senior creditor.

In junior bond issues subordinated to all other debt, including future debt, the question does not arise and there is no limit on the amount of future senior debt.

In purchase price financings, such as leveraged bids, many compromises are possible, e.g. the senior debt may be increased by a specified amount over the originally contemplated commitments in the senior credit agreement less any actual repayments of the senior debt.

The senior creditors ought also to be entitled to defer payments of the senior debt and to increase the interest rate without prejudicing the subordination, and the definition of senior debt should cover refinancings or refundings of the senior debt in order to facilitate restructurings and to enable the senior creditors to arrange take-out finance.

It is not usual to provide that, if the senior creditors extend a payment date, the junior creditors will similarly extend. Nor is it usual to establish that if the senior creditors convert into equity, e.g. on a work-out, the junior creditors must convert into a lower-ranking class of equity. The reason is that it is too complicated to legislate in advance and too difficult to impose those requirements ahead of the actual facts: one has to leave them to work-out negotiations or to the operation of a rehabilitation plan in bankruptcy proceedings.

10–9 **Covenants in junior debt agreement** The covenants by the debtor in the junior debt agreement have three main repercussions:

- Breach generally entitles the junior creditor to refuse to lend further advances under a conditions precedent clause in the junior credit agreement, thereby removing the expected cushion and turnover of proceeds to the senior creditor. Because of this and other factors, in mezzanine finance the junior loans should be advanced at the outset of the transaction or pro rata with the senior loans, and should not be revolving.

- Breach will usually be an event of default empowering the junior creditor to accelerate. This is discussed below.

- The junior creditor can enjoin the debtor or the senior creditor from entering into a transaction, as on a work-out, which infringes a covenant. Any violation resulting from a transaction with the senior creditor may render the senior creditor liable to the junior debtor for the tort of inducing a breach of contract. In practice the ability of the junior creditor to enjoin a transaction is a more powerful weapon than the sanction of acceleration. This is because an acceleration is adverse to the junior creditor since it is likely to put the debtor out of business (by virtue of fraudulent trading rules) and will crystallise the subordination on the resulting insolvency or under an express term freezing junior payments on an acceleration by the junior creditor. A veto does not of itself bring about this cataclysm.

10–10 In mezzanine finance, junior institutional lenders seek greater covenant protection than is appropriate for insider subordinations and junior bond issues. The object of the senior creditor is to denude the junior creditors of as much as possible of their covenant protection so as to prevent the junior creditors holding the senior creditors to ransom. The junior creditors on the other hand will seek to protect their debt by normal credit covenants, so that they can force a restructuring before the debtor's financial condition deteriorates so as to prejudice the junior debt. The presence of any significant covenants in the junior debt instrument is likely to seriously hamper work-out negotiations.

Nobody is likely to object to routine covenants of the debtor in the junior credit agreement, such as the provision of financial information and compliance certificates, the maintenance of consents for the finance, the maintenance of corporate existence and of insurances, the prompt payment of taxes, a restriction on dividends and a prohibition on mergers or consolidations.

From the point of view of the senior creditors, the more sensitive coven-   **10–11**
ants in the junior debt instrument for mezzanine finance include:

- **Negative pledge** A negative pledge prohibits the grant of security by the debtor. Normally the senior creditors resist a negative pledge in the junior debt instrument. But if such a clause is included, the debtor may be entitled to secure the senior debt since the junior creditor is benefited, or if the junior creditor is secured on the same assets in a junior position and on the basis that the rights of the junior creditor are restricted along the lines indicated in chapter 11. Many work-outs involve the grant of security.

- **Restriction on substantial disposals** Senior creditors often resist an anti-disposal covenant in the junior debt instrument. Work-outs or adverse conditions may necessitate a disposal programme. Further, senior bank loans for leveraged bids are often made in the expectation of significant disposals of assets of the acquired company in order to repay the senior loans quickly. The senior creditors sometimes have power to consent to disposals by the debtor (and to override any contrary covenants in the junior credit agreement) if the disposal is at fair value and the proceeds are applied in reducing the senior debt.

- **Restriction on changes in business** A period of difficulty may necessitate a slimming down of the debtor's lines of business.

- **Borrowing limits and financial ratios** These may restrict new money: see para 10–8. Borrowings in excess of the limit are often allowed if they are used to repay the senior debt within a specified period.

As a matter of drafting, one technique is to permit extensive covenants in the junior credit agreement and to provide in an intercreditor agreement that the senior creditors can compel the junior creditors to waive their covenants except for those which are to be entrenched. This technique maintains the junior covenants if the senior debt should be paid off leaving the junior debt intact.

In **insider subordinations**, there are either negligible covenants in the   **10–12**
junior debt instrument (since the insiders commonly control the debtor) or, in the rare case that there are any, the senior creditor should have complete freedom to override the debtor's covenants given to the junior debtor.

In **junior eurobond issues**, particularly debt issues by banks, the bond-holders' covenant protection is virtually non-existent. They are treated almost as preferred equity, though without a vote or the ability to participate in profits or capital appreciations.

Remedies of junior creditor generally

10–13   The main remedies of the junior creditor on an event of default are to accelerate the junior debt, to enforce a judgment by execution against assets of the debtor, and to initiate insolvency proceedings. The exercise of any of these remedies could prejudice the senior creditor's efforts to see the debtor through a downturn in its fortunes if there is a light at the end of the tunnel. One argument is that a junior creditor is likely to be quicker to exercise remedies to prevent further erosion of the junior debt by further trading at a loss. The contrary, and more convincing, argument is that junior creditors are most unlikely to enforce when the inevitable result is that they will be subordinated and that they are more likely to favour a restructuring. The play of the bargaining chip in the form of an ability to bring the house down may result in a Pyrrhic victory indeed.

In any event, in insider subordinations, the junior creditor is generally barred from exercising any of these remedies.

In junior bond issues, the events of default are commonly very light and in some extreme forms (particularly junior bond issues by banks qualifying as capital for capital adequacy purposes) the remedies of the junior bondholders are limited to liquidating the debtor – a nuclear bomb they are not likely to drop if the only result is that they are so deeply subordinated to all other creditors that they will receive nothing.

Controls on the junior creditor's remedies in mezzanine finance can be more complicated.

10–14   Sometimes, the mezzanine creditor's events of default are emasculated by the usual techniques of long grace periods, materiality tests, exclusion of subsidiaries other than major subsidiaries, high thresholds and high acceleration majorities. There can be much discussion about the triggering of the mutual cross-defaults which give each set of creditors the right to accelerate. Sometimes non-payment of junior interest is excluded as a default if the debtor has insufficient net earnings and is not paying dividends. But these will not normally be enough to neuter the events of default altogether and to prevent fragility. There may also be a "poison pill" (change of control of the debtor) or an event of default if the junior issue or the debtor is downgraded by a rating agency.

Sometimes, the junior acceleration and enforcement rights are stayed during a standstill period to give the senior creditors time to negotiate a cure. But usually junior creditors are permitted to petition for a reorganisation or a liquidation if the debtor is insolvent. In that event the junior creditors stand to lose the most and hence are more likely to support a rehabilitation plan.

Variations of junior debt and desubordinations

In the case of subordinations where the senior creditor is a party, the debtor   **10–15**
and the junior creditor will typically agree with the senior creditor in an intercreditor agreement not to amend key provisions in the junior credit agreement, including the definition of junior debt; the subordination clauses; the amount and time of payment of principal and interest of the junior debt (so as, e.g. to ensure that senior debt matures before the junior debt if the junior payments are allowed prior to an event of default); the covenants, events of default and acceleration rights (including majorities) in the junior debt instrument (so that the junior creditors do not enhance their ability to bring the house down); and the currency of the junior debt.

Where the senior creditors are not parties to an intercreditor agreement with the junior creditors, as in the case of subordinated bond issues, the senior creditors are vulnerable if the debtor and the junior creditor can, between themselves, agree to de-subordinate the junior debt without the consent of the senior creditor.

The senior creditor could object to a de-subordination only if some obligation by the junior creditor in favour of the senior creditor not to do so can be established.

The answer to this depends on the local efficiency of contracts conferring benefits – whether by way of a trust of proceeds or a simple contract – upon strangers, i.e. the law of gifts, third party beneficiary contracts, collateral warranties inviting reliance, and promissory estoppel, e.g. because the debtor recorded the subordination in its accounts and hence invited reliance. Probably English law is the most conservative, with the Franco-Latin systems being much more accommodating and with the United States in an intermediate position. But even in English-based systems, the hostility to the third party beneficiary contract has suffered defeats, e.g. the New Zealand Contracts (Privity) Act 1982. In England a deed poll (just an ordinary deed) expressed to be in favour of the senior creditors is sufficient to give them the benefit of the contract, even though they have not signed and even though they are not specifically named, provided the class intended to be benefited can be identified.

A subordination trust will be alterable without the senior creditor's   **10–16**
consent if the trust deed expressly allows alterations, e.g. by bondholder majorities. The senior creditor contracts on the basis of the power of alter-

ation. If the senior creditor wishes to inflict a sanction against desubordination, he should require the debtor in the senior credit agreement to agree not to desubordinate.

If there is a provision in the subordination agreement whereby the junior creditor offers to maintain the subordination on the basis that the senior creditor can accept the offer by lending senior debt to the debtor, the senior creditor may become a party to the contract by accepting the offer by conduct without notifying the acceptance on the basis of the engaging case of *Carlill v Carbolic Smoke Ball Co* [1893] 1 QB 256.

10–17 Some stand-alone subordination agreements provide:

> "The junior creditor declares that this subordination is an inducement and consideration to each senior creditor to give or continue credit to the debtor or to acquire senior debt. The senior creditor may accept the benefit of this subordination by giving or continuing credit to the debtor or acquiring senior debt. The junior creditor waives reliance and notice of acceptance."

Language similar to this was held in a US decision to constitute a waiver by the junior creditor of the defence of reliance: *Re Discon Corp*, 346 F Supp 839 (SD Fla 1971).

Capital adequacy subordinations sometime provide that the junior creditor may not de-subordinate without the consent of the regulatory authority. Senior creditors rely on this practical protection.

Transfers of junior debt and priorities

10–18 If a junior creditor transfers his debt, is there a risk that the assignee will take free of the subordination?

Simple debts In the case of subordination trusts, the junior creditor might create a subordination trust of proceeds of the same debt in favour of another creditor or might transfer the junior debt without disclosing to the assignee the presence of the intercreditor agreement under which the junior creditor agrees to transfer the proceeds of the debt to the senior creditor.

Most legal systems give effect to prohibitions on assignments of debts. An intercreditor agreement may restrict the various potential forms of disposal as follows:

> "So long as any senior debt is outstanding, the junior creditor will not:
>
> (a) create or permit to subsist any security in favour of any person over any of the junior debt or its proceeds or any interest in the junior debt or its proceeds;

(b) assign or otherwise dispose of any of the junior debt or its proceeds or any interest in the junior debt or its proceeds to any person;

(c) transfer by novation any of its rights or obligations in respect of the junior debt to any person; or

(d) subordinate any of the junior debt or its proceeds to any other person,

unless in each case that person agrees with the senior creditor that he is bound by all the terms of this subordination in manner satisfactory to the senior creditor or by the execution of an accession agreement in the form set out in the schedule hereto."

Of course junior debt is often intended to be fully marketable, such as subordinated bond issues and institutional loans for change of control transactions.

If there is no prohibition, and the junior creditor assigns, the English **10–19** priorities between assignees depend primarily on who is the first to give notice to the debtor: *E Pfeiffer Weinkellerei-Weinenkauf GmbH & Co v Arbuthnot Factors Ltd* [1988] 1 WLR 150. Whether notice to the debtor of an assignment of proceeds has the same effect as notice of an assignment of the debt itself is unclear. The sensible solution is that the senior creditor ought to be able to protect his priority by notice to the debtor because an assignment of proceeds carries with it the entire commercial value of the claim and is therefore substantially the same as a full assignment. If this is incorrect (and there is much case law on the inefficiency of notice of assignment of future claims), there would seem to be no fool-proof method of protecting the priority unless the assignee can be put on notice of the subordination.

If the junior creditor receives the proceeds which he is to hold on trust but then diverts the proceeds, the senior creditor has a right to trace as a proprietary claim. The right to trace is lost if, e.g. the proceeds are paid into an overdrawn account of the junior creditor at a bank which does not know that the moneys are trust moneys at the time of payment and has given value before notice: *Thomson v Clydesdale Bank Ltd* [1893] AC 282, HL.

If the subordination is contractual and is contained in a separate agreement from the junior debt, whether the assignee takes free of the subordination will presumably depend on cases submitting assignees to the existing relationship beween assignor and debtor. In English parlance, assignees take subject to "equities".

In *Mangles v Dixon* [1852] 3 HLC 702, a shipowner assigned a charter to a bank without disclosing a separate agreement reducing the charter-hire by half. *Held*: the bank as assignee was subject to the undisclosed separate agreement, in the absence of collusion by the charterer.

10–20   **Negotiable instruments** If the junior debt is evidenced by a negotiable instrument not recording the subordination, then a holder in due course of the negotiable instrument should take free of the subordination on usual principles of negotiability. Whether under English law an express subordination provision in a promissory note itself would destroy its strict negotiability should depend upon the terms of the subordination, e.g. as to whether the note is thereby made conditional or uncertain in amount. But there ought to be no objection to referring to the subordination effected by the intercreditor agreement on the face of the instrument so as to notify it to holders provided that this does not qualify the obligation to pay: consider the Bills of Exchange Act 1882 s 3(3). Subordination of a bearer bond (either directly or by virtue of a trust deed for bondholders) does not destroy negotiability because negotiability of bearer bonds is sanctioned by commercial usage which (unlike bills of exchange legislation) does not insist on unconditionality. The bond is negotiable if the market treats it as negotiable: *London Joint Stock Bank v Simmons* [1892] AC 201.

In the United States, a holder of negotiable instrument takes subject to a subordination stated on the instrument: see UCC ss 3–302 and 3–306.

10–21   The senior creditor should, if possible, take possession of any negotiable instruments evidencing the junior debt. The agreement may provide that if any junior debt is subsequently evidenced by a negotiable instrument, the instrument will be deposited with the senior creditor.

A purchaser of a subordinated debenture or negotiable bond will plainly be on notice of a subordination noted on the instrument. In the United States, s 202(1) of the UCC will render a purchase of an investment security subject to a subordination noted on or referred to in the security.

One purpose of requiring assignees of the junior debt to agree the subordination is to bind the assignees to positive covenants in the subordination agreement and to establish privity between assignees and the senior creditor, e.g. in relation to covenants to pay amounts equal to set-offs realised by the junior creditor and covenants not to accelerate or vary the junior debt. Further, the transferring junior creditor will wish to be released from liability to the senior creditor for breaches by the assignee. An intercreditor agreement can set up a procedure for novations of senior and junior debt to incoming lenders.

Forms of accession agreement can provide for the accession of new debtors, e.g. new subsidiaries.

Extra default events in senior credit agreement

A number of additional events of default may be appropriate in the senior   **10–22**
credit agreement. These include:

— non-compliance by the junior creditor or the debtor with the terms of
   the subordination agreement;

— breach of representation or warranty by the junior creditor or the debtor
   in the subordination agreement;

— inefficacy or termination of the subordination agreement for any reason;

— occurrence of an event of default under any agreement evidencing junior
   debt and entitling the junior creditor to accelerate the junior debt;

— occurrence of any other event allowing premature acceleration of the
   junior debt, e.g. under an illegality clause.

The occurrence of one of these defaults should normally by the terms of
the subordination agreement freeze any further permitted payments by the
debtor to the junior creditor, either permanently until cured or during a payment freeze period: para 10–13 *et seq.*

Protective clauses: the guarantee analogy

Turnover subordinations and guarantees

A turnover subordination is similar in substance to collateral security   **10–23**
granted by the junior creditor over the junior debt to secure the senior debt.
Because the junior creditors pays the debt owed by the debtor to the senior
creditor, it is likely that the technicalities of guarantee law (as applied to collateral security) will be attracted to some turnover subordinations. This
should be so even though a turnover subordination is not characterised as a
security interest, but rather as an absolute transfer. The reason that the
guarantee analogy seems broadly appropriate is that both guarantees and
turnover subordinations involve a situation where one person (the guarantor or junior creditor) is obliged to pay a debtor's debt owed to another (the
beneficiary of the guarantee or the senior creditor) and the law is protective
of those in that position.

Some of the principles set out in this section are unlikely to apply to
contractual subordinations to all debt but should apply only to turnover
subordinations.

Subrogation by junior creditor

10–24   A junior creditor who has turned over dividends to a senior creditor probably has a right of subrogation to the senior debt and all securities for the senior debt.

This flows from the general rule that if one person at the request of a debtor pays the debtor's debt owed to a third party creditor then the payer is entitled to be subrogated to the creditor who has been paid and for this purpose the creditor's claim is not deemed to be extinguished. The classic examples are guarantees and liability insurance. Because in effect a turnover subordination amounts to the junior creditor using his asset to pay the senior creditor, the same doctrine of subrogation should apply.

Subrogation by law is somewhat technical (especially when the debtor did not request that his debt be paid by a third party) and hence a subordination agreement should confirm the position by providing that the junior creditor is entitled to be subrogated to the senior creditor's claim and any guarantees or security for the claim if and when the senior debt has been paid in full. The doctrine of subrogation in relation to both guarantee and insurance law generally requires that the guarantor or insurer must have paid the claim in full before he is entitled to be subrogated to the creditor paid. In order to avoid any question of whether the junior creditor can come alongside the senior creditor on the senior creditor's security after a partial payment only (or after a full turnover of the junior debt which is insufficient to pay the senior debt), the subordination agreement should expressly exclude the junior creditor's right to subrogation until the senior debt has been paid in full. A general non-competition clause is desirable, e.g. the junior creditor agrees that he will not claim subrogation, contribution or indemnity or otherwise claim against a debtor by virtue of a turnover if this could result in the junior creditor claiming in competition with the senior creditor.

Suspense account

10–25   If the turnover by the junior creditor is insufficient to pay the senior debt, the senior creditor should be entitled to place the turnover amounts on suspense account and not apply them towards the reduction of the senior debt. In this way the senior creditor maximises his proof against the debtor on an insolvency. The suspension should naturally terminate once the senior creditor has received proceeds from whatever source equal to the senior debt. The validity of suspense accounts is well documented in English case law on guarantees, e.g. *Commercial Bank of Australia v Wilson* [1893] AC 181, PC.

Waiver of defences clause

A "waiver of defences" clause adapted from guarantees should normally be   **10–26**
included in turnover subordination agreements, except subordinations to all
other debt.

Under such a clause, the junior creditor agrees that the subordination and
his obligations under the subordination are not to be affected by, for
example, waivers granted to or compositions with the debtor or any other
person, variations of the senior debt or of any security or guarantees for the
senior debt, or releases or non-perfection of any security or guarantees for
the senior debt.

Under guarantee law, waivers in relation to or variations of the guaranteed claim release the guarantor unless he agrees to them. The same might
apply to variations of the senior debt, such as extensions of the due date for
payment for it might be said that the junior creditor's position is prejudiced
or that he agreed to be subordinated only to the specified senior debt and
not some varied senior debt.

Releases of security or guarantees for the senior debt by the senior credi-   **10–27**
tor may allow the junior creditor to treat his obligation to turn over proceeds under the subordination as diminished to the extent that the junior
creditor's rights to the security on subrogation are thereby lost to him.
Further, the junior creditor's risk of loss by virtue of his obligation to turn
over recoveries is increased if the senior creditor diminishes his own potential recoveries. These principles are well established in guarantee law.

In the case of contractual subordinations, the question of whether variations of the senior debt release the junior creditor should primarily depend
upon whether the junior creditor agreed to be subordinated only to some
specific senior debt and not a varied senior debt. Since a contractual junior
creditor should not have a right of subrogation, releases of security and the
like by a senior creditor should not normally weaken the subordination.

The waivers should not be necessary in subordinations to all present and
future debt of all other creditors since the consent to subordination to all
creditors ought to carry with it a consent to variations and releases by a
particular senior creditor.

Contribution between junior creditors

If there are two equal junior issues constituted by a turnover subordination   **10–28**
and one of the junior creditors turns over dividends to the senior creditor
but the other does not, then the paying junior creditor should as a matter of

law have a right of contribution against the other junior creditor to the extent the paying junior creditor has paid more than his share.

The junior creditor should be prohibited from claiming contribution from another junior creditor in competition with any claim by the senior creditor against the contributing junior creditor.

Some junior issues state that a junior creditor is obliged to turn over only its own proportion of the senior debt so as to avoid one set of junior creditors being obliged to sue the other. This is because contribution actions against anonymous bondholders may be impractical. An analogy is to be found in rateable proportion clauses in insurance contracts.

In contractual non-turnover subordinations, no junior creditor should be liable to contribute to another because no junior creditor is obliged to pay a senior creditor.

Duration of subordination

10–29   In appropriate cases a subordination agreement should provide that the subordination is a continuing subordination and applies to the ultimate balance of the senior debt, notwithstanding any intermediate payment in whole or in part of the senior debt.

Where the senior debt is revolving, such as fluctuating debit balances on bank current account, then, by analogy with guarantee law and on the basis of the rule in *Clayton's Case*, the subordination of junior debt may cease as soon as the senior debt is reduced to zero even though subsequently the senior debt springs up again by new advances.

10–30   Where the junior creditor subordinates all present and future debt owing to him to all present and future debt owing to a particular senior creditor, such as a bank, consideration should be given as to whether there should be some provision for termination of the subordination by the junior creditor as regards senior debt incurred after notice of termination lest the courts imply that the junior creditor has the right to cancel the subordination on reasonable notice. A termination of the subordination could effectively deter the senior creditor from making new advances and hence restrict the senior creditor's ability to finance a work-out. In an appropriate case it should be an event of default in any senior debt instrument that a termination of the subordination is to entitle the senior creditor to accelerate the senior debt concerned.

It should not be necessary in bond issues which are subordinated to all other present and future debt to provide that the subordination is continuing or to include provisions for termination, since the subordination avails all senior debt so long as the junior bond is outstanding.

Exhaustion of recourse by senior creditor

A subordination agreement may provide that the senior creditor is not **10–31** obliged to exhaust recourse against securities or guarantors or the debtor before claiming the benefit of the turnover of proceeds under the subordination. This is probably the law in any event.

Senior debt non-provable

The subordination agreement may provide that the junior creditor is obliged **10–32** to turn over recoveries on the junior debt even though the senior debt is invalid, unenforceable or non-provable and even though the senior creditor has agreed to a composition reducing or renouncing the senior debt, as if there were no such defect.

In principle there is no objection to such a term and indeed many guarantees validly provide that the guarantor must pay the principal creditor even if the principal creditor is unable to claim from the principal debtor, as where the guaranteed debt turns out to be ultra vires.

A disadvantage for a junior creditor is that, having turned over proceeds to pay the invalid or non-allowable senior claim, the junior creditor has nothing to be subrogated to.

Under the insolvency laws of many countries post-insolvency interest is not recoverable by a creditor. In three US cases the courts have held that a senior creditor could not claim a turnover of dividends by the junior debtor to cover post-insolvency interest on the senior debt unless the subordination agreement expressly so provided: *Re Kingsboro Mortgage Corp*, 541 F 2d 400 (2d Cir 1975); *Re Time Sales Finance Corp*, 491 F 2d 841 (3d Cir 1974); *Re King Resources Co*, 385 F Supp 1269 (D Colo 1974).

Return of preferential payment of senior debt

It should be made clear that if the debtor makes a payment of the senior **10–33** debt which the senior creditor must subsequently return as a preferential payment or for any other reason, the junior debt continues to be subordinated to the new senior debt when it springs up again.

A similar situation might arise if the senior creditor is a trustee of another debt issue and must disgorge a payment on the private senior debt on the ground that the senior creditor acted in conflict of interest in recovering its own private debt ahead of the claims of the creditors for whom the senior creditor is a trustee. The junior debt should be expressed to remain junior to the senior debt which is reinstated after the disgorgement.

Appropriation of payments

10–34 A clause should provide that the senior creditor may appropriate receipts and apply the proceeds of security towards a debt owed to the senior creditor other than the senior debt. This is to negative the possibility, that, where a senior creditor receives a payment from the debtor which he could appropriate either to the senior debt or to some other debt, the law might imply that he must appropriate first to the senior debt so as to exonerate the junior creditor as "guarantor" of the senior debt.

A similar possibility might apply if the senior creditor has general security which he could apply either to the senior debt or some other debt. If the senior creditor can apply the security proceeds to his other debt, he maximises his recoveries.

CHAPTER 11

SECURED SUBORDINATED DEBT; TRUSTEES

Secured senior and junior debt

Generally

If both the senior and the junior debt are secured, the subordination of the   **11–1**
junior creditor is effectively achieved by the junior priority of his security.
Subordination of the debt as well as the security remains necessary since, if
the security is insufficient, both claims would be unsecured and would rank
equally on the bankruptcy of the debtor unless the junior creditor had
agreed to be subordinated. Further, the security for the senior debt may turn
out to be invalid.

   In a US case the court forced a subordinating secured lender to remain
subordinated where the senior security failed for lack of perfection. The
court inferred an intention from the priority agreement that the debt was
subordinated as well as the security: *General Electric Credit Corp v Penn-
sylvania Bank & Trust Co*, 11 UCC Rep 858 (Pa 1972).

   In any event an intercreditor agreement is highly desirable to regulate the
rights of the creditors as secured creditors in order to protect the senior
creditor.

Variation of law of priorities

In the absence of a mandatory statute, secured creditors can normally agree   **11–2**
between themselves to vary the priorities between successive security interests which would otherwise apply, e.g. the first in time rule, or the rule that
the first to get the legal (namely, the best) title for value without notice ranks
ahead. There is much English case law on conduct by a mortgagee leading to
a loss of a priority he would otherwise have, e.g. if he leaves the title deeds
with the mortgagor. If a mortgagee can lose priority by conduct, he can lose
it by agreement.

   Where a registration statute provides that the securities rank according to

---

the order of registration – particularly registration regimes for assets (as opposed to registration by mortgagor) such as those applicable to land, ships and aircraft – then register the senior security first and then the junior, or vest the security in a common trustee. If neither route is possible, and the statute is mandatory, this should normally affect third parties only and not a different ranking agreed between mortgagees.

11–3   Section 9–316 of the UCC comes to the rescue in relation to personal property security interests by providing that nothing in Article 9 "prevents subordination by agreement by any person entitled to priority". The re-ordering of priorities will be upheld on a US bankruptcy. Section 510(c) of the Bankruptcy Code of 1978 provides that, "a subordination agreement is enforceable in a case under this title to the same extent that such agreement is enforceable under applicable non-bankruptcy law". This should apply to the subordination of security as well as to unsecured debts. In Germany, the ranking of land mortgages may be changed and registered pursuant to BGB s 880.

In the case of security over receivables, insurance or other intangibles, notices and debtor (or insurer) acknowledgements should reflect the agreed ranking.

It appears to be a general rule in the developed jurisdictions that the ranking can be altered by agreement although generally this does not affect third parties. The junior secured creditor can usually enforce his rights independently but can waive enforcement in favour of the senior creditor. This appears to be the position, for example, in Belgium, Finland, France, Greece, Italy, Luxembourg, the Netherlands and Sweden.

> In *Cheah v Equiticorp Finance Group Ltd* [1991] 4 All ER 989, PC, the Privy Council decided on appeal from New Zealand that mortgagees of shares could change their priorities without the consent of the mortgagor: the mortgagor had to pay all his secured liabilities and was not affected by ranking.

Common trustee

11–4   The security may be given to each creditor separately or ideally granted to a common trustee for both sets of creditors: para 11–12 *et seq.*

Restrictions on rights of junior secured creditor generally

11–5   An intercreditor agreement between the secured creditors should regulate the matters discussed in chapter 10 such as permission for the senior creditor to add new money qualifying as senior debt, controls on the covenants in the junior debt agreement, and restrictions on the junior creditor's rights of enforcement. These and certain other matters require further discussion.

The scope of the senior creditor's protections depend on the class of transaction. In insider subordinations, the junior creditor can expect to have no, or very few, rights. His security is there only to put him ahead of trade creditors but otherwise the senior creditor is to have complete freedom in the management of the security and as to whether to add new money. However in transaction finance involving secured mezzanine debt provided by institutions, the junior creditor commonly requires greater protections.

New money advanced by senior creditor

The intercreditor agreement should permit the senior creditor to add **11–6** additional debt to his security ranking prior to the junior debt since otherwise the junior creditor might block a work-out and, further, revolving advances under the senior credit agreement might not rank ahead as a matter of law. Normally a first mortgagee cannot add on uncommitted further senior advances after he has notice of a second mortgage; see s 94 of the Law of Property Act 1925; s 30 of the Land Registration Act 1925; compare UCC s 9–312.

If the senior creditor is permitted to advance senior-ranking new money up to a limit only, then any excess over the limit should be expressed to rank after the junior creditor who should be limited as to the amount of the junior debt.

Enforcement rights of junior creditor

Under English security law, the junior creditor has virtually the same rights **11–7** of enforcement as the senior creditor – namely, rights to sue for the debt, to foreclose (an unusual remedy), to sell, to appoint a receiver and to take possession. If the senior creditor is to have any peace, these rights should be severely curtailed by the intercreditor agreement lest the senior creditor be forced into an inopportune realisation or the bargaining power of the junior creditor be disproportionately enhanced on a work-out or change of business plan. In relation to mezzanine transactional finance, see paras 10–13 *et seq* for common formulations.

For example, under English law a junior mortgagee can exercise the powers of sale conferred on him by his mortgage, by statute or by the court. He does not have to obtain the concurrence of the first mortgagor if he sells subject to the prior mortgage (*Manser v Dix* (1857) 8 De GM & G 703) but of course he can only sell subject to the first mortgage and in practice purchasers may be reluctant to buy on these terms. If the second mortgagee wishes to sell free of the first mortgage on terms that the proceeds are paid first to the prior mortgagor, he must obtain the concurrence of the first mortgagee or a court order.

11–8   In addition, the second mortgagee should be obliged to release his security in the event of a private sale at fair value by the first mortgagee or by the mortgagor with the consent of the first mortgagee. The first mortgagee should be given power of attorney to release if the second mortgagor fails to do so. The purpose of this is: (a) to prevent the second mortgagee from blocking a private sale by the mortgagor at the insistence of the first mortgagee in those jurisdictions where only judicial sales or sales by public auction are permitted; (b) to forestall the necessity for applications to the court if the second mortgagee refuses to comply or delays the sale; and (c) to allow the first mortgagee to persuade the mortgagor to sell if the position is hopeless, instead of compelling the mortgagee to be put to the trouble and expense of a forced sale.

The intercreditor agreement should normally exclude any right the junior mortgagee may have to insist that insurance policy moneys be applied in reinstatement of the mortgaged property, e.g. under the Fires Prevention (Metropolis) Act 1774 s 83. Insurance policies are often in any event payable only against reinstatement.

11–9   As to receivers, a second mortgagee in England can appoint a receiver if he has the power by the mortgage or by statute and if the first mortgagee has not already done so. The court may appoint in suitable cases. In practice, apart from sale, this is the most commonly exercised power and is the remedy almost exclusively exercised where the security comprises a floating charge. There could be conflict between a senior and junior creditor as to whether an administrative receiver should be appointed under a floating charge in order to block an administration order – the English equivalent of the US Chapter 11.

Senior creditor's responsibilities to junior creditor

11–10   In the case of subordinated debt, the junior creditor has an interest in ensuring that the senior creditor preserves and maximises the security. The less that the senior creditor receives out of the security, the greater is the turnover obligation of the junior creditor to the senior creditor and the smaller are the proceeds available to the junior creditor.

With insider subordinations, the insider can expect no reassurance from the senior creditor. But with transaction finance, such as loans to finance a bid, the position may be different. A junior creditor might seek duties of the senior creditor to perfect his security by registration or filing, not to release any security, to maintain deposited title deeds and the like in safe custody, and the like.

If the junior creditor has separate security, the senior creditor also has an interest in ensuring the validity of the junior security since the junior security enhances the turnover to the senior creditor: para 6–20.

Registration of intercreditor agreements

In the United States, no UCC filing of intercreditor agreements is required,   **11–11** although some states permit a creditor to subordinate his security by filing a UCC amendment statement (commonly known as a UCC–2 or UCC–3) indicating an intent to subordinate. In England, an intercreditor agreement which simply re-orders the priority of security and which does not of itself create security does not have to be registered in England under the provisions for the registration of company charges. Only charges have to be registered. But under s 401 of the Companies Act 1985 as amended (amendments not yet in force) any variation of the registered particulars of a charge should be registered. There is provision for the registration of priority for further advances in charges relating to registered land: Land Registration Act 1925 s 30.

Trustees for junior debt

If the junior debt is an issue of securities which will be broadly held or if   **11–12** both classes of debt are secured, it is usually preferable to appoint a trustee and, in some cases, a trustee is essential. Trustees are not available in most civil code jurisdictions.

Turnover subordinations

In the case of issues of junior debt securities subordinated by a turnover subordination to specific senior creditors, it would be impracticable for the junior creditors to seek out and claim turnover proceeds from each junior creditor. If the junior securities are bearer bonds, the junior creditors will be anonymous.

On the other hand, if the subordination of the junior issue is achieved by a contractual subordination to all creditors without any turnover obligation, this pragmatic factor does not arise and a trustee need be appointed only if local law requires a trustee. Many international issues of junior euro-bonds by banks subordinated contractually to all other unsubordinated creditors have been made without a trustee.

Secured debt

11–13   If the senior and junior debt are secured, then a trustee is useful to hold the benefit of the security for the benefit of both creditors. While separate secur-ity could be given to each creditor and the priority and remedies regulated by an intercreditor agreement, the advantages of a common trustee include: (a) the assets covered by the security are the same for both creditors; (b) the enforcement remedies are the same; (c) if there are many creditors, it is not necessary to vest security in numerous mortgagees or to grant subsequent additional security to all the creditors: it is enough to grant the security to the trustee alone; (d) proceeds of realisation can be applied by the trustee in the prescribed order without the necessity for any turnover from the junior creditor; (e) the trustee is responsible for perfecting the security and holding title deeds and the like on deposit; (f) the insurance is common; (g) there is no conflict with mandatory "order of registration" priorities; and (h) a trustee is necessary if the creditors wish to transfer their claims by novation: see below.

In the case of security for senior and junior debt involving many credi-tors, it would generally be hopelessly cumbersome to grant the security to each creditor separately.

Aspects of debt trusteeship are considered in another work (in chapters on bond issues) in this series on international financial law.

11–14   If the debts are secured and the senior and junior credit agreements allow substitution of creditors by novation, then a trustee is necessary to preserve the security on a novation. This is because the old debt in favour of the out-going creditor is cancelled and replaced by a new debt in favour of the incoming creditor. Without a trustee the security would have to be recreated in favour of the incoming creditor. With a trustee the security is created once and for all in favour of the trustee for the benefit of a class of creditors, including future creditors who become beneficiaries by novation. There is no English objection to creating a trust for future beneficiaries who are unidentified when the trust is created provided that it is possible to deter-mine whether a particular claimant is within the intended class of benefici-aries when the trust property vests.

Novations are commonly employed as a method of transferring a partici-pation in a syndicated credit as a means of enabling the outgoing bank to transfer its commitment to make new loans: various fiscal and regulatory factors have also influenced this method of transfer.

Conflicts of interest

As to conflicts of interest, normally it would be difficult for a trustee to act   **11–15** for both a secured and an unsecured issue of debentures. But there should be no objection to a common trustee holding the security for both the senior and the junior creditors in, say, a financing of a leveraged bid. In order to resolve the potential exposure of the trustee to divided loyalties, the trust deed should specifically direct the trustee to exercise his discretions (e.g. to accelerate and the timing or manner of enforcement) in accordance with the directions of the majority senior creditors by value. There can only be a conflict if the trustee has a discretion, not where he has a duty to act as directed. The trust deed should absolve the trustee from taking any action if the majority senior creditors fail to give instructions when requested.

PART III

STATE LOANS

CHAPTER 12

INTRODUCTION TO STATE LOANS

Introduction

Comparison with corporate loans

While law and practice have tended to treat state borrowers like other parti-   **12–1**
cipants in the market arena, the legal aspects of sovereign risk are still quite
distinct. The reasons are not hard to find.

Law-making sovereignty A state is in charge of its own law-making machinery and can therefore change its laws unilaterally and compel its courts to
give effect to the changes.

Sovereign immunity Until the last quarter of the twentieth century state
obligations were effectively binding in honour only on account of the doctrine of sovereign immunity whereby a sovereign could not be sued in the
courts of a foreign power. Immunity is no longer a significant impediment in
many developed jurisdictions if the transaction is commercial. Sovereign
immunity is reviewed in subsequent chapters.

State insolvency The essentials of insolvency are a freezing of piecemeal seiz-   **12–2**
ure by creditors, the realisation of the assets, the distribution of the proceeds
amongst claiming creditors and finally the release of the insolvent so that he
can start again with a clean slate.

Although states can and do become insolvent, there is no international
insolvency machinery which imposes equity and order upon creditors, least
of all one which enables the assets to be realised and the proceeds to be distributed to creditors, followed by a release of the debtor. At one time this
did not matter greatly because, as states were protected from being sued
abroad by the sovereign immunity doctrine, they could pay in their own
time or not pay at all. However, the erosion of immunity has made it more
difficult for defaulting states to trade internationally and the repercussions
could be serious where unpaid creditors resolve upon the pursuit of their
claims. But protections to states are still available.

12–3 Constitutional prohibitions In a few countries there are constitutional objections to foreign governing law, submission to foreign courts and waivers of immunity. This problem is particularly acute in the case of South American countries adopting the Calvo doctrine formulated by an Argentinian of that name in 1868 as a result of the intervention of France and Great Britain in the Argentine, Uruguay and Mexico with the intention of protecting their national creditors. Examples are Brazil and Venezuela.

Economic controls Although the documentation for sovereign credits has increasingly become assimilated to that for commercial loans, the national interest and prerogatives of sovereignty of militate against the policy controls and covenants which lenders normally look for. Governments do not usually countenance significant contractual fetters on economic policy. IMF credits are an exception, as are restructuring agreements rescheduling an insolvent state's external debt.

Conflict of laws

12–4 The conflicts rules applying to state obligations are different in some respects from those applying to creatures of municipal law.

Status and recognition A state has no status in foreign courts unless it is recognised as a legal person. The question of recognition of states is considered in chapter 15.

12–5 Powers and authorisations It is considered that sovereign states have inherent power to borrow and that constitutional limitations are matters of authorisation. The powers of political subdivisions such as members of a federation may be constitutionally limited.

In many countries foreign borrowings by the government or political subdivisions require sanction by the legislature or other executive action. Such sanction may have to be specific on each occasion or may take the form of general enabling legislation permitting borrowings up to a specified ceiling or for specified purposes.

There does not appear to be any reported English authority as to whether a loan contracted in excess of the powers of a state or a constituent territory in its constitution would be ultra vires and therefore void.

State succession Principles of state succession apply where a state breaks up, or is absorbed by another state, or becomes independent: see chapter 18.

Contents of state loan agreements

On the whole, loan agreements with states are very similar to corporate loan   12–6
agreements which are discussed in detail in another work (on international
loans, etc., in this series of books). The main differences are noted below
(see the Appendix for various forms).

Representations and warranties The import of representations and warranties is discussed generally in another work in this series on international
financial law. These cover: constitutional power; authorisations; legal validity; non-conflict with laws, the constitution and other agreements; all
official consents obtained; pari passu ranking; and a statement that the loan
is a commercial act and not governmental and the state is not entitled to
immunity: see para 13–39. There are usually no warranties as to litigation
or financial condition, although there may be a warranty as to the correct-
ness of any information memorandum produced to solicit a syndicated loan.

Covenants There will invariably be (1) a negative pledge (which may extend   12–7
to the central bank and public state bodies) though it may be limited to debt
payable, or optionally payable in foreign currency or to a foreign creditor)
(2), a pari passu clause, and (3) possibly a covenant to maintain IMF membership in good standing. These covenants are examined elsewhere in this
series. There are no financial ratios or economic covenants.

Events of default The events of default will usually include: non-payment;
non-compliance; incorrect representation and warranty; cross-default
(often limited to debt payable or optionally payable in foreign currency);
rescheduling of debt or actual or announced moratorium on foreign currency debt or non-payment of foreign currency debt as it falls due; creditor's
executions; and a material adverse change clause. For events of default
generally, see elsewhere in this series.

Other clauses The credit agreement will invariably contain a waiver of   12–8
immunity from suit, pre-judgment proceedings, and enforcement.
   The agreement will select a foreign governing law and foreign jurisdiction. A choice of external law and forum is often essential to insulate the
obligations from changes of law by the debtor country, e.g. exchange
controls. Arbitration is almost never accepted by commercial banks, and
has only been allowed by international development agencies, such as the
World Bank, and in a few exceptional cases where the state's constitution
prohibited a submission to a foreign forum, e.g. Brazil. Insulation by the
choice of an external governing law and the implications of arbitration are
also discussed elsewhere in this series.

12–9 In other respects all the normal clauses typical of international loans will appear, e.g. substitute basis, increased costs, illegality, tax grossing-up, assignments and set-off.

Syndicated credits will contain the usual syndicate provisions, e.g. severality of commitments, syndicate democracy, agent bank provisions and a pro rata sharing clause. See elsewhere in this series for detailed discussions.

CHAPTER 13

SOVEREIGN IMMUNITY GENERALLY

Generally

Sovereign states have long been privileged subjects of international law. **13–1** Before the twentieth century hardly any country in the world would permit its courts to entertain actions brought by a private citizen against foreign sovereigns. The traditional view is illustrated by Lord Campbell's strictures in the English case of *De Haber v The Queen of Portugal* (1851) 17 QB 171, 207: "to cite a foreign potentate in a municipal court . . . is contrary to the law of nations and an insult which he is entitled to resent".

The immunity which one sovereign accorded to another in his own courts has been justified on doctrines of independence and dignity, but in practice was probably based on the expedient of gaining reciprocity and because judicial actions caused diplomatic antagonisms. However as states became increasingly involved in ordinary commercial activities, the maintenance of sovereign immunity has resulted in substantial injustice to private contractors. Most commercially significant jurisdictions now hold that if the sovereign descends to the market place, he must accept the sanctions of the market place.

Nevertheless, deimmunisation has a potentially profound effect on insol- **13–2** vent states because there is no bankruptcy statute which can protect them from their creditors by imposing a freeze on proceedings, still less a statute which can discharge them from their debts so that they can start afresh or write down their debts by majority creditor votes which bind dissentient creditors. State immunity is therefore to some extent a corrective protection to the exposure of states to their creditors. On the other hand, the need for that protection has to be balanced against the reality that insolvent states do not have to realise their assets, mainly their territory, for the benefit of creditors as is the case with corporations and individuals.

The degree to which immunity has been restricted varies greatly amongst the several jurisdictions. A degree of statutory deimmunisation has been achieved by the US Foreign Sovereign Immunities Act of 1976, the UK State Immunity Act of 1978, the Singapore State Immunity Act of 1979, the South African Foreign States Immunity Act 1981, the Canadian State

---

Immunity Act of 1982, the Pakistan State Immunities Ordinance 1981, and the Australian Foreign State Immunities Act 1985. By contrast, in other countries, deimmunisation has been achieved by case law. Before a more detailed examination of the statutes in the United Kingdom and the United States, it is worth briefly reviewing in a general way the principal issues likely to be involved.

13–3   The main areas are:

- the distinction between foreign governments and the home government

- the distinction between governmental and commercial acts

- the position of states, political sub-divisions and state-owned corporations

- immunity from enforcement

- jurisdictional nexus

- arbitration

- deimmunisation of state-owned ships

- waivers of immunity; and

- the enforcement of foreign judgments.

Foreign governments and home government

13–4   A distinction must be drawn between suing a foreign government and suing the home government. Because a home government ultimately controls its courts and because no embarrassing foreign relations issues are involved, the right of action by a private citizen against his own government in domestic courts has been more quickly acknowledged than the impleading of foreign states.

On the other hand, most jurisdictions do not permit a successful judgment creditor to enforce his judgment against the local government by levying execution on state assets. It is assumed that the government will as a matter of course satisfy the judgment forthwith. The right of local suit and the expectation of payment are of course theoretical if a state borrower annuls the claim by legislation.

13–5   A review of the attitudes of a number of jurisdictions shows considerable similarity. In the United Kingdom the old rule that the King could do no wrong and could not be sued in his own courts was overruled by the Crown Proceedings Act 1947, whereby claims can be made against a department of state in the United Kingdom, such as HM Treasury, through ordinary civil proceedings in the United Kingdom courts. No execution of the judgment against Crown property is permitted. Instead the department in question is required to satisfy any claim made against it out of moneys made available by Parliament.

Spanish law provides in effect that the courts are to be entitled to grant declaratory judgments declaring the rights of the parties and may order these declarations to be complied with. Execution orders against the state are not permitted and payment of the claim must be authorised by the government: see Art 15 of the Law on State Administration and Accounting of 1911, and Art 18 of the Law on State Property of 1964.

In the Netherlands the Hoge Raad has held that it is constitutionally empowered to deal with a claim for damages against the government, even if the wrong was committed in the public sphere: HR August 18, 1944 NJ 1944, 455. In Belgium the Cour de Cassation decided in the case of *Ville de Bruges v Société La Flandria*, Pasicrisie Belge 1921, I.114 that the Belgian government is not immune from suit whenever the controversy involves "civil rights". The right to bring an action against the Belgian government is not limited to Belgian nationals but is available to foreigners (Art 128 of the Belgian Constitution). It is thought unlikely that a judgment creditor could enforce his judgment against the Belgian state by levying execution: he must rely on the government to budget a payment. In Germany the Constitution of 1949 and the BGB probably allow actions against the state in civil matters. In France *execution forcée* against the French state is not possible.

Similar patterns are observable in Latin America. In Argentina only a **13–6** very limited category of state assets are theoretically subject to attachment, namely those which are not used in public services and which the state holds in the same capacity as would a private party. Venezuela does not allow the attachment of state assets but the Ministry of Finance is statutorily obliged to make provision in the state budget for the payment of judgment debts.

The position of state entities and political subdivisions is variable. In Quebec, a provincial official must consent to any execution over the assets of a Quebec municipality.

Governmental acts and commercial acts

The most important distinction in sovereign immunity questions is that **13–7** between public and governmental acts of a sovereign (acts *jure imperii*) and its commercial or private acts (acts *jure gestionis*). Under the restrictive view of immunity courts will arrest suit or prevent execution only where the activity or property is of a governmental nature. This is the descent to the market place doctrine.

The restrictive view of immunity appeared in Italy in 1886, in Belgium in 1903, in Switzerland in 1918 (an action involving Dreyfuss and the Austrian Ministry of Finance), in France in 1929, in Austria in 1950, in the United States (as a result of a change in executive policy) in 1952 and in the United Kingdom in 1977. These dates are of course somewhat arbitrary because of the patchy way in which the restrictive view was adopted: this depended on the accidents of litigation. Civil code countries seem to have found it easier to give effect to the distinction because of the more familiar division between public and private law.

13–8   One suspects that the adoption of the restrictive review is now very wide since it represents the current international consensus. It would be surprising, e.g. if the 70 or so English-influenced states or if the same number of Franco-Latin states or the two dozen Germanic states did not find the judicial shift in favour of deimmunisation in the leading jurisdictions wholly convincing. The English adoption of the restrictive doctrine was initially non-statutory: see *Trendtex Trading Corpn v Central Bank of Nigeria* [1977] QB 529, CA. Former Soviet states in Central and Eastern Europe, which previously adhered to the absolute view, have now probably changed their minds. The position in Japan remains to be seen and it is said that Korea adheres to the absolute view. Possibly some Latin American states, such as Brazil and Ecuador, might retain the absolute view.

Apart from international sea and ship conventions, the main international convention is the rather timid European Convention on State Immunity of 1972 (para 14–64), plus numerous bilateral treaties, promoted notably by the US, Switzerland and the former USSR. State immunity is covered by the Convention on Private International Law of 1926 (the Bustamente Code) between certain Latin American States.

13–9   **Characterisation** The characterisation of governmental activity is controversial although there has been increasing convergence over recent years. Divergent views were in the past propounded by national courts as to whether one has regard to the purpose of the transaction or to its nature. Was a loan to construct a government building an act *jure gestionis* on grounds of its intrinsic nature as a commercial transaction or were the courts to take into account the fact that the transaction is associated with an activity which is essentially governmental? A US court held in 1918 that a contract for the purchase of army boots was governmental while an Italian court held in 1925 that it was not. The French Cour de Cassation held that a contract to supply cigarettes to the Vietnamese army was governmental: *Guggenheim v State of Vietnam*, Clunet, Vol 89 (1962), p 433. Further, there was no general agreement on the characterisation of public loans. If the "purpose test" is followed, how would one characterise a loan used partly for governmental and partly for commercial purposes? Ultimately it is arguable that all state business activities are indirectly for the public welfare. But in the main commercial jurisdictions, the purpose test is now discarded. The United Kingdom, Australia and the United States by statute adopt the "nature of the activity" test. In the Swiss case of *Republique Arabe Unie v Dame X* (Judgment of February 10, 1960, Tribunal Federal, ATF 85, I 23), the court held that the distinction between commercial and governmental acts is to be decided according to Swiss law, not the law of the state involved. In *Republic of Italy v Beta Holdings SA*, 65 ILR (1984) 394, the Swiss court emphasised that although an act may have a public purpose, recourse to private means to achieve it will lead the courts to treat it as a commercial act and therefore not immunised.

Relevant transactions In the context of international finance, the main contracts likely to be relevant include: **13–10**

(1) **Borrowings** and guarantees of borrowings, including bond issues. Borrowings are expressly commercial in the case of the UK State Immunity Act 1978 s 3 and the Australian Foreign State Immunities Act 1985 s 11, and have been held to be so in France (*Societe Basue-Marchal et cie v Turkey*, 47 ILR (1974) 155 (Court of Appeal, Rouen)) and Italy: *Consorzio Agrario della Tripolitania v Federazione Italiana Conzorzi Agrari*, 65 ILR (1984) 265 (Court of Cassation). The international consensus is that borrowings are commercial and therefore deimmunised, even if the proceeds are to be used for a government purpose (e.g. a balance of payments loan) and even if the default is by political act not related to solvency, e.g. trading with the enemy legislation.

(2) **Contracts for the purchase of goods** or commercial services, e.g. take-or-pay contracts by state entities in relation to project finance and construction contracts. Sale of goods contracts have been held to be commercial in the United States even if for military purposes (*McDonnell Douglas Corp v Iran*, 758 F 2d 341, 349 (8th Cir 1985)) and in decisions in Switzerland, the Philippines, the Netherlands, France and Italy. This has been applied even to purchase, building and leasing contracts in relation to embassies in Denmark, England, Germany, Greece, Italy and Switzerland, and after some hesitation, probably now France: *Spanish State v SA L'Hotel George V*, Court of Cassation 1973, 65 ILR (1984) 61 (lease of Spanish tourist office).

(3) **Concessions**, e.g. in relation to project finance. Economic development programmes may be regarded as governmental.

Thus in the US case of *Practical Concepts Inc v Bolivia*, 613 F Supp 863, 615 F Supp 92 (DDC 1985), the US firm was to supply consulting services to Bolivia.

Held: the agreement was governmental because it contained provisions as to tax exceptions, immigration privileges and diplomatic immunities which were not typically commercial.

But in French, Danish and German decisions, the activities of state oil and gas companies (in Iran and Algeria) were commercial sale of goods and building. Contrast the following:

In *Mol Inc v Bangladesh*, 736 F 2d 1326 (9th Cir 1984) cert denied 105 S Ct 513, Bangladesh granted a foreign company a licence to catch and export rhesus moneys. Bangladesh unilaterally terminated the agreement. *Held*: the transaction was governmental and Bangladesh was immune. A right to regulate natural resources is a sovereign function and no private party could have made such an agreement.

But in South Africa a contract for survey and planning work relating to Mozambique's agricultural and water development was treated as commercial: *Inter-Science v Mozambique*, S Ct 1979, 64 ILR (1983) 689.

The regulation of prices for natural resources has been held in a series of cases in the United States to be governmental, e.g. *Int'l Association of Machinists & Aerospace Workers v OPEC*, 477 F Supp 553 (CD Cal 1979); 63 ILR (1982) 284.

(4) **Transport operations** The operation of railways has been held to be governmental in Swiss and Dutch decisions, but not in France. The US courts treat the operation of a state airline as commercial, e.g. *Sugarman v Aeromexico*, 626 F 2d 270 (3d Cir 1980); ILR (1982) 446.

13–11   An acute question is whether a default under a commercial transaction for governmental reasons can immunise the act, even though the original transaction was commercial, or whether the maxim, "once a trader, always a trader", should apply. The matter arose in England at common law in *I Congreso del Partido* (1983) AC 244, where Cuba stopped ships of state-owned entities from delivering sugar to Chile because of a right wing *coup d'etat* in Chile, but was not resolved. But at least one member of the House of Lords opined that it was precisely to protect traders against politically-inspired breaches that the restrictive theory was developed. The better view is that a default for political reasons does not immunise if the transaction was originally commercial: see the decision of the Swiss Federal Tribunal in *Central Bank of Turkey v Weston*, 65 ILR (1984) 417.

13–12   **Country survey** Examples of the adoption of the restrictive doctrine in various jurisdictions are noted below.

Austria In *Dralle v Republic of Czechoslovakia*, 17 ILR (1950) 155, the Austrian Supreme Court upheld a claim against a Czech nationalised firm to restrain the use in Austria of certain trademarks. The activity was held to be commercial and not in the exercise of sovereign authority. In the *Collision with Foreign Government-owned Motor Car (Austria) Case*, 49 ILR (1961) 73, the court held that an action was not to be judged by its aim or purpose but "from the inherent internal character of the transaction or from the legal relationship created". The question was whether the plaintiff was claiming against the state on the strength of a private law relationship or one in its sovereign domain. Damages caused by driving an embassy car were of a private law nature.

Belgium Belgian courts have since at least 1879 deimmunised states in respect of commercial activities. Decisions ordering deimmunisation relate to building contracts for a railway station and the purchase of guano, and even contracts for the sale of arms, but not the lease of a building for an embassy and not films made for the purposes of government information.

Canada The Canadian State Immunity Act 1982 is largely based on the UK   **13–13** legislation. Under the Act a state loses its immunity where it "explicitly submits to the jurisdiction of the court by written agreement or otherwise either before or after the proceedings commence": s 4. A state can "explicitly or by implication" waive its immunity from "attachment, execution, arrest, detention, seizure or forfeiture": s 11. However, a waiver in relation to central bank property must be explicit. As with the UK and US legislation, process can be served through diplomatic channels but the parties are free to agree to any other method of service: s 9. A default judgment may be signed against the state after appropriate delays: s 9. The state may consent to relief by injunction or specific performance including presumably prejudgment injunctions to prevent assets from being moved from the jurisdiction: s 10. Subject to an exemption for military property, property which is used or intended to be used by a state for a commercial activity loses its immunity from attachment and execution without a formal waiver: see s 11. Where a state does not waive its immunity from jurisdiction, a state may still be deimmunised if the proceedings relate to a commercial activity, meaning "any particular transaction or course of conduct that by reason of its nature is of a commercial character". Borrowings are not expressly stated to be a commercial activity but, having regard to trends in international law, one would be surprised if a Canadian court would put the clock back on this issue.

Denmark In *Czechoslovakia v Jens Nielsen Bygge Enterprises A/S*, Supreme Ct, 1982, III JPI (1984) 639, a contractor claimed for breach of a contract to build an embassy. The contract provided for the jurisdiction of the Danish courts. It was held that the state was deimmunised.

13–14 **France** The French courts have historically viewed the restrictive doctrine narrowly but this is changing. In *Société Transhipping v Federation of Pakistan*, 47 ILR (1966) 150, the Cour de Cassation held that a contract for the survey and construction of water distribution and drainage works was a contract for public works and hence a public act. The Cour de Cassation held in *Administration des Chemins de Fer du Government Iranian v Société Levant Express Transport*, 52 ILR (1969) 315 that foreign states and entities acting at their behest or on their behalf enjoy immunity from jurisdiction only insofar as the act which gives rise to the dispute constitutes an act of public power – *act de puissance publique* – or was performed in the interest of a public service. But in *Spanish State v SA L'Hotel George V*, 65 ILR (1984) 61, the court held in the 1970s that Spain was not entitled to immunity in respect of a lease of premises to the Spanish Tourist Office in Paris since the entering into of the lease was not an act of sovereign authority. In 1961 Turkey was deimmunised on a guarantee of a bank loan to Constantinople: 45 ILR 74.

13–15 **Germany** Article 25 of the Basic Law of the Federal Republic of Germany provides that "The general rules of international law shall form part of federal law. They shall take precedence over the laws and create rights and duties directly for the inhabitants of the federal territory." Hence the German courts have felt free to apply their view of trends in customary international law on the matter of sovereign immunity. The statute constituting the German courts does not prohibit the exercise of jurisdiction over persons except insofar as they are immune by virtue of general rules of public international law, of international agreements or of other legal rules: s 20 of the *Gerichtsverfassungsgezetz*. In the *Claim v Empire of Iran Case*, 45 ILR (1963) 57, the court upheld a claim for the cost of repairs carried out at the Iranian Embassy at the ambassador's request. The court held that the repairs were a non-sovereign activity; "one should refer to the nature of state transactions, and not to the motive or purpose of the state activity". In 1974 a Munich court (1977 ELD 23) allowed a claim for an estate agent's commission due from a foreign government on the purchase of land for a consulate. Courts have held the letters of credit opened to buy cement for an army barracks (*Central Bank of Nigeria Case* 65 ILR (1975) 131), and a contract for building of an oil pipeline (*NIOC Pipelines Contracts Case*, 65 ILR (1982) 212) are deimmunised commercial transactions.

13–16 **Greece** In 1949 the Athenian Court of Appeal (Annual Digest 6 (1949) 291) permitted an action in relation to the Romanian envoy's premises in Athens. The court held that immunity did not extend to matters which arise from such activities as the administration of property which do not concern the sovereignty of the state.

Italy Italian jurisprudence was amongst the forerunners in the adoption of the restrictive view. Italian decisions have deimmunised commercial transactions, such as building contracts on the land of foreign armed forces (*US v Irsa*, 65 ILR (1963) 262), and farming loans to a Libyan state consortium: *Consorzio Agrario di Tripolitania Case*, 65 ILR (1966) 265. There are numerous decisions involving state employees.

Netherlands The Netherlands adopts the restrictive view and has deimmu-   13–17
nised a railway building contract even though it had military value: *Société Européenne d'Etudes v Yugoslavia*, 65 ILR (1973) 356. Ditto a contract for the purchase of onions: *Parsons v Malta*, 65 ILR (1977) 371.

Singapore Singapore has a State Immunity Act 1979 which is based upon the UK legislation.

South Africa South Africa has the Foreign State Immunities Act 1981, which is similar to the UK legislation.

Switzerland Switzerland has ratified the 1972 European Convention on the   13–18
Immunity of States (para 14–64 *et seq*) but Switzerland has, since at least 1918, been one of the leaders in the development of the restrictive theory of sovereign immunity. Unlike the United Kingdom, but like the United States, the Swiss courts require substantial connection between the act performed by the state and the exercise of Swiss jurisdiction. Some leading Swiss decisions are mentioned in subsequent paragraphs.

States, political sub-divisions and state-owned corporations

Generally Jenkins LJ remarked in the English case of *Baccus SRL v Servicio*   13–19
National del Trigo [1957] 1 QB 438 at 466:

> "In these days the Government of a Sovereign State is not as a rule reposed in one personal sovereign: it is necessarily carried out through a complicated organisation which ordinarily consists of many different ministries and departments. Whether a particular ministry or department or instrument, call it what you will, is to be a corporate body or an unincorporated body seems to me to be purely a matter of governmental machinery."

The question is whether all public bodies which carry out administrative functions or are owned by the state can borrow sovereign immunity by virtue of their sovereign connection. If so, a state could in effect immunise its entire economy by pursuing a policy of political corporatism.

At the top of the pyramid, there is the central government itself. Then there are departments of state which may be separate and enjoy a measure of independent legal personality, either because they can sue and be sued in their own name (as in the United Kingdom) or because they have been granted separate legal personalities. Next rung down are political sub-divisions (such as states which make up a federation) and dependent territories. Beneath these are cities, municipalities and other administrative divisions. Finally there is a huge population of state corporations – central banks, state trading corporations, airlines, development agencies, public utilities and nationalised industries. In communist countries the whole economy was nationalised and the same was more or less true of numerous collectivist states outside the communist bloc. The only connection between these institutions and the state lay in the ultimate (and sometimes remote) ownership or control by the state.

13–20   **Political subdivisions** Generally the immunity of political subdivisions is restricted. The Brazilian state of Bahia was denied immunity in Belgium although it undoubtedly exercised a measure of delegated sovereignty: *Feldman v Etat de Bahia*, AJ Vol 26 (1932) 484. In France the State of Ceara was denied immunity in an action claiming payment of bonds on a gold basis on the ground that, whatever the internal powers of the state, it did not enjoy external sovereignty in the field of international relations: *Ministere Public v Etat de Ceara*, Colmar, June 27, 1928, Clunet 1929, 1040. The United Kingdom and the United States have restricted the immunity of political subdivisions by legislation. Under the European Convention on State Immunity constitutent states of a Convention federation do not enjoy immunity from suit, but by Art 28 of the Convention a contracting state can by declaration designate that a particular constituent territory can share in the immunities granted to sovereign states.

13–21   **State-owned corporations** Some state-owned corporations are ordinary companies with a share capital, but many more are statutory corporations or even divisions of the government with varying degrees of independence. Some are commercial (trading corporations, airlines), some semi-commercial (central banks, development organisations), while others are governmental and political. The key determinants are whether the entity has a separate legal personality and whether it is carrying out purely governmental functions or is acting commercially. The trend seems to be that a separate legal entity is immune only if it is acting in the exercise of sovereign authority, although practice is not uniform.

The United Kingdom and the United States have statutorily restricted the immunities of government corporations: see the review in the next chapter.

In Switzerland it seems that the courts look to the nature of the act rather than the legal status of the state entity. Foreign state entities which are separate personalities enjoy immunity only if the act is in the exercise of sovereign authority, e.g. *Banco de la Nación (Lima) v Banca Cattolica de Veneto*, BGE 110 1a 43.

The German courts have also held that it is enough that an entity enjoys a **13–22**
personality distinct from the state according to the law of the place of its
domicile for that entity to be refused immunity: Judgment of June 7, 1955,
Federal Court, 22 ILR 17; *Central Bank of Nigeria Case*, Frankfurt, 1975,
ILR (1984) 131. This was repeated in cases involving the National Iranian
Oil Company.

Switzerland and the United States have many bilateral treaties deimmu-
nising state entities (including deimmunisation from enforcement), as did
the former USSR.

Immunity from enforcement

Generally Obtaining a judgment is one thing, enforcing it is another. Forced **13–23**
execution against a state has frequently aroused diplomatic antagonisms.

However a judgment is futile unless there are means to enforce it.
Commercial embarrassment is not of itself always a powerful factor in the
conduct of international relations. Amongst the solutions commonly found
to reduce this privileged position is to permit enforcement in four main
cases:

1. Where the sovereign state has consented to the enforcement, such as by
    a waiver of immunity.

2. Where the assets concerned are purely commercial assets and not pub-
    lic assets used in the administration of the state. This solution is found
    in statutory codes and in decisions in Austria, Germany, the
    Netherlands and Switzerland (subject to Swiss nexus). Hence embassy
    bank accounts are commonly immunised.

3. Where the action is an action in rem, e.g. in respect of an asset such as
    land or a ship, provided that it is used for ordinary trading purposes.
    Thus in the Hong Kong case of *The Philippine Admiral* [1977] AC 373,
    the Privy Council refused immunity for an action brought against a
    ship owned by the Government of the Philippines which was being
    operated as an ordinary trading ship.

4. Where the defendant is a state entity. Here the diplomatic objections
    are less prominent because state entities generally perform commercial
    and trading functions so their assets are more likely to be of a private
    nature.

The position in the United Kingdom and the United States is governed by the legislation reviewed in the next chapter. As to the position under the European Immunity Convention, see para 14–64.

13–24   Some countries insist on an executive authorisation for enforcement measures against the property of a foreign state. This is so in Greece: Emergency Law No 15/1938 Art 1(1). In Italy Law No 1263 of July 15, 1926, provides that, subject to reciprocity, no measures of execution nor preventive measures can be levied upon the property of foreign sovereigns without obtaining the prior authorisation of the Ministry of Justice. Evidently this is never granted. Apparently in France and the Netherlands, the executive can intervene, but this is not binding on the courts. A leading German case is the decision of the Federal Constitutional Court of December 13, 1977, in the *Philippines Embassy Case* (UN Doc A CN 4 343 and 142).

> A landlord of the Philippines Embassy in West Germany successfully sued for rent arrears and obtained a garnishee order on two bank accounts which the Philippines Embassy held with a local bank in Germany. *Held*: German law incorporates the general rules of international law on the subject of sovereign immunity. Property is immune if it serves the sovereign purposes of the sovereign state. Waivers of immunity should in principle be irrevocable. However embassy bank accounts for an embassy's costs and expenses are not subject to execution, nor should a sending state be required to provide details about its bank accounts.

> In the German *National Iranian Oil Co Case* (1983) reported at 65 ILR 215, creditors attached funds of the NIOC in German banks. The funds represented proceeds of sale of oil. The NIOC alleged that the funds belonged to the Iranian government. *Held*: the attachments should be upheld. The funds were commercial, even though they were to be transferred to the state for budget expenditure.

13–25   An early leading case in Belgium is the *Socobelge Case*, 18 ILR (1951) 3:

> In 1925 Socobelge of Belgium agreed with the Greek government to repair a Greek railway. The Greeks stopped payment in 1936. In 1936 an arbitral tribunal awarded just short of 7,000,000 gold dollars to Socobelge, which remained unpaid. In 1939 the PCIJ confirmed the arbitral award, but the Greeks insisted that the claim was subject to a moratorium. In 1950 Socobelge attached about US$7,000,000 held by Belgian banks and others for the account of the Greek government and the Greek National Bank. *Held*: the attachment was good on the ground that both the transaction and the assets were commercial and therefore not immune.

13–26   In France, the result of the cases appears to be that execution against the property of a sovereign state, including prejudgment attachments, is possible if the use of that property is commercial and, possibly, is used for the transaction concerned. Where the property is a bank deposit or accounts receivable it has to be shown that they were allocated towards a commercial activity.

In *Englander v Banque d'Etat Tchecoéslovaque* (Court of Cassation, 1970, Rev Crit 101) the plaintiff was allowed to attach bank funds placed with a French commercial bank and belonging to the Czech State Bank. See also *Braden Copper Company v Groupement d'Importation de Metaux*, 12 ILM 182 (1973).

In *Eurodif v Iran* (March 1984) 77 ILR 513, Iran contracted to buy power from a nuclear power project and repudiated. *Held*: Iran was deimmunised in respect of a pre-judgment conservatory attachment (*saisie conservatoire*). Immunity from execution is not available if the attached asset is employed in a private commercial activity which gives rise to the claim in question. The same applies to post-judgment execution (*saisie éxécution*). But the assets of commercial public entities are deimmunised completely in respect of all their commercial assets: *Société Sonatrach v Migeon* (October 1985) 77 ILR 525; *Société Air Zaire v van Impel*, 77 ILR 510.

In Switzerland if there is no immunity from suit, there is no immunity **13–27** from provisional prejudgment attachments or from execution.

In *Republique Arabe Unie v Dame X* (TF Febuary 10, 1960 , RO 86 I 23; Clunet, 1961, 458), a Swiss citizen who had leased property to a minister from the United Arab Republic attached UAR funds with a Swiss bank after a dispute on the lease. *Held*: the attachment was upheld. The Federal Tribunal asserted that "where there is no immunity from suit there should be no immunity from execution". On the other hand the court appeared to acknowledge that if the funds were to be used for governmental purposes they might be immune. In the instant case however, although the funds were originally intended for military expenditure, that purpose had fallen away and they were left idle without being earmarked.

This case followed the earlier decision of *Kingdom of Greece v Julius Bar & Co* (Federal Tribunal, June 6, 1956) where the court said that if execution could not follow judgment, the judgment would lack the essential attribute that it can be executed against the will of the party against whom it is rendered. The court decision would, the court said, be reduced to a mere "legal opinion." See also *Republic of Guinea v M*, 1985, SchwJIR 42 (1986) 69.

The Netherlands allows enforcement against commercial assets if the **13–28** transaction was commercial.

In *NV Cabolent v National Iranian Oil Co*, 5 ILM 4 (1975) 77, assets of NIOC in Holland were attached in enforcement of an arbitration award. The court upheld the attachment on the grounds that the activities of NIOC were of a commercial nature and that its assets were not public funds of Iran.

In *Société Européenne d'Études et d'Entreprises v Socialist Federal Republic of Yugoslavia*, 14 ILM (1975) 71, the Hoge Raad upheld enforcement proceedings in a case involving the enforcement of an arbitration award for the payment of construction moneys for a railway in Yugoslavia. Notwithstanding the argument of the Yugoslavs that the railway had a military character, the court said that the contractual relationship was *acta gestionis*.

13-29 **Governmental property** Generally as mentioned, developed states tend to allow enforcement against commercial property, but not governmental property. Clearly, embassy buildings and military property are governmental, including military software, such as clothing and fuel. Shares in public international organisations may be: the Swiss Federal Court so held in 1966 in the case of an attempt to attach Italy State railway shares in Eurofima, formed by 14 European States, on the grounds that the company was established in the public interest: *Republic of Italy v Beta Holding SA*, 65 ILR (1984) 394. Perhaps artefacts within the national cultural heritage are immune.

13-30 **Bank accounts** The main targets of attachments are bank accounts. The problem is that the nature of the account leads to a question of the future use of the account and whether it is possible to split it between governmental and commercial portions. States have an interest in alleging future governmental use. Decisions in Germany, the Netherlands and Switzerland have required that, to be immune, the moneys must be specifically allocated to a public purpose and mere statements that they will be so allocated in the future were not enough: *Central Bank of Nigeria Case*, Frankfurt 1978, 65 ILR (1984) 131; German and Dutch decisions involving the National Iranian Oil Company; *Republic Arabe Unie v Dame X*, Swiss Federal Tribunal 1960 RO 86 I 23, 65 ILR (1984) 385. The Australian Foreign State Immunities Act 1985 states that property that is apparently vacant or not in use is commercial, unless the contrary can be shown: s 32(3)(b), but see s 41. The UK State Immunity Act 1978 reverses the onus of proof if the chief UK diplomat certifies that the property is not commercial: s 13(5). But moneys in diplomatic accounts are generally regarded as governmental, thereby generally immunising the whole of embassy accounts: see, e.g. Germany: *Philippines Embassy case*, Constitutional Court, 1977, 65 ILR (1984) 146; England: *Alcom v Colombia* [1984] 2 All ER 6; 23 ILM 719 (1984). Diplomatic bank accounts are not protected by the Vienna Convention on Diplomatic Relations, but may be by customary law.

If the accounts are mixed, there are problems of proof. The US deimmunised the whole of an embassy bank account which was partly for commercial purposes: the state should have segregated the account: *Birch Shipping Corp v Tanzania*, 507 F Supp 311 (DDC 1980); 63 ILR (1982) 524. Both the German and British courts have rejected pro rating an embassy account and immunised the whole account: see above. This may simply be a reflection of the attitude to diplomacy and is probably not general for all sovereign accounts.

Central banks Central banks commonly perform both governmental and   **13–31**
commercial functions, e.g. they issue currency and hold the foreign currency reserves, but carry out commercial banking transactions. Typically, they hold their foreign currency resources with banks abroad. Decisions in England (prior to the State Immunity Act 1978), Switzerland, France and Germany have not immunised central bank accounts if there was no evidence they were used for public purposes. Often the funds are used to pay foreign loans, to buy foreign investments or to pay the foreign liabilities of state-owned corporations.

But immunity statutes have specially immunised central bank property in the absence of an express waiver in the United Kingdom and the United States. The Australian Foreign State Immunisation Act 1985 treats a central bank in the same way as a state for enforcement purposes so that governmental property is immunised: s 35(1).

Prejudgment attachments States differ according to whether or not prejudg-   **13–32**
ment attachments are permitted in the absence of an express consent by the state concerned. In the United Kingdom a Mareva injunction to restrain the removal of assets from the jurisdiction requires an express consent. This is to avoid frivolous arrests and diplomatic antagonisms. But it means the assets can be switched. Similarly in the United States a prejudgment attachment also requires an express consent. Decisions in Belgium, the Netherlands, Switzerland and Germany, however, go the other way. In *Royaume de Grece v Julius Bar & Cie* (Judgment of June 6, 1956, Tribunal Federal, ATF 82, I, 75) the court held that deimmunisation from attachment must inevitably follow from deimmunisation from jurisdiction, otherwise the court's decision is a "mere legal opinion". Many of the Swiss cases have in fact been concerned with prejudgment attachments. In the *Philippines Embassy* case cited in para 13–24 above, the District Court of Frankfurt said that if exercise of jurisdiction is permissible, attachment on the local assets of a foreign state is also admissible and only those assets which are dedicated to a public service of the state are to be exempted from forcible attachment and execution. France does not distinguish between pre- and post-judgment attachments: para 13–26.

Jurisdictional nexus

13–33   Some states require that the act which is the subject of the proceedings must have some substantial connection with the state of the forum. This is to prevent forum-shopping and the use of a country's courts for embarrassing disputes having no substantial connection with the country. There are more likely to be diplomatic repercussions if there is no local direct effect. This jurisdictional nexus requirement is at the heart of the US Foreign Sovereign Immunities Act 1976: para 14–38 *et seq*. Nexus is also required by the European Convention on State Immunity: see Arts 4 and 7 (para 14–64 *et seq*). Switzerland too requires a substantial connection between the act performed by the state and Swiss territory.

> In the decision of the Federal Tribunal of June 19, 1980, in *Libya v Libyan American Oil Company*, 20 ILM 15 (1981), Liamco sought an attachment against Libyan assets located in Switzerland to satisfy an arbitral award made in favour of Liamco against Libya relating to the nationalisation of certain petroleum concessions. The arbitration was held in Geneva. *Held*: attachment was refused on the ground that the case did not have sufficient connection with Switzerland. But Liamco succeeded in Sweden in the enforcement of the same arbitral award on the basis of a Swedish jurisdictional act relating to foreign arbitration agreements: see 20 ILM 893 (1981).
>
> In *République Hellénique v Walder*, Tribunal Federal, RO 56, I 237, repayment of a loan to the Greek Government was to be made abroad. *Held*: the Federal Court declared itself incompetent to rule on the matter because it could find no connection between the contract and Swiss territory.

It is not enough that a foreign state holds assets in Switzerland. Swiss courts will exercise jurisdiction only where the legal relationship which is the subject of the litigation arose in Switzerland or is to be performed there or the debtor has acted in such a way to indicate that Switzerland is to be the place where the agreement is to be carried out.

13–34   In Germany, on the other hand, no substantial connection need be established between a claim against a foreign state and Germany. According to s 23 of the German Code of Civil Procedure, jurisdiction in respect of money claims against persons having no domicile in Germany is vested in the court of the place in Germany where the defendant has any assets of whatever description (the "tooth-brush" jurisdiction) or where the object of the claim is located. Like the English courts, therefore, the German courts do not have any regard to subject-matter jurisdiction in immunity matters and will apply their normal long-arm jurisdictional rules in claiming *in personam* jurisdiction over the defendant state: see the 1977 Frankfurt decision in the *Central Bank of Nigeria Case*, 65 ILR (1984) 131. Similarly the Netherlands did not require some special nexus in a 1973 case, *Société Euro-*

péenne d'Études v Yugoslavia, 65 ILR (1984) 356. No connecting link is required in the UK and Australian statutes beyond the ordinary jurisdictional rules.

Arbitration

Although arbitration is unusual in financial contracts for the reasons given   13–35
elsewhere in this series on international financial law, arbitration is common in state concessions and state trading contracts, e.g. in relation to project finance. Arbitration awards can ultimately end up in court enforcement, either in the municipal courts or in recognising courts, e.g. under the New York Arbitration Convention of 1958. There is much international case law on whether a submission to arbitration is a waiver of immunity from jurisdiction and enforcement, but the cases are not consistent. The Australian, UK and US statutes deal with arbitration expressly.

Deimmunisation of state-owned ships

The Brussels Convention for the Unification of certain rules concerning the   13–36
Immunity of State-Owned Ships of 1926 (together with the Protocol of May 1934) assimilates the position of state-owned ships and cargoes used for commerce to that of the private vessel.

Article 1 provides:

> "Sea-going ships owned or operated by States, cargoes owned by them, and cargoes and passengers carried on State-owned ships, as well as the States which own or operate such ships and own such cargoes shall be subject, as regards claims in respect of the operation of such ships or in respect of the carriage of such cargoes, to the same rules of liability and the same obligations as those applicable in the case of privately-owned ships, cargoes and equipment."

Article 2 provides:

> "As regards such liabilities and obligations, the rules relating to the jurisdiction of the courts, rights of action and procedure shall be the same as for merchant ships belonging to private owners and for private cargoes and their owners."

Article 3 preserves immunity in respect of non-commercial vessels and their cargoes.

> "The provisions of the two preceding Arts shall not apply to ships of war, State-owned yachts, patrol vessels, hospital ships, fleet auxiliaries, supply ships and

other vessels owned or operated by a State and employed exclusively at the time when the cause of action arises on Government and non-commercial service, and such ships shall not be subject to seizure, arrest or detention by any legal process, nor to any proceedings *in rem*."

It is further provided:

"Nevertheless, claimants shall have the right to proceed before the appropriate courts of the State which owns or operates the ship in the following cases:
  (i) Claims in respect of collision or other accidents of navigation
  (ii) Claims in respect of salvage or in the nature of salvage and in respect of general average
  (iii) Claims in respect of repairs, supplies or other contracts relating to the ship
and the State shall not be entitled to rely on any immunity as a defence."

The rules for state-owned cargoes on board such ships are different: see Arts 3(2) and 3(3). See also the Montevideo Treaty on International Commercial Navigation Law of 1940.

Waivers of immunity in financial agreements

13–37 **Waiver clauses** It appears to be universally recognised that a state may irrevocably waive immunity by express contract in advance and there is some support for the principle that a waiver from jurisdiction is not a waiver from enforcement.

The practice in financial agreements where a state or state entity is the borrower is to set out an elaborate waiver of immunity clause whereby the borrower:

— waives immunity from jurisdiction in relation to the agreement (often not necessary because the act is commercial);

— waives immunity from enforcement, execution and attachment of its assets as regards any judgment in relation to the agreement. In the United Kingdom, but not the United States, this waiver will deimmunise military assets such as defence contracts;

— waives immunity from prejudgment proceedings, relief and attachment in relation to its assets such as Mareva injunctions or other prejudgment injunctions or attachments. An express written consent is necessary in both the United States and the United Kingdom;

— appoints an agent for service of process within the jurisdiction so as to avoid the slow-moving procedures for diplomatic process under relevant immunity legislation and to confer relatively automatic jurisdiction.

In the case of both the US and UK legislation, an express waiver of immunity from enforcement is required in the case of a central bank, i.e. its assets are, generally speaking, deemed to be governmental as opposed to commercial and therefore immune from suit.

After a submission to the jurisdiction and appointment of an agent for process, a waiver of immunity might read: 13–38

"The State irrevocably waives all immunity to which it may be or become entitled in relation to this Agreement, including immunity from jurisdiction, enforcement, prejudgment proceedings, injunctions and all other legal proceedings and relief, both in respect of itself and its assets, and consents to such proceedings and relief."

Warranties In loan agreements these jurisdictional waivers are often buttressed by a warranty to the following effect: 13–39

"The Borrower is subject to civil and commercial law with respect to its obligations under this Agreement. The execution, delivery and performance of this Agreement by the Borrower constitute private and commercial acts rather than governmental or public acts. The Borrower and its property do not enjoy any right of immunity from suit, set-off or attachment or execution on judgment in respect of the obligations of the Borrower under this Agreement. The waiver contained in this Agreement by the Borrower of any such right of immunity is irrevocably binding on the Borrower."

Apart from the event of default "trigger" effect of the warranty if it should be incorrect, such a warranty may assist in estopping the borrower from alleging that the transaction was governmental and not commercial and therefore immunised. Whether the courts would permit the parties to characterise the legal nature of a transaction by private contract is an interesting question.

Warranties of this type are almost never inserted in bond issues, other than in the subscription agreement.

The protective effect of warranties is discussed in another work (on international loans, etc.) in this series of works.

Enforcement of foreign judgments

Notwithstanding deimmunisation and endemic state defaults, there have been few actions against states on loan contracts in recent years and hence little opportunity for development in the area of the reciprocal enforcement of judgments. Presumably states will apply their own rules but it should be noticed that under the European Judgments Conventions, a judgment   13–40 against a defendant (presumably including a foreign state) in any of the contracting states will enjoy full faith and credit throughout all of the other contracting states. However, in England s 31 of the Civil Jurisdiction and Judgments Act 1982 provides that a judgment against a foreign state will be enforced only if:

(a) the debtor is not the United Kingdom nor the state of the forum;
(b) the judgment is not for a fine, taxes or penalty and (subject to exceptions) is final and conclusive; and
(c) the forum court had jurisdiction corresponding to the jurisdictional rules over foreign states set out in the State Immunity Act 1978, e.g. the debtor state submitted to the jurisdiction or the transaction was a commercial one.

There are special rules under the European Convention on State Immunity regarding the recognition and enforcement of judgments rendered against a contracting state by a court in another contracting state: para 14–66.

CHAPTER 14

UK AND US IMMUNITY LEGISLATION; EUROPEAN CONVENTION

UK State Immunity Act 1978

Introduction

The State Immunity Act 1978 adopts the restrictive theory of immunity as **14–1** opposed to the previous absolute theory developed by the courts. The Act enabled the United Kingdom to ratify the International Convention for the Unification of Certain Rules relating to the Immunity of State-owned Vessels of 1926 as well as the European Convention on State Immunity of 1972.

States and state entities

States There is a difference in treatment between states, constituent terri- **14–2** tories of a federal state, "separate entities" and central banks. As to "State", s 14(1) provides that the immunities and privileges conferred by Part I of the Act "apply to any foreign or commonwealth State other than the United Kingdom". It is further provided that references to a state include references to

(a) the sovereign or other head of that state in his public capacity (sovereigns in any event enjoy personal immunity: see s 20). A sovereign presumably acts in a public capacity when he contracts a loan on behalf of his state but not a loan for private purposes;

(b) the government of that state; and

(c) any department of that government.

But they do not include a "separate entity": these are dealt with separately.

There is no comprehensive definition of "State", but s 21 provides that a certificate by or on behalf of the Secretary of State shall be conclusive evidence on any question whether any country is a state for the purposes of Part I of the Act, whether any territory is a constituent territory of a federal state for those purposes or as to the person or persons to be regarded for those purposes as the head or government of a state.

UK colonies and certain other dependent territories are not states within the Act and can be sued in the United Kingdom (if at all) only by the ancient petition of rights procedure because they are not within the Crown Proceedings Act 1947. HM Dominions, such as Australia or New Zealand, are states within the Act.

There is power to restrict or extend immunities by Order in Council in certain cases: s 15(1).

14–3   Separate entities Separate entities enjoy a lesser immunity than is available to states. A separate entity is defined by s 14(1) of the Act as any entity "which is distinct from the executive organs or the government of the State and capable of suing or being sued": para 14–20 *et seq.*

Immunity from jurisdiction

14–4   The Act distinguishes between immunity from jurisdiction (the claim itself) and immunity from enforcement.

Section 1 of the Act provides that a state is immune from the jurisdiction of the courts of the United Kingdom except as provided in Part I of the Act. Hence the Act establishes the general principle of immunity but goes on to provide wide exceptions to the general rule.

Exceptions to immunity from jurisdiction

14–5   Submission to jurisdiction Section 2(1) provides that a "State is not immune as respects proceedings in respect of which it has submitted to the jurisdiction of the courts of the United Kingdom" (reflecting Art 2 of the European Convention).

Section 2(2) provides that a "State may submit after the dispute giving rise to the proceedings has arisen or by a prior written agreement; but a provision in any agreement that it is to be governed by the laws of the United Kingdom is not to be regarded as a submission." In order to deimmunise the state, it is not necessary in addition for the state to appoint an agent for service within the jurisdiction. However such appointment is desirable so as to confer the relatively automatic jurisdiction of the English courts.

Section 17(2) provides that "references to an agreement include references to a treaty, convention or other international agreement".

Section 2(3) provides that a State is deemed to have submitted in the fol- **14–6**
lowing cases (reflecting the European Convention on State Immunity of
1972 Arts 1(1) and 13):

(a) it has instituted the proceedings; or

(b) it has intervened or taken any steps in the proceedings, except:

  (i) where the intervention or step is taken for the purpose only of
      claiming immunity or "asserting an interest in property in cir-
      cumstances such that the State would have been entitled to
      immunity if the proceedings had been brought against it" (an
      example is the action *in rem*), or

  (ii) where the step is "taken by the State in ignorance of facts enti-
      tling it to immunity if those facts could not reasonably have
      been ascertained and immunity is claimed as soon as reasonably
      practicable". It is difficult to foresee circumstances in which this
      might apply: note that the ignorance must be of "facts" not law.

Section 2(6) provides that a "submission in respect of any proceedings
extends to any appeal but not to any counterclaim unless it arises out of the
same legal relationship or facts as the claim" (reflecting the European Convention on State Immunity of 1972 Art 1(2)). The "head of a State's diplomatic mission in the United Kingdom, or the person for the time being
performing his functions, shall be deemed to have authority to submit on
behalf of the State in respect of any proceedings; and any person who has
entered into a contract on behalf of and with the authority of a State shall be
deemed to have authority to submit on its behalf in respect of proceedings
arising out of the contract": s 2(7).

Commercial transactions Section 3 provides that a state is not immune as **14–7**
regards proceedings relating to a "commercial transaction entered into by
the State".

This provision does not apply if the parties to the dispute are states or if
the parties to the dispute have otherwise agreed in writing: s 3(2). Hence the
parties can contract out.

The section also does not apply to certain Admiralty and related proceedings if the state in question is a party to the Brussels Immunity Convention
for State-Owned Ships of 1926: s 10(6). This is to avoid conflict between the
Brussels Convention and the Act.

"Commercial transaction" For the purposes of s 3(1) a "commercial trans- **14–8**
action" means:

(a) any contract for the supply of goods or services;

(b) any loan or other transaction for the provision of finance and any guar-
    antee or indemnity in respect of any such transaction or of any other
    financial obligation; and

(c) any other transaction or activity (whether of a commercial, industrial,
    financial, professional or other similar character) into which a State
    enters or engages otherwise than in the exercise of sovereign authority.

There are special rules for contracts of employment: see s 4.

This wide exception treats states in the same way as private persons
engaging in commercial transactions and adopts the approach that it is the
nature rather than the purpose of the transaction which is relevant. It
follows that where a state contracts a loan it is immaterial if the loan is for a
military airport or for an engineering project. If this were not the case,
immunisation would depend upon how the state actually applied the proceeds of a loan. Further, confusion would result if the state spent a loan
partly on, say, a naval port and partly for a commercial harbour.

It is also considered irrelevant that the breach of the contract, initially a
commercial transaction, was an act of sovereign authority, e.g. for foreign
policy reasons.

14–9   It should be noted that in (a) and (b) it is irrelevant that the state is
involved in the transaction in the exercise of sovereign authority, but the
exercise of sovereign authority immunises in the case of (c): see *Alcom Ltd v
Republic of Colombia* [1984] AC 580 at 603, HL. The term "the exercise of
sovereign authority" implies the distinction between sovereign and non-
sovereign acts (acts *imperii* rather than acts *gestionis*) but is not defined. No
doubt the courts will be influenced by international case law on the matter.

There is nothing in the European Convention of State Immunity of 1972
similar to s 3.

14–10   **Contracts to be performed in the United Kingdom** Section 3 further provides that a state is not immune as respects proceedings relating to "an obligation of the State which by virtue of a contract (whether a commercial
transaction or not) falls to be performed wholly or partly in the United
Kingdom". As to the extension of the United Kingdom to certain dependent
territories, see s 17(3). See s 17(4) as to extension to adjacent waters. As to
place of performance, a contract to pay money is generally performable
where the money is to be paid: see, e.g. *Ralli Bros v Cia Naviera Sota y
Aznar* [1920] 1 KB 614.

Section 3(1)(b) applies regardless of the nature of the transaction, i.e.
whether or not it is commercial or in the exercise of sovereign authority,
provided that the obligation arises under a contract to be performed wholly
or partly in the United Kingdom.

However, this deimmunisation does not apply in four cases: 14–11

(a) if the parties to the disputes are states;

(b) the parties to the dispute have otherwise agreed in writing;

(c) if the provision mentioned in para 14–13 relating to the Brussels Convention applies: see s 10(6);

(d) if (i) the contract is not a commercial transaction, and (ii) the contract was made in the territory of the state concerned and (iii) the obligation in question is governed by its administrative law: s 3(2).

Arbitration Section 9 (reflecting the European Convention on State   14–12
Immunity of 1972 Art 12) provides that where "a State has agreed in writing to submit a dispute which has arisen, or may arise, to arbitration, the State is not immune as respects proceedings in the courts of the United Kingdom which relate to the arbitration". Enforcement of the award is governed by the principles set out in s 13: para 14–15 *et seq*.

The deimmunisation, however, is subject to any contrary provision in the arbitration agreement, and does not apply to any arbitration agreement between states: s 9(2).

Ships used for commercial purposes Section 10 applies to Admiralty pro-   14–13
ceedings and proceedings on any claim which could be made the subject of Admiralty proceedings. Section 10(2) provides that a state is not immune as respects an action in rem (for Scotland, see s 17(5)) against a ship (which is defined to include a hovercraft – s 17(1)) belonging to that state or an action in personam for enforcing a claim in connection with such a ship, if, at the time when the cause of action arose, the ship was in use or intended for use for commercial purposes. By s 17(1) "commercial purposes" means purposes of such transactions or activities as are mentioned in s 3(3): para 14–8 Actions *in rem* include mortgage actions: see the Supreme Court Act 1981 s 20.

Subject to special rules for cargo set out in subsection (4), this s 10(2) applies to "property other than a ship" as it applies to a ship.

As regards "sister ship" action when the cause of action arises both ships must be in use or intended for use for commercial purposes: s 10(3).

References to a ship belonging to a state include references to a ship in its possession or control or in which it claims an interest: s 10(5).

Other cases There are also special deimmunisation provisions for proceed-   14–14
ings in respect of (among other things):

(a) contracts of employment: s 4;

(b) death or personal injury or damage to or loss of tangible property caused by an act or omission in the United Kingdom: s 5;

(c) any interest of the state in, or its possession or use of, immovable property in the United Kingdom or any obligation of the state arising out of its interest in, or its possession or use of, any such property, e.g. mortgage actions: s 6;

(d) the membership of a state in a body corporate, an unincorporated body or a partnership in certain circumstances: s 8.

Immunity from enforcement

14–15   As regards the more sensitive matter of enforcement, the deimmunisation is less dramatic. By virtue of s 13(2), subject to the exceptions mentioned below, the following remedies are not available against a state:

1.   injunctions (or interdicts in Scotland). For example, a prejudgment conservatory Mareva injunction would not be available;

2.   orders for specific performance;

3.   orders for the recovery of land;

4.   orders for the recovery of other property;

5.   all proceedings against property of the state for the enforcement of judgments or arbitrations awards;

6.   actions *in rem*, orders for the arrest, detention or sale of the property of the State. Section 3(6) adapts the language to take account of the procedure in Scotland.

Exceptions to immunity from enforcement

14–16   **Written consent** By s 13(3) any relief may be given or process issued with the written consent of the state concerned. This consent may be given by prior agreement. This includes agreement in a treaty – see s 17(2). The consent may be expressed so as to apply to a limited extent or generally. It follows that a state can by agreement deimmunise some property but not other property e.g. defence or heritage assets. The Act thereby preserves contractual freedom. If a general consent is given it would seem that military assets are deimmunised. But see s 16(2) as to proceedings relating to anything done by or to the armed forces of a state within the United Kingdom. Section 13(3) provides that a provision merely submitting to the jurisdiction of the courts is not to be regarded as a consent for the purposes of the subsection.

By s 13(5) the head of the State's diplomatic mission in the United Kingdom or the person for the time being performing his functions shall be deemed to have authority to give on behalf of the state any consent referred to in s 13(3).

Commercial property By s 13(4) the remedies listed in para 14–15 above   **14–17**
under (5) and (6) (and only those remedies) are available against the property of the state used or intended for use for commercial purposes. Hence a Mareva injunction is not available even against commercial assets without a written consent.

By s 17(1) "commercial purposes" means purposes of such transactions or activities as are mentioned in s 3(3): para 14–8.

By s 13(5) the certificate of the head of the state's diplomatic mission in the United Kingdom or the person for the time being performing his functions to the effect that any property is not in use or intended for use by or on behalf of the state for commercial purposes shall be accepted as sufficient evidence of that fact unless the contrary is proved.

Often the main assets of a state abroad are investments and money in   **14–18**
bank accounts. This provision, however politically understandable, seems to put it in the hands of the state concerned whether its assets can be attached. The onus of proof might be particularly difficult to discharge in the case of money in bank accounts claimed to be intended for, say, military purposes: money is fungible.

> In *Alcom Ltd v Republic of Columbia* [1984] AC 580, HL, a creditor of the Republic obtained summary judgment against the Republic for failure to pay a commercial debt and sought to garnish the embassy bank account. The Colombian ambassador provided a certificate under s 13(5). Notwithstanding this, it was shown that money in the embassy account was used for defraying expenditure of the embassy of a commercial nature, e.g. supplies for the embassy, paying wages and making loans to Colombian students to enable them to get home. *Held*: the embassy account was immunised. A judgment creditor seeking to attach a credit balance by garnishee proceedings has to show that the state's bank account is earmarked by the foreign state *solely* for the settlement of liabilities incurred in commercial transactions and is immunised if it is partly used for sovereign purposes. The account is indivisible.

A wide interpretation of the decision is that, if a creditor seeks to attach a bank account of a foreign state, all that the foreign state has to do is to show that *some* of the money is intended for sovereign purposes, e.g. (perhaps) payments for military contracts. This broad view would make it much more difficult to achieve a remedy against credit balances which are often the main foreign asset of a state or a state entity.

On the other hand, a narrow interpretation would confine the decision to *embassy* bank accounts as opposed to *general* accounts in the name of the state. Support for this narrower view may be derived from the fact that the court based its argument not merely on the State Immunity Act but also on the Vienna Convention on Diplomatic Relations and from international law trends regarding embassy accounts: para 13–30.

Nevertheless, the decision does underline the importance of securing an express waiver of immunity from enforcement in contracts with states.

Special immunisation for European Convention States

14–19   However, in cases where the defendant state is a party to the European Convention on State Immunity of 1972 (not being cases within s 10 of the Act (mainly Admiralty proceedings)) the remedies in para 14–15 under 5 and 6 will only be available if:

(a) the process is for enforcing an arbitration award; or

(b) the process is for enforcing judgments that are final within the meaning of s 18(1)(b) of the Act and the defendant state has made a declaration under Art 24 of the European Convention on State Immunity of 1972. The reason for this exception is that the European Convention generally permits no execution against property of the defendant state. However, a state can deimmunise itself in this respect by a declaration under Art 24 of the European Convention that execution against the property of the state is permissible: para 14–64 *et seq*. The policy is that, if a state applies its wider exemptions to the immunity doctrine to other contracting states, that state should be willing to accept the possibility of execution against its commercial assets.

State entities

14–20   **Definition** State entities enjoy a lesser immunity protection than states themselves. Separate entities are defined by s 14(1) of the Act as any entity "which is distinct from the executive organs of the government of the State and capable of suing or being sued". There is therefore a double test:

(a) ability to sue or be sued. Presumably one looks to the law of the state concerned to ascertain this aspect of legal personality, but the position is not clear: the lex fori may also play a part.

(b) distinctness from government in the sense that it is not a department of state. It remains for the court to settle the criteria of distinctness: the

approach of the courts in common law cases may be useful in this connection.

In *Mellenger v New Brunswick Development Corpn* [1971] 2 All ER 593,
[1971] 1 WLR 604, the court granted immunity to the New Brunswick Corporation because it never pursued any ordinary trade or commerce, but promoted
the industrial development of the province in the way that a government
department does. Apart, however, from the statute, the functions of the corporation, as carried out in practice, showed that it was carrying out the policy of
the Government of New Brunswick itself. It was its alter ego.

In *Trendtex Trading Corpn v Central Bank of Nigeria* [1977] QB 529, CA, it
was held that the Central Bank of Nigeria was not a department of state and
was not entitled to immunity.

In *Czarnikow Ltd v Rolimpex* [1979] AC 351, the defendant was a Polish state
enterprise. The House of Lords endorsed the effect of the arbitrators' finding
that Rolimpex, though set up and controlled by the Polish state, was not so
closely connected with the government as to be an organ or department of the
state, since the state enterprise could run its own commercial business.

In *The Playa Larga* [1983] 2 Lloyd's Rep 171, [1983] Com LR 58, CA, a
Cuban state trading enterprise agreed to deliver a quantity of sugar to a Chilean
company with state connections. Following a right-wing coup in Chile, Cuba
broke off diplomatic relations with Chile and ordered the sugar-bearing ships
out of Chilean waters. *Held*: the sugar contract was effectively frustrated and
that it was not a self-induced frustration on the basis that the Cuban state trading enterprise was a separate legal entity. This ruling appears to give a state
trading enterprise a readily available way out of embarrassing contracts.

It is thought unlikely that international organisations are separate entities
within the Act: para 19–13 *et seq.*

Immunity from jurisdiction Section 14(2) provides: **14–21**

"A separate entity is immune from the jurisdiction of the courts of the United
Kingdom if, and only if:
(a) the proceedings relate to anything done by it in the exercise of sovereign
authority; and
(b) the circumstances are such that a State (or, in the case of proceedings to
which section 10 above applies [mainly Admiralty proceedings], a State
which is not a party to the [Brussels Ship Immunity Convention 1926])
would have been so immune."

In other words, generally speaking, a separate entity is immune only
where the state itself would have been immune and the separate entity is
exercising sovereign authority.
The meaning of "exercise of sovereign authority" involves the distinction

between *acta imperii* and *acta gestionis* which has been elaborated on in numerous international decisions and also by the English courts, particularly in *I Congreso del Partido* [1983] 1 AC 244, [1981], HL; *Trendtex Trading Corpn v Central Bank of Nigeria* [1977] QB 529, CA, and *The Philippine Admiral* [1977] AC 373, HL.

It seems possible that in the case of s 14 it may be relevant that the breach of the contract giving rise to the proceedings was *acta imperii* even though the contract itself was commercial.

14–22 **Immunity from enforcement** Section 14(3) provides that if a separate entity submits to the jurisdiction in respect of proceedings in the case of which it is entitled to immunity by virtue of s 14(2) (para 14–21) then it is entitled to the same immunity from enforcement and the other procedural privileges afforded by s 13(1) to (4): para 14–14. This is subject to a special exception in favour of central banks and other monetary authorities: para 14–23.

It is suggested that immunisation applies only if the state submits and that the state is deimmunised from execution where the separate entity is otherwise deimmunised from the jurisdiction of the United Kingdom courts, e.g. because the transaction is a commercial one under s 3. It is probably the case that the Act sets out a complete code of immunity so that if there is no express enforcement immunity in the Act, then the separate entity will not be entitled to immunity.

14–23 **Special immunisation of central banks** A state's central bank or other monetary authority is given special favourable treatment as regards enforcement. The reason is that, without such immunisation, foreign central banks might have been discouraged from depositing foreign reserves in the United Kingdom and hence lose the safe haven afforded by a country traditionally providing that protection.

Section 14(4) provides that where a central bank is a "separate entity" (as defined) it has the same advantages as a state under s 13(1)–(3), e.g. no penalties for failure to discover for the purposes of proceedings, immunisation from injunctions, specific performance and certain recovery actions and from the enforcement of judgments and arbitration awards against its property without its consent or prior agreement: para 14–14 *et seq*.

14–24 Under s 13(4), a state's property is in any event deimmunised if it "is for the time being in use or intended for use for commercial purposes", but by virtue of s 14(4) the property of a state's central bank or other monetary authority is not to be regarded as in use or intended to be in use for commercial purposes. This applies whether or not the bank or authority is a separate entity. As a result enforcement actions against any property of a central bank or other monetary authority, commercial or public, require its consent.

The immunisation from enforcement of a judgment, etc., applies only if the property is that of a central bank or monetary authority. If the property is that of the state itself, e.g. because (perhaps) it acts as agent for the state, then possibly the special characterisation of that property as being non-commercial and therefore immunised from enforcement would be forfeited. If so, the property will be treated in the same way as that of a state and subject to enforcement of a judgment if it is in use or intended to be used for commercial purposes: see s 13(4).

Private company acquired by the state It seems possible that a private corporation may benefit from immunity as a "separate entity" if it is subsequently brought into the public sector after the contract is entered into and the proceedings relate to anything done by it in the exercise of sovereign authority. Specific consents to relief and issue of process are not therefore necessarily irrelevant in the case of private corporations.   **14–25**

Constituent territories Constituent territories of federal states are treated in the same way as separate entities and therefore have a lesser immunity protection than states, subject to the following exceptions: **14–26**

(a) a constituent territory is entitled to the s 12 procedural privileges (mainly, service of process through diplomatic channels and an extended two months to acknowledge the writ);

(b) an Order in Council may provide for the provisions of Part I of the Act to apply to that particular territory as they would apply to a state: s 14(5). In other words a constituent territory can be upgraded to a state for immunity purposes.

Dependent territories It has been noted (para 14–2) that by s 14(1) a "State" means "any foreign or commonwealth State other than the United Kingdom". Section 23(7) provides that Orders in Council may extend any of the provisions of the Act, with or without modification, to any dependent territory of the UK, e.g. the Channel Islands and Colonies.   **14–27**

Procedure

The Act sets out a number of procedural privileges available to states: **14–28**

Discovery Section 13(1) provides that no penalty by way of committal or fine shall be imposed in respect of any failure or refusal by or on behalf of a state to disclose or produce any document or other information for the purposes of proceedings to which it is a party.

14–29 **Service of process** The Act sets out rules for service of process upon foreign states and state entities.

Section 12(1) provides that any writ or other document required to be served for instituting proceedings against a state shall be served by being transmitted through the Foreign and Commonwealth Office to the Ministry of Foreign Affairs of the state and service shall be deemed to have been effected when the writ or document is received at the Ministry. For the procedure, see RSC Ord 11, r 7.

> In *Westminster City Council v Government of the Islamic Republic of Iran* [1986] 3 All ER 284, [1986] 1 WLR 979, service through diplomatic channels was impossible due to the discontinuance of diplomatic relations. *Held*: this did not allow the court to dispense with the requirement of service. Accordingly, since it was not possible to serve the Iranian Government, the court could not consider the matter.

Where the writ cannot be served upon states within the jurisdiction, the effect of s 12(7) is that it may still be necessary to bring the matter within the provisions of RSC Ord 11 whereby the court can exercise a discretion (which is by no means automatic) to serve a writ outside the jurisdiction in a limited number of cases. This underlines the desirability of the appointment of an agent within England for service of process against the state, so as to take advantage of s 12(6): para 14–30.

The state has two months to acknowledge the proceedings, thereby preventing quick summary proceedings by a default judgment.

14–30 **Alternative service by agreement** By s 12(6) the method of service through diplomatic channels set out in s 12(1) "does not prevent the service of a writ or other document in any manner to which the State has agreed". Hence the parties can agree on a different method of service. In this case there are two significant procedural advantages:

(a) the two-month grace period for acknowledging service of the writ as set out by s 12(2) does not apply: s 12(6);

(b) the provisions of s 12(4) as to proof of diplomatic service and expiry of the two month period in the case of default judgments do not apply.

A further advantage is that, if an agent for service of process is appointed within England, the virtually automatic jurisdiction of the English courts will be available and it would not be necessary to apply for leave to serve process outside the jurisdiction.

Some states prefer to appoint their ambassador to the Court of St James as agent for service of process. The question arises whether an ambassador would be immune. The matter seems to slip between the State Immunity Act

1978 and the Diplomatic Privileges Act 1964. In the absence of authority, it is thought that the immunity of an ambassador is a privilege of his state which may waive it.

Counterclaims and actions *in rem* Section 12(7) provides that the section **14–31** "shall not be construed as applying to proceedings against a State by way of counterclaim or to an action *in rem*". A state which itself institutes proceeding will therefore be subject to counterclaims.

Diplomatic and taxation immunities

Certain matters are excluded from the Act by s 16. The most important of **14–32** these in the present context are diplomatic immunities and taxation.

Diplomatic immunities Part I of the Act does not affect any immunity or privilege conferred by the Diplomatic Privileges Act 1964 or the Consular Relations Act 1968. These immunise such assets as diplomatic premises and archives. Section 20 deals with the immunisation of heads of state acting in their private capacity in certain circumstances.

Taxation Part I of the Act does not apply to any proceedings relating to tax- **14–33** ation other than those mentioned in s 11 of the Act (VAT, customs or excise duty, agricultural levies and certain rates). It is thought that a contractual indemnity in respect of taxes or a grossing-up clause is not a claim for taxes but a claim for compensation and therefore not specially immunised.

United States Foreign Sovereign Immunities Act of 1976

Generally

The US Foreign Sovereign Immunities Act of 1976, amended in 1988, is **14–34** similar in many respects to the UK State Immunities Act 1978. Prior to the Act the US courts generally favoured restrictive immunity but the State Department could "suggest" to the court that the foreign state was immune and the courts generally deferred to that suggestion. Although under the doctrine enshrined in the 1952 "Tate Letter" the State Department espoused the restrictive principle of immunity, the State Department was frequently embarrassed by attempts by foreign states to bring diplomatic pressures to bear upon the determination. In the result the position of the private litigant was unpredictable.

As with the State Immunity Act 1978, the general plan of the Act is to affirm the general principle of immunity of a foreign state from jurisdiction and from execution on a judgment and then to set out wide exceptions to the rule. The action must be within one of the exceptions if the foreign state is to lose its immunity.

The immunity provisions of the Act are subject to "existing international agreements to which the United States is a party". The United States has negotiated numerous treaties of Friendship, Navigation and Commerce and the terms of these will need to be borne in mind since they override the Act.

14–35   The deimmunisation under these treaties usually applies only to "business activities in the United States" and may apply only to commercial state enterprises, not the state itself. Although one of the purposes of the Act was to enable the State Department to withdraw from involvement in litigation against foreign states, the Act has not reduced the powers of the President to intervene in the resolution of major foreign policy disputes or emergencies between one country and another.

> In *Dames & Moore v Reagan*, 101 S Ct 2972 (1981), the Supreme Court held that the President of the United States has the executive power to suspend the claims of a US national against a foreign sovereign and to terminate such claims through the imposition of binding arbitration in an international claims tribunal (in this case the Iranian Hague Tribunal). See also *Charles T Main International Inc v Khuzestan Water & Power Authority*, 651 F 2d 800 (1st Cir 1981).

The case law on the Act is substantial.

Definitions (s 1603)

14–36   The definitions used in the Act are of great importance in following the tenor of the legislation.

A *"foreign state"* includes a political subdivision of a foreign state or an agency or instrumentality of a foreign state. The term *"political subdivision"* would presumably include all governmental units beneath central government, such as federated states, provinces and (perhaps) municipalities.

An *"agency or instrumentality of a foreign state"* is defined to mean any entity which is a separate legal person, corporate or otherwise, and which is either an organ of a foreign state or one of its political subdivisions or a majority of whose shares or other interests is owned by the foreign state or political subdivision, e.g. state trading corporations, mining enterprises, shipping lines or airlines, central banks, export associations, government procurement agencies or a department or ministry which acts and is suable in its own name. The definition of agencies and instrumentalities does not include foreign-owned US corporations nor entities created under the laws of a third country, which are in any event not entitled to immunity in the US courts.

If an entity is within the definition of a foreign state, then it is entitled to immunity unless one of the exceptions applies. If it is not within the definition then it is not entitled to immunity. Unless otherwise stated, the term "foreign state" will be used in this review in the sense defined by the Act to include political subdivisions, agencies and instrumentalities.

An entity is not within the Act unless it performs governmental functions and is subject to direct governmental control. A Yugoslav workers organisation established for the purpose of constructing and operating a nuclear-power generating facility was not an agency or instrumentality of a foreign state: *Edlow International Co v Nuklearna Electrarna Kisko*, F Supp 827 (DDC, 1977). The following have been held to be within the term: Novosti, "an information agency of Soviet public organisations", on account of its essentially public functions: *Yessenin-Volpin v Novosti Press Agency*, 443 F Supp 849 (SDNY, 1978); the Soviet Tass Agency; and a Chilean company 95 per cent owned by a wholly-owned Chilean state entity.

"*Commercial activity*" means either a regular course of commercial conduct or a particular commercial transaction or act. The House Report on the Act opines that the borrowing of money would be included within the definition. Nature, not purpose, is the test so that the mere fact that the loan proceeds are to be used for a public purpose will not be fatal to the commercial nature of the transaction. Case law has held that the following are commercial activities: sale of cement, even if for army barracks; operation of a state airline; and the issue of certificates of deposit by a state-owned bank.   **14–37**

"*A commercial activity carried on in the United States by a foreign state*" means a commercial activity carried on by the state and having substantial contact with the United States. It is thought that points of contact might be negotiation and signature of the financial contract in the United States, participation by United States banks, and the making of payments in the United States. Decisions have brought commercial banking businesses carried on by state-owned banks within this provision, e.g. *State Bank of India v Chicago Joint Board*, 16 ILM 853 (1977).

Immunity from jurisdiction (s 1605)

A foreign state (including political subdivisions, agencies and instrumentalities) is not immune from jurisdiction: **14–38**

(a) Where it has expressly or impliedly waived its immunity. A foreign state can waive for a governmental entity. The scope of the implied waiver is not defined.

(b) Where the action is based upon acts enjoying a prescribed nexus with the United States, i.e. based upon:

 (i) a commercial activity carried on in the United States by the foreign state, or

 (ii) an act performed in the United States in connection with a commercial activity of a foreign state elsewhere, or

 (iii) an act outside the territory of the United States in connection with a commercial activity of the foreign state elsewhere and that act causes a direct effect in the United States.

The nexus requirement was intended to prevent an avalanche of sovereign litigation which did not enjoy substantial US contacts.

In 1988 an amendment to the Act provided that, usually, a foreign state will not be entitled to immunity in actions brought either to enforce an agreement to arbitrate in the United States or to confirm an award made pursuant to such an agreement: s 1605(a). Enforcement is not to be refused on the basis of the act of state doctrine: 9 USC s 15.

14–39   There is substantial case law on these provisions. For example:

> In *Carey v National Oil Corpn*, 453 F Supp 1079 (SDNY 1978); affirmed 592 F 2d 673 (1979) it was held that the "direct effect" requirement was not satisfied in the case of an alleged breach by Libya or its National Oil Company of crude oil supply contracts between the National Oil Company and the Bahamian subsidiaries of a New York corporation, even though the claims had been assigned to a New York resident and the refined products from the oil were to be used in the United States.

> On the other hand the breach of a letter of credit having a New York beneficiary, advised by and payable through New York banks, would satisfy the criterion: *National American Corpn v Federal Republic of Nigeria*, 448 F Supp 622 (SDNY 1978).

A foreign borrower's failure to pay a New York bank in US dollars payable in New York probably constitutes a "direct effect".

As to (i), a commercial activity in the United States has been held to include: a US representative office; regular flights into the United States; publication of an invitation to bid in the United States; and substantial negotiations in the United States, but not isolated meetings, telex contacts nor a promissory note payable in New York. See, e.g. *Gemini Shipping Inc v Foreign Trade Organisation for Chemicals and Foodstuffs*, 647 F 2d 317 (2d Cir 1981); *Maritime International v Nominees v Republic of Guinea*,

693 F 2d 1094 (DC Cir 1982), cert denied, 104 S Ct 71 (1982); *East Europe Domestic International Sales v Terra*, 467 F Supp (SDNY), affirmed without opposition, 610 F 2d 806 (2d Cir 1979). There are many other cases, though some, e.g. tort actions, have no relevance in this context.

There has been little case law on (ii).

As to (iii), numerous cases have established that financial loss incurred by a US corporation through commercial contacts with a foreign state abroad fulfils the criterion of direct effect.

Immunity is also removed in the case of certain expropriations and commercial ships (including enforcement of maritime liens and US and foreign ship mortgages). As to ships, see ss 1605(b) and 1610, amended in 1988.

A selection of a foreign law and a submission to a foreign court are not an express waiver: *Eaglet Corpn Ltd v Banco Central de Nicaragua*, 839 F Supp 232 (SDNY 1993).

Immunity from execution (ss 1608 and 1609)

Exceptions to immunity The property in the United States of a foreign state   **14–40** or a political subdivision, agency or instrumentality of a foreign state (if, and only if, "used for a commercial activity in the United States") is not immune where any of the following apply:

(a) Immunity is expressly or impliedly waived. Note that a waiver can only apply to commercial property;

(b) The property concerned is or was used for the commercial activity upon which the claim is based. This latter exemption is not likely to be of much help in financial transactions. The exemption is a compromise between the wish to afford relief and the wish not to discourage investment in the United States by exposing all the state's commercial property to attachment. The degree of connection appears unclear – must the property be used for the very transaction on which the claim is based, for a series of connected transactions, or for the whole commercial business of which the transaction is only one part?

(c) Where the execution relates to a judgment establishing rights in property which has been taken in violation of international law.

Agencies and instrumentalities The exceptions to immunity from execution   **14–41** and attachment in aid of execution are widened in the case of an agency or instrumentality which is therefore less protected than a foreign state or political subdivision. Any property of the agency or instrumentality can be attached or be executed upon if the agency or instrumentality is engaged in a commercial activity in the United States and either:

(a) the agency or instrumentality has expressly or impliedly waived its immunity, or

(b) the judgment relates to a claim for which the agency or instrumentality is not immune from jurisdiction by virtue of the United States links mentioned in s 1605: para 14–38. In this case it is not necessary to show that the property sought to be seized was used for the activity upon which the claim is based. Any property is caught. The court has a discretion to suspend the attachment and execution and can therefore take into account arrangements necessary for the making of the payments including legislation.

Property "of a central bank or monetary authority held for its own account" is immune in the absence of an explicit waiver: s 1611(b)(1). Perhaps central banks cannot waive immunity from a prejudgment attachment, but commentators differ. The better view is that they can.

14–42 **Prejudgment attachments** The attachment of assets prior to the entry of judgment, e.g. to prevent the state from in the meantime removing the property to frustrate satisfaction of a judgment, requires an express waiver. An implied waiver will not suffice. Further, the property concerned must be property used for a commercial activity in the United Sates and the purpose of the attachment must be to secure satisfaction of a judgment that might be entered against the foreign state and not for the purpose of obtaining jurisdiction. There are several decisions construing whether waivers of immunity in treaties extended to prejudgment attachments. A waiver from "any right or immunity from legal proceedings including suit, judgment and execution" deimmunises a prejudgment attachment: *Libra Bank Ltd v Banco Nacional de Costa Rica*, 676 F 2d 47 (2d Cir 1982). See also *S&S Machinery v Masinexportimport*, 706 F 2d 411 (2d Cir 1983).

14–43 **Retained immunity** Section 1611 retains immunity for certain classes of property such as military property and the property of certain international organisations and of central banks. Unlike the United Kingdom, if an embassy account includes moneys intended for both governmental and commercial purposes, the identifiable commercial portion is attachable: *Birch Shipping Corpn v Tanzania*, 63 ILR (1980) 524.

Remedies (s 1606)

14–44 Section 1606 establishes that a deimmunised foreign state is liable as if it were a private party in like circumstances (except for punitive damages). It seems therefore that a court could grant an injunction or order specific performance although such orders may be difficult to enforce if the foreign state fails to comply and has no local assets.

Service of process (s 1608)

If the parties agree on a special arrangement as to service, then such service   **14–45** is sufficient for jurisdictional purposes. Lenders relying on, say, the New York courts will therefore request the appointment of a local agent for service of process and also back this up with procedures for the mailing of process.

If no special arrangement exists, then the Act sets out a hierarchy of methods which are to be followed. These include service under international convention or, if none, by registered mailing the prescribed documents to the Foreign Ministry of Affairs, or through diplomatic channels. All of these failed in the Iranian case of *New England Merchants National Bank v Iran Power Generation and Transmission Co*, 495 F Supp 73 (SDNY 1980), by reason of the disorder then prevailing in Iran. But the court was co-operative and devised another invention to serve process: telexes in Farsi and English.

Once service has been made then a foreign state must serve its answer within 60 days.

The court cannot enter a judgment by a default where the state fails to appear unless the plaintiff establishes his claim by evidence satisfactory to the court.

Comparison of United Kingdom and United States Immunity Legislation

While the State Immunity Act 1978 ("the UK Act") and the Foreign Sover-   **14–46** eign Immunities Act of 1976 ("the US Act") adopt the same principle of restrictive immunity, there are significant differences in the implementation of that general doctrine. While the divergences are of little importance where the loan instrument contains a specific submission by the borrower to the desired courts coupled with a procedure for the service of process within the jurisdiction and the borrower expressly waives immunity from suit and execution, the Acts yield different results where the borrower is not prepared to or does not have the constitutional power to submit to the jurisdiction of foreign courts or to grant express waivers. Without being exhaustive, some of the differences are set out below.

14–47 **Jurisdiction** The US Act creates jurisdiction in the Federal district courts. If a foreign state loses immunity by virtue of the Act, the US court will have subject-matter jurisdiction. The UK Act does not contain jurisdictional requirements but the court must have judicial jurisdiction over the foreign state under the English jurisdictional rules before the Act can come into effect.

The difference is apparent where the borrower is not prepared to waive immunity or specifically to submit to the jurisdiction. The English courts could nevertheless claim jurisdiction if, inter alia, the loan agreement is expressly or impliedly governed by English law: they could then apply the UK Act. In the United States however it is doubtful whether an express choice of, say, New York law, let alone an implied choice, would be adequate to confer jurisdiction for the purposes of the US Act.

14–48 **Commercial activity** The US Act does not expressly characterise borrowings as commercial activities although the legislative history of the Act and the commentaries tend to the conclusion that borrowings will fall within the definition. There seems little doubt about the matter. The UK Act removes all doubt by specifically including borrowings and guarantees within the commercial activity definitions. Further, under the US Act, commercial activity has to have the prescribed contact with the United States. Contact is not necessary in the United Kingdom. It follows that under the UK Act, state transactions enjoying no relation to the United Kingdom are justiciable and may be deimmunised.

14–49 **Contracting out** Under the UK Act a borrower can expressly contract out of the UK Act if it wishes to preserve its immunity from suit. Under the US Act perhaps a borrower cannot do so if the contract satisfies the prescribed contacts.

14–50 **Political subdivisions** Under the UK Act a constituent territory of a federal state is assimilated to public entities and therefore has lesser immunity protection. Municipalities and all political subdivisions will always be treated like separate entities unless (in the case of constituent territories) they are immunised by Order in Council. Under the US Act political subdivisions of all kinds, whether or not states in a federation, are assimilated to and benefit from the wider immunity accorded to foreign states.

14–51 **State entities** Under the UK Act "separate entities" need not be owned by the state to enjoy immunity. Under the US Act an "agency or instrumentality, of a foreign state" must be an organ of government or majority-owned. In practice there is probably little difference since a "separate entity" is immunised under the UK Act only if it is acting "in the exercise of sovereign authority" which is unlikely unless it is state-related. In both cases, central banks are in a privileged position.

Enforcement Under the UK Act, in the absence of a consent, property of a   **14–52**
state "for the time being in use or intended for use for commercial purposes" is not immune. Under the US Act in the absence of a waiver, the
deimmunised property of a state is (generally) limited to property used for a
commercial activity in the United States and which is or was used for the
commercial activity on which the claim is based.

Where a state waives immunity from enforcement, the waiver in the case
of the US Act applies (generally speaking) only to property in the United
States used for a commercial activity in the United States. In the case of the
UK Act a consent by a state to execution applies to all property of that state
anywhere and whether or not commercial. Naturally this is subject to the
practical limitation that the English courts cannot enforce an execution on
property abroad. The comparison in the case of state entities is rather more
complex.

Under the UK Act a consent to enforcement can (subject to very limited
exceptions) deimmunise military assets. Under the US Act military assets are
generally exempt from enforcement: see s 1611 of the US Act.

Central banks Assets of a central bank are in both cases specifically immu-   **14–53**
nised from enforcement unless there is an express waiver.

European Convention on State Immunity of 1972

Generally

This Convention was the first major international treaty on sovereign   **14–54**
immunity and has been ratified by at least six states: Austria, Belgium,
Cyprus, the Netherlands, Switzerland and the United Kingdom.

The purpose of the Convention is to remove the immunity from suit of
contracting states if the required jurisdictional criteria are met and to establish the reciprocal recognition and enforcement of judgments obtained
against a contracting state. It does not enlarge the possibilities of enforcement.

Immunity from suit

The Convention provides that if proceedings are brought against a contract-   **14–55**
ing state in the courts of another contracting state, then the defendant state
will not be entitled to immunity if the case falls within the catalogue in Arts
1 to 14, e.g. where a contracting state submits to the jurisdiction of the

courts of another contracting state (Art 2); or if it counterclaims (Art 1) or takes any step in the proceedings relating to the merits (Art 3); or if the proceedings relate to an obligation of the contracting state which is to be discharged in the territory of the forum state (Art 4); or where a contracting state participates in a company, association or other legal entity having its seat, registered office or principal place of business in the territory of the state of the forum (Art 6). Further a contracting state cannot claim immunity if it has in the territory of the state of the forum an office, agency or other establishment through which it engages "in an industrial, commercial or financial activity," and the proceedings relate to the activity of the office, agency or establishment: Art 7.

The essence of the catalogue is to establish reasonable jurisdictional links between the transaction and the courts concerned and thereby to avoid the implementation of exorbitant jurisdictional bases. If the case does not fall within the catalogue, then the state is immune: Art 15.

Reciprocal recognition and enforcement

14–56　The Convention establishes that execution may not be had in the state of the forum against the property of the contracting states. However in return for this immunity from enforcement, each contracting state accepts an obligation, subject to certain safeguards, to give effect to judgments given against it by the courts of another contracting state if the case falls within the catalogue of cases of non-immunity set out in the Convention: Art 22.

The effect therefore is that, although each contracting state has an international obligation to give effect to judgments rendered against it by the courts of another state where the judgment satisfies the relevant criteria, there is no direct enforcement: Art 23. Since private litigants might be prejudiced if a state gives too wide an interpretation to the overriding provisions which allow it to refuse implementation (e.g. on grounds of public policy) and because of the absence of the machinery for direct enforcement, Art 21 introduces a procedure for judicial control. The dissatisfied litigant can litigate the refusal before the courts of that state, for what that is worth. However under an optional additional protocol he can alternatively submit his case to an international European Tribunal composed of seven members of the European Court of Human Rights. The United Kingdom was not a signatory to this Protocol.

Optional regime

14–57　The immunity rules are more conservative than those applying in a number of European countries, such as the United Kingdom, Belgium, Germany and Switzerland. There is therefore an optional regime whereby contracting states can follow their own more progressive rules and declare that they will entertain proceedings against contracting to the extent that they entertain proceedings against third states, and limit their own immunity as against contracting states which reciprocate.

The effect of the optional regime differs according to whether the contracting state against whom the proceedings are brought has or has not also made a declaration under the optional Art 24.

If it has made a declaration, then it has an obligation to give effect to the judgment if certain jurisdictional requirements are met. Further, subject to certain conditions, property in the state of the forum can be levied against if that property is used exclusively in connection with an industrial or commercial activity in which the state has been engaged in the same manner as a private person and if the proceedings related to that activity. The United Kingdom has made such a declaration.

If on the other hand the other contracting state has not made a declaration, then, although it can still be sued under the more extensive deimmunisation rules in the state which has made such a declaration, there is no obligation to give effect to the judgment. In addition its property in the state of the forum cannot be subjected to forced execution.

Chapter 15

STATE INSOLVENCY

Meaning of state insolvency

15–1 A state is insolvent when it is unable to meet its foreign currency liabilities as they fall due.

The alternative test of deficiency of assets to cover liabilities is not appropriate because most of a state's assets are not realisable. The inability to pay relates to foreign currency obligations only: a state need never be bankrupt by reason of liabilities denominated in its domestic currency because it can create its own currency.

State insolvency is to be distinguished from the repudiation of foreign debt. A state repudiates where, whether or not in a position to meet its foreign currency liabilities as they fall due, it declares it will not meet those foreign currency liabilities or adopts other legislative measures which have the effect of expropriating its creditors. Such measures include whole or partial cancellations, the imposition of excessive exchange controls or taxes, conversion of foreign debt into irredeemable local currency scrip and other acts amounting to a constructive taking.

15–2 A declared repudiation cannot cancel the legal claim – at least if it is governed by an external law. The legal effect of a repudiation is to give a right to the creditor to treat the contract as at an end and to call in the loan.

The most prominent examples of outright repudiations were the repudiation of Confederate bonds by the carpetbagger governments, the repudiation of Tzarist and Kerensky issues by the former USSR, the effective repudiation in the late 1940s of Chinese foreign debt in arrears since before the war, and the various constructive or declared repudiations of debt on Communist takeovers by some Eastern European countries after World War II (although some of these were subsequently settled), by Cuba in the 1960s and by Vietnam in the 1970s. The 1917 Russian repudiation amounted to £944,813,762 plus a further £850,000,000 in Treasury Bonds issued as cover for advances made by the Allied Powers during World War I.

Outline history of state insolvency

15–3 Pre–1950 data in this section are based mainly on Borchard & Wynne, *State Insolvency and Foreign Bondholders* (1951) 2 vols, Yale University Press.

State insolvency has been a feature of international lending from time immemorial. The banks of Bardi and Peruzzi were ruined by the defaults of King Edward III on his Italian debts after his accession in 1327. The Medici Bank had to write off most of its loans to King Edward IV following his expensive embroilment in the Wars of the Roses.

Since the Napoleonic Wars, four decades of widespread default are discernible.

1825–1835 The first foreign bond default on the London Stock Exchange   15–4
was an 8 per cent £500,000 loan to Joseph I, Emperor of Germany, floated in 1706 and raised at the suggestion of the Duke of Marlborough. Apparently that was paid. It was only after the Napoleonic wars that London was besieged by states desirous of obtaining bond loans, with unhappy results. In the decade beginning in 1825 the London bond issues raised on the basis of colourful prospectuses by the newly independent South American republics (notably Colombia, Chile, Peru, Buenos Aires, Brazil, Mexico and Guatemala) quickly went into default and remained so episodically throughout much of the nineteenth century. Spain defaulted in 1823. Portugal repudiated the Don Miguel loan in 1832 on the grounds, unmeritorious in international law, that Don Miguel was a usurper. Greece was soon in default on its romantic independence loans of 1824 and 1825. The Greek default was hardly surprising. The nominal amount of the 1825 loan was £2 million. It was issued at $56\frac{1}{2}$. After deduction of this and that, only £275,000 reached Greece, £60,000 of it in stores. The loan remained dishonoured until 1879.

1870s The 1870s brought to an end another period of foreign loan mania.   15–5
Again most of the defaulters were Latin American states (including Honduras, Paraguay, Santo Domingo, Costa Rica and Venezuela) joined now by Turkey and Egypt (in 1862). Some investors had purchased £200,000 of bonds secured on the wealth of Poyais. Poyais was in fact a swamp in South America.

The scandals generated by the speculative fever led to the House of Commons Select Committee Report of 1875. Portugal and Greece again went into default in 1892 and 1893 respectively. Between 1870 and 1914 Britain exported about £3,500 million capital.

Governmental interventions In principle a default by a state is not, under   15–6
public international law, in itself an international delinquency which the state of the creditor is called upon to vindicate: see the *Colombian Bond cases (US v Colombia)* (1868), cited in Moore B, *History and Digest of the International Arbitrations to which the United States has been a Party,* 5

vols, I (1898) p 3612; *Ballistini Case, Italy v Venezuela*, UN Rep, Vol X, p 18 (1903). States become engaged to protect their nationals only in the case of an international wrong, such as denial of injustice, expropriation without compensation or unjustifiable discrimination.

As to state practice, the attitude adopted by Canning in 1824 and more or less by states ever since (although the practice has not been uniform) is that foreign offices are not debt-collecting agencies.

But direct intervention by foreign powers in the financial administration of insolvent states and the appointment of customs or other receiverships was not uncommon. The measures included participation by bondholder representatives in the financial agencies of the debtor state, the establishment of foreign financial commissions, and receiverships of customs duties and other revenues. Classic examples were the Ottoman Debt Council (1881–1944) controlled by foreign allied powers, and the Egyptian Caisse de la Dette Publique (1880–1940) instituted initially by five European powers and performing functions similar to a trustee in bankruptcy. Other debtors subjected to foreign financial control included Tunis (1869), Greece (1898) and Morocco (1902). The US established customs receiverships in respect of Santo Domingo (1907), Haiti (1916), Nicaragua (1911), Panama, Cuba and Liberia. International financial control was established by the League of Nations over some of the lesser European states in the Inter-War period, especially Austria, Hungary and Greece. For a review, see Borchard & Wynne, *State Insolvency and Foreign Bondholders* (1951) vol I p 277 *et seq*.

Much of this intervention was motivated by political considerations rather than solicitude for bondholders. In the post-colonial period, such intervention became politically unacceptable and was replaced by the orderly, voluntary intervention achieved through IMF economic stabilisation programmes as a condition of IMF standby arrangements for member states.

Military intervention (Mexico, 1861; Venezuela, 1902) to secure payment is patently unlawful.

15–7   **1930s** The third general collapse on foreign debt payments took place in the 1930s largely as a result of the Depression which itself was partially influenced by the post-War dislocation and the running sore of German reparations. World War I itself had generated relatively few defaults on foreign public debt except for the (not unexpected) suspension of payments by belligerents. The principal exception was the Soviet repudiation of the Tzar's foreign debt: this had the most impact on French investments. The United States replaced Britain as the main provider of foreign capital.

During the 1930s all European countries (except Finland) defaulted on World War I loans made by the United States thereby provoking much US resentment, a resentment captured by President Coolidge's remark: "They hired the money, didn't they?" Seventeen out of 20 Latin American states (not Venezuela, Argentina and Honduras) fell into arrears on their external bond issues: all except three had settled bondholder claims by 1950. New South Wales was one of a number of British Commonwealth territories which imposed a moratorium or reduced foreign claims by legislation. On occasion bondholder claims were diminished by other means, notably the outlawing of gold clauses by the United States and other states. A list of states abrogating gold clauses appears in Nussbaum, *Money in the Law, National and International* (2nd ed 1950) pp 280–283. Another example was the German conversion in the 1930s of foreign currency claims into local currency payable locally, a legislative act which gave rise to much litigation in Europe and elsewhere.

1945–1980 After World War II, a number of outstanding defaults remained   15–8
unsettled. Two important milestones in debt rescheduling were the Anglo-American Financial Agreement of 1946 and the Multilateral London Conference on German External Debt of 1953 which adjusted and reduced the German foreign debt. This latter agreement was highly concessionary (partly as a reaction to the vengeful post-World War I Treaty of Versailles) and was remarkable for its espousal of the concept that a renegotiation should take into account what a debtor can pay as opposed to what it ought to pay.

The 1950s also saw settlements of the external debt of Japan, Italy and Austria. For details of these and the 1953 German Settlement, see GR Delaume, *Legal Aspects of International Lending and Economic Development Financing* (1967) pp 337 *et seq.*

State defaults accelerated in the 1960s and 1970s. Countries which, between 1956 and 1980 entered into multilateral debt relief agreements include Argentina, Brazil, Chile, Ghana, India, Indonesia, Pakistan, Peru, Turkey, Sierra Leone, Zaire, Liberia, Madagascar, Senegal, Togo, Uganda and Poland. India and Turkey were chronically insolvent during most of the 1970s. The first Argentinian insolvency of this period was in 1956.

Detailed tables may be found in Hardy, *Rescheduling Developing Country Debts 1956–1980: Lessons and Recommendations*, February 1982, Working Paper No 1, Overseas Development Council; Cizauskas, *International Debt Renegotiation, Lessons from the Past*, World Development, vol 7 1979.

1980s State insolvency in the 1980s dwarfed all previous eras. Nearly all   15–9
the countries in Africa, Latin America and the independent Caribbean and most in Sovietised Central Europe became insolvent in the 1980s. Other countries included Egypt and North Korea.

The new features of state insolvency in the 1980s compared to, say, a century before that included the following (amongst others):

1. The **deimmunisation** of states from judicial process in many jurisdictions, thereby replacing diffuse financial sanctions by compelling legal sanctions. Most credit contracts contain express waivers of immunity which are effective in most developed countries. However, since there is no international bankruptcy machinery as such, debt settlements must still be achieved by agreement between creditors and the debtor state. A review of state insolvency remains largely a narrative of debt relief negotiations as opposed to a description of rules of law.

2. The replacement of direct foreign intervention in the management of a country's finances (customs receiverships, foreign financial control, military pressures) by the orderly and voluntary economic intervention achieved through **IMF programmes.**

3. **Limitations on the monetary sovereignty** of states resulting from global economic interdependence and, at the legal level, from international treaties, in particular the Articles of Agreement of the IMF. Until the establishment of the IMF, international monetary law (as opposed to episodic co-operative practices) was negligible.

15–10 4. Change in the **identity of creditor,** namely the replacement of public bond debt (as the main category of foreign borrowing) by government or government-insured credits by commercial bank loans. In addition, after World War I, and particularly in the 1960s and 1970s the industrialised countries promoted exports by providing insured, subsidised export credits and thereby built up large contingent claims on foreign countries. The explosion of commercial bank loans was in the 1970s fuelled by the need to recycle OPEC deposits. A large proportion of state debt was comprised of short to medium-term floating rate bank credits as opposed to the relatively long term fixed rate bonds which formed the main mode of private foreign investment prior to, say, the 1930s. Banks are sophisticated institutions and are more amenable to official pressures: in practice therefore the rescheduling process became much easier and better organised.

5. The relatively non-competitive, coordinated efficiency of ad hoc or permanent **negotiating committees** to deal with state insolvency, notably the Paris Club and commercial bank steering committees.

6. The proliferation of **state agencies and instrumentalities** as state borrowing arms. These state entities may be subject to the conventional bankruptcy jurisdiction. The state may benefit from the veil of incorporation. See para 15–22 *et seq.*

Causes of state insolvency

States become insolvent for much the same reasons as do corporations: mis-   **15–11**
management or misfortune or both.

Mismanagement includes over-borrowing, governmental over-spending, poor financial management, inadequate financial statistics, and, in some cases, particularly with despotic governments, official embezzlement and fraud on a gigantic scale.

Misfortune outside the reasonable control of the state have included wars, economic slumps, increases in interest rates, collapse of commodity prices (important for commodity producing countries), and uplifts in oil prices (as in the 1970s as a result of the OPEC cartel).

Comparison with municipal bankruptcy

Although recent trends have tended to approximate states increasingly to   **15–12**
the legal status of other subjects of law commensurate with the extensive participation by states in commercial activities, a great and inevitable disparity still exists between a municipal bankruptcy and the bankruptcy of a state. Some of the differences may be listed as follows:

– **Realisation** In contrast to a municipal bankruptcy, the fixed assets of a state, such as its land, cannot be realised for division amongst the creditors. The emphasis must therefore be on rehabilitating the state's foreign earning capacity out of which the external debt must be paid and encouraging the necessary internal economic disciplines. In other words, final liquidation is not available – only a consensual debt reorganisation.

– **Management** The economic affairs of the state cannot be taken over and managed by a receiver, trustee in bankruptcy, judicial manager or other representative of the creditors. The debtor stays in posession. Direct intervention, as adopted by capital exporting countries in the nineteenth and early twentieth centuries, is now generally unacceptable on political grounds. In the post-colonial era, creditors have to rely on other indirect means, e.g. IMF stabilisation programmes. The IMF is the only company doctor available and has less authority than a new chief executive installed by the creditors. The continued authority of the government may be threatened by the insolvency, a factor which has to be taken into account in rescheduling negotiations. Chaotic and rapidly changing management is quite usual.

– **Freeze on creditor suits** Creditor suits or attachments in external courts   **15–13**
cannot be frozen by a bankruptcy order or judicial moratorium to prevent piecemeal seizures in the interests of equality and an orderly realisation. There are no freezes on contract cancellations, accelerations,

---

set-off or security enforcement or title finance repossessions on the lines of those found in the more draconian judicial reorganisation laws for corporate debtors.

– **Dissenting creditors** In contrast to municipal laws allowing judicially approved creditor plans, debt reorganisations of state debt cannot be imposed on dissenting creditor minorities by majority creditor vote or judicial sanction. Consensus is needed. This has to be achieved by peer pressure, recognition of mutuality, and official arm-twisting.

– **Disclosure** Apart from statistics resulting from treaty arrangements, e.g. the International Financial Statistics collected by the IMF, there are no internationally enforced disclosure obligations.

– **Preferences** There are no statutory rules for the recovery of preferential payments or transfers to a creditor while the state is insolvent and no statutory disgorge of fraudulent preferences.

15–14　– **Security** Most state debt is unsecured, although security is sometimes found, e.g. over crop receivables, foreign investment securities or bullion. Any restructured debt cannot in practice be secured.

– **Priorities** Priority or equality of payment must be settled by the difficult process of agreement.

– **Discharge** A bankrupt individual can secure a discretionary discharge. A company can be dissolved. But a state cannot obtain a discharge for debts which it cannot and is unlikely to be able to pay except by agreement with the creditors prepared to cancel debt and except in certain cases where the debt is governed by the state's own law. Hence a state cannot usually wipe the slate clean of the misfortunes or excesses of previous administrations. Strictly the abstract claim for the debt can remain for ever, assuming creditors take appropriate action to keep the claim alive under limitation or prescription legislation. This must inevitably be the case since the state does not realise its assets to pay its creditors.

– **Delinquencies** The management of a state is not generally subject to municipal rules imposing personal liability or sanctioning delinquencies or the negligent assumption of liabilities where there is no reasonable prospect of their being paid as and when due. But the citizenry can sometimes express their views.

15–15　– **Currency** On a muncipal bankruptcy, foreign currency claims are commonly converted compulsorily into local currency. This does not occur on state insolvency – fortunately for creditors. But this means that currencies may not receive equal treatment.

– **Interest** Interest continues to run. On a muncipal bankruptcy, post-insolvency interest is usually not claimable or (what amounts to the same thing) is subordinated to other creditors. As a result, the interest piles up and massively increases the defaulted capital.

— **Set-off** Set-off continues to be available on the basis of the solvent rules. On a municipal bankruptcy, some states enhance the ordinary set-off, while others forbid it altogether.

— **Debt/equity conversions** The state cannot be rendered solvent by a conversion of debt into equity. But there are rough approximations: see para 16–18 *et seq.*

Claims commissions

Governments have intervened in the past to regulate the claims of their   15–16
creditor nationals by the establishment of claims commissions. These have taken a number of forms, e.g. (i) commissions to realise local enemy property taken into custodianship or seized in war-time or in the case of other diplomatic collapse and to distribute the proceeds to national creditors; (ii) mixed commissions established by treaty between a creditor and debtor state to consider and settle the claims of nationals out of lump sum payments by a debtor state. The latter class have been used more for expropriation and tort claims than for loans in default.

An important commission is the Foreign Claims Settlement Commission of the United States charged with the responsibility of determining the validity of claims brought by US nationals against specified foreign governments for failure to pay compensation for the expropriation of the property of US nationals. An instance of the establishment of a mixed arbitral tribunal for the settlement of claims was the Algiers Agreement signed between the United States and Iran in January 1979.

One question is whether a court of a foreign country not party to the treaty would regard the national's claim as liquidated by the settlement. On normal principles of composition law, a creditor should be bound by the settlement if he assented to it, e.g. by claiming or receiving a benefit: see *Dunlop Rubber Co v WB Haigh & Sons* [1937] 1 KB 347. If he did not assent to it and his claim is governed by another system of law, the legislation establishing the Commission may not be recognised by a foreign court as discharging the claim on usual principles of private international law.

Protections to insolvent states

Now that states have been deimmunised in most developed states in relation   15–17
to commercial credits and in view of the widespread use and validity of contractual waivers of immunity in credit agreements, a state which defaults on

its foreign obligations is exposed to judicial action by foreign creditors and to execution over foreign assets. No bankruptcy law can intervene to protect the state by imposing a freeze on creditor actions. Nevertheless, substantial protections of a legal and practical nature still remain.

15–18 **Local assets inviolable** A major difference between a municipal bankruptcy and a state bankruptcy is that most of a state's assets are inviolable from legal process. Creditors cannot seize and sell off portions of territory. A state can pass legislation, binding on its courts, immunising domestic assets from execution, and many have done so. It is hence only the foreign assets which are potentially exposed, such as bank accounts, foreign investments, bullion and trading contracts. In practice some of these foreign assets are likely to have been run down by the state in an attempt to ward off the insolvency.

15–19 **Monetary sovereignty** A state may, by the exercise of its monetary sovereignty over its own currency, depreciate the claims of creditors denominated in that currency, e.g. by inflationary monetary policies (printing more money) or devaluations. But this does not help with foreign currency loans.

15–20 **Legislative sovereignty** When the obligation in question is governed by the state's own system of law, then a unilateral moratorium postponing that obligation may be recognised by external courts. Other measures which have been recognised by external courts in these circumstances include exchange controls, the imposition of withholding taxes and forced conversion of the debt into scrip payable domestically in the domestic currency.

The efficacy of these measures depends upon contract conflicts rules. The English principle is that an exchange control or the like will be ineffective if it does not arise not under the governing law of the contract so that an external governing law provides insulation. This is the position adopted by the 1980 Rome Convention on the Law Applicable to Contracts which is discussed elsewhere in this series on international financial law.

15–21 **IMF Articles of Agreement, Article VIII, s 2(b)** Under Art VIII, s 2(b) of the Bretton Woods Agreement establishing the IMF, there is provision for mutual recognition by the courts of IMF members of each others exchange controls applicable to "exchange contracts" if the controls are consistent with the IMF Agreement. This provision has had a limited reception by municipal courts. England, Belgium and the United States will not normally regard a loan contract as being within this provision, but the courts of Germany, Luxembourg and France may do so. This topic, too, is discussed elsewhere in this series.

Sovereign immunity Foreign assets may be protected by the immunity doctrine, especially central banks and embassy accounts. However many state loan agreements contain elaborate waiver clauses which, as it has been seen, now achieve wide recognition in industrialised countries where a state's foreign assets may be situate. The availability of sovereign immunity has been reviewed above.

State entities and veil of incorporation Where the foreign debt is owed by a separate state entity as opposed to the state itself, the state has a greater freedom in readjusting their obligations and greater protection against foreign creditor remedies. The state entity itself is in a worse position. See the next section.

Insolvency of state entities

Generally Where the borrowing entity is separate from the state itself and is **15–22** not merely an organ or alter ego of government, the strictly legal position of the state is decidedly improved. This is so even though the deimmunisation of state entities is more complete than in the case of the state itself.

Public corporations include those which perform governmental functions (such as central banks), those which are financial organisations, such as foreign trade or investment banks, those which are part of the basic administration or infrastructure of the state (post offices, railways, forests, mines) and those which are purely commercial enterprises (such as state holding companies). They may be run as arms of government (financed by government appropriations and managed by government officials) or they may enjoy commercial autonomy. They may be formed as statutory corporations without shares or as ordinary joint-stock companies under general company legislation. The constitution and functions of the state entity have a crucial effect on its status under local law and also under the laws of other states.

Where a state entity is in law treated as an autonomous entity separate from the state itself and not merely part of the state, the state may be shielded from the legal consequences of a default by that entity and may enjoy an enlarged legislative ability to impose debt relief upon foreign creditors. One may note some of the consequences if the state entity is indeed a separate autonomous corporation enjoying independent legal personality.

Veil of incorporation The state itself cannot be sued for a default on the **15–23** obligations of the state entity. Subject to exceptions, a shareholder, even a sole shareholder, is not liable for the debts of the company except in exceptional cases, e.g. agency or excessive commingling.

Conversely, the assets of a state entity, such as an airline or central bank are not available to satisfy the obligations of the state. See, e.g. France: Judgment of July 21, 1987, Cass (*Société Ltd Benvenuti v Banque Commerciale Congolaise*), 115 Clunet 108 (1988); US: *Letelier v Republic of Chile*, 748 F 2d 790 (2d 1984), cert denied, 105 S Ct 2656 1985; *Hercaire International Inc v Argentina*, 821 F 2d 559 (11th Cir 1987). But in Switzerland, see the Judgment of April 24, 1985, TF (*Socialistiche Libysche Arabishe Volks-Jamahirya v Actimon SA*), 108 La Semaine Judiciaire 33 (1986). The veil of incorporation was lifted in *First National City Bank v Banco Para el Comercio Exterior de Cuba*, 462 US 611 (1983) (veil could be pierced if the state entity is a mere agent of the government or if the corporate form was abused to work fraud or injustice).

As a matter of international law, a state does not, in the absence of wrongful interference, incur international responsibility for subordinate political sub-divisions, e.g. a municipality: see *Winget Claim*, 26 ILR (1957) 255. Various claims commissions have upheld this rule, e.g. the 1920s Anglo-Turkish Mixed Arbitral Tribunal (Turkey not liable for debts of Vilayet of Adrianople) and the Romanian-German Mixed Arbitral Tribunal (Germany not liable for the debts of Hamburg). The US Supreme Court refused to exercise jurisdiction where the Prince of Monaco bought up Confederate repudiated bonds and, as a sovereign and equal, invoked the original jurisdiction of the Supreme Court: *Monaco v Mississippi*, 292 US 313 (1934).

15–24   **Set-off** Bank deposits for the account of the state's central bank or another state entity cannot be used by way of set-off against the obligations of the borrowing state entity. It is universally true that mutuality is required for set-off.

15–25   **Transfers of assets** The state can pass reorganisation legislation providing for the transfer of the assets of the state entity to another state organisation. In 1971 the United Kingdom passed a statute purporting to transfer assets from the troubled Rolls-Royce. Asset-strips run into difficulties. They may be regarded as a preference under foreign municipal law. The statute transferring the assets may not be recognised by external courts if the asset concerned is treated as being outside the territorial jurisdiction of the legislating state or is otherwise contrary to the public policy of the forum. Foreign judicial recognition of expropriatory devices is discussed elsewhere in this series of works. The English courts will recognise a transfer of corporate assets only if the transferee is universal successor to the assets and liabilities of the transferor: *National Bank of Greece and Athens v Metliss* [1958] AC 509 (universal succession recognised); contrast *Re United Railways of Havana etc Warehouses Ltd* [1961] AC 1007, HL, where an attempted novation of the debt by Cuban legislation was held ineffective to discharge the debtor under a contract governed by Pennsylvanian law in the absence of universal succession.

Exchange controls Where a state itself imposes restrictions which inhibit its   15–26
own obligations, the state itself is unilaterally purporting to alter its contracts and it is possible that foreign courts will be less inclined to recognise the effect of the exchange restrictions. This limitation is less apt where the state entity is the obligor and the state interferes with its obligations by an embargo or exchange control or price regulation or export ban. One arm of the state is imposing force majeure on another in the general interests of the state.

> In *Czarnikow Ltd v Rolimpex* [1979] AC 351, HL, a Polish state entity contracted to sell sugar. A serious sugar shortage arose in Poland. The government imposed an export ban. The state entity claimed this was government intervention beyond its control rather a force majeure clause. *Held* by the House of Lords: the state entity was relieved because it was distinct from the state. They had not colluded in the ban.

> In *The Playa Larga* [1983)] 2 Lloyd's Rep 171, CA, a Cuban state trading enterprise agreed to deliver a quantity of sugar to a Chilean company with state connections. Following a right-wing coup in Chile, Cuba broke off diplomatic relations with Chile and ordered the sugar-bearing ships out of Chilean waters. *Held*: the sugar contract was effectively frustrated. It was not a self-induced frustration, since, said the court, the Cuban state trading enterprise was a separate legal entity. This ruling appears to give a state trading enterprise a readily available way out of embarrassing contracts.

The US Act of State cases involving Costa Rican and Mexican state banks in the 1980s on this topic are reviewed elsewhere in this series of works.

Domestic liquidation of state entities A state may endeavour to secure a dis-   15–27
charge of the foreign obligations of an insolvent state entity by liquidating the entity under local law. The liquidation of a government instrumentality or a statutory corporation may require a special local decree.

In practice, the most important impact of a local liquidation is that usually foreign currency debts are compulsorily converted into local currency. If the local currency is depreciating rapidly – which it usually is if the state is insolvent – the effect is to expropriate the foreign currency creditor to the great advantage of the state itself.

Foreign liquidation of state entities Neither the UK State Immunity Act   15–28
1978 nor the US Foreign Service Immunities Act of 1976 deal with bankruptcy specifically so recourse must be had to the general deimmunisation rules in those Acts.

Where the state entity is formed under the ordinary laws of a country other than the debtor state, it will usually be subject to local bankruptcy procedures in the same way as other municipal companies. The most common state entities incorporated abroad and likely to incur foreign debt are state-owned or joint venture banks and government trading organisations. The state entity may be incorporated under the laws of the debtor state but have branches or assets abroad. In most countries, the presence of local assets is sufficient to confer insolvency jurisdiction on the foreign court where the assets are. Insolvency jurisdiction is examined elsewhere in this series.

One question is whether the state entity is subject to foreign municipal bankruptcy law. Aside from questions of immunity, the general tendency of bankruptcy legislation appears to be to exclude foreign state agencies and public corporations from the general bankruptcy jurisdiction exercisable over foreign entities. Recourse must be had to case law to define the characteristics of a public body sufficient to exempt it from jurisdiction.

15–29   In **England,** it would seem that a corporation must share the characteristics of a company formed under the Companies Acts before it can be wound-up under the provisions of the Insolvency Act 1986 applying to the liquidation of foreign companies: see s 220 *et seq.* It is considered that administrative corporations such as municipalities will usually be outside the Act and it is possible that state corporations exercising governmental functions may also be outside the Act.

Some of the indicia of a public administrative corporation might include: establishment by special statute, rather than registration under ordinary local company legislation; performance of governmental or administration functions as opposed to commercial activities; responsibilities of the management owed to the government; finance provided by government appropriations; governmental control of borrowings and other finance; no shareholders as such, and appointment of government nominees to the directorate. There is much English case law: see, e.g. *Tamlin v Hannaford* [1950] 1 KB 18, CA (UK public corporation); *Canno Brewery Co Ltd v Central Land Board* [1919] AC 744; *International Railway Co v Niagara Parks Commission* [1941] AC 328; *Pfizer Corpn v Ministry of Health* [1965] AC 512, HL; *Mellenger v New Brunswick Development Corpn* [1971] 1 WLR 604.

15–30   In the **United States** it appears that foreign states and departments, agencies or instrumentalities of a foreign state or other foreign government entities are excluded from the jurisdiction of the Bankruptcy Reform Act of 1978: see s 109 when read with s 101(30).

In **Germany** the bankruptcy jurisdiction is of wider scope and applies to all natural persons and corporations whether or not commercial. It appears uncertain whether foreign public corporations are subject to the jurisdiction. Section 213 of BA 1877 as amended extends the bankruptcy jurisdiction to persons and associations which can be sued in their collective name under civil procedure legislation, but it may be that these are limited to German judicial persons. A new German bankruptcy act has been enacted and will come into force on January 1, 1999.

In **Italy,** Art 1(1) of BA 1942, as amended, explicitly excludes public bodies from bankruptcy proceedings. The exclusion would extend to both Italian and foreign public bodies.

CHAPTER 16

RESCHEDULING OF STATE DEBT

Introduction

16–1 A state whose credit is deteriorating commonly experiences a rapid shortening of its credit terms, a rapid increase in short-term liabilities and finally a complete drying-up of credit. The pattern has been that the state then consults with its main bank and government creditors and issues a moratorium request. This "cut-off request" is significant because it stabilises the situation by assuring creditors that they are to be equally treated and ends the "pay now" demands.

Debt is usually rescheduled on the "short-leash" approach. Under the short-leash, the amount of debt which is rescheduled is limited to a proportion of the amount of existing or imminent arrears. The rescheduled debt is defined as arrears at the cut-off date plus payments falling due over, say, the next six to 18 months.

The objectives of the short-leash approach in the eyes of the creditors are (a) to encourage the debtor state to adopt an austerity programme to improve its capacity to pay; (b) to enable the creditors to monitor performance and to ascertain whether additional relief in future years will be warranted; (c) to maintain the creditors' bargaining power; and (d) to discourage an over-easy debt relief.

Hierarchy of creditors

16–2 There is generally a hierarchy of creditors:

1. **Supranational creditors** These are generally the IMF, the World Bank and regional development organisations. Theoretically, supranational creditors do not reschedule (although the IMF may roll over one standby into another). The argument is that either they are lenders of last resort or provide development loans which are the foundation of a nation's credit. The real reason perhaps is that they have the necessary diplomatic power to resist wholesale rescheduling.

2. **Government debt** This is either direct inter-governmental debt or debt

produced by the calling of export credit guarantees. Government debt is generally rescheduled on Paris Club principles formulated since an Argentine insolvency in 1956 when the Club, formed of the finance ministers of leading industrial nations, was established under the chairmanship of the French Minister of Finance. The rescheduling is not development aid and is not concessional; access to the Club is available only in an emergency; and the debtor country must undertake an IMF programme, i.e. Paris Club members do not monitor the debtor state's economy themselves. Each member of the Club reschedules on a comparable basis implemented by bilateral treaties within the multilateral guidelines laid down by the Club minutes, and other countries are expected to do the same. The Club has no set rules or formal constitution.

3. **Public bond issues** Public bond issues are difficult to reschedule. In practice, the amounts are usually fairly small in relation to the rest of the defaulted debt because financially weak states have not usually been able to borrow publicly in the Eurobond market. Government bond issues do not generally have a trustee, and corporate bondholder community statutes will not usually apply. Hence it is not possible to stop a single bondholder from suing for his money and thereby disturbing the equality principle. A paradoxical effect of the absence of a trustee and trust deed (which commonly contains a "no-action" clause) is to enhance the position of holders of the public debt of a state. Prior to 1950 most of the external debt of insolvent states took the form of public bonds: these were rescheduled by exchange or consolidation schemes negotiated with quasi-official foreign bondholder councils, most of which are now defunct.

4. **Commercial bank debt** Because commercial banks are well organised and subject to official and commercial pressures and because the amount of the debt, if written off, may have a devastating effect on their balance sheets, the international banking community can quickly be organised into rescheduling agreements. Whether short-term debt or letter of credit debt is rescheduled depends upon the severity of the insolvency. The negotiation is effected through a steering committee comprised of the main bank creditors who perform a liaison role. 16–3

5. **Trade debt** Trade debt is usually not rescheduled, partly for pragmatic reasons and partly because trade debt can usually be unilaterally "pipelined" by the introduction of exchange controls by the debtor state. Because the debt concerned is generally governed by the law of the debtor state, the modification of maturities by the exchange control will generally be recognised by foreign courts. Sometimes this pipelining of trade debt is put on an orderly basis under a supplier's arrears

programme, e.g. Turkey (1970s) and sometimes the debt may be the subject of a formal scheme, e.g. Nigeria (1980s) , where trade debt was assumed by the central bank which issued medium-term notes to the foreign creditors in exchange for the trade debt.

Rescheduling agreements

16–4   A rescheduling agreement itself is very similar to a gigantic syndicated credit containing clauses found in normal syndicated credits but much elaborated. All bank creditors sign and it is generally a condition precedent to the effectiveness of the agreement that a high threshold of eligible debt is attained, e.g. 90 per cent. Often new money is required: this has sometimes been used to pay defaulted interest so as to relieve the balance sheets of the banks, since otherwise a major series of reschedulings resulting in necessary writedowns of non-performing loans might have threatened the solvency of international banks. The new money participations are pro-rated according to exposures. The grant of security, the sale of territory and the transfer of producing assets to a state corporation issuing shares to foreign creditors are all theoretically possible, but politically out of the question.

16–5   If the mechanics of the rescheduling involve a refinancing of the defaulted debt, the roll-over may technically spark off pro rata sharing clauses in syndicated credits if not all members of the syndicate choose to reschedule (generally they have little choice in commercial terms). Objections by sub-participants in loans which have been laid off by untidy sub-participation methods have given rise to a little litigation but have commonly been resolved by negotiation. The main difficulties are that the technical roll-over might be deemed to be a repayment compelling a lead bank to pay the sub-participant, and that it is difficult to commit the sub-participant to any new money. Contractual clauses dealing with these situations are reviewed elsewhere in this series.

Apart from deimmunisation by comprehensive waiver clauses and the usual submissions to external law and forum, the exposure of the state to foreign creditors is increased by virtue of requirements for centralisation of the international monetary assets with the central bank so as (inter alia) to render them more accessible; and cross-guarantees of the state, the central bank and certain public sector entities, thereby removing the effect of the veil of incorporation.

This increase in technical legal exposure is compensated by majority bank controls of acceleration and by pro rata sharing clauses which together seriously inhibit unilateral action.

Reconciliation of debts The debtor state will usually appoint a firm of inter- **16–6**
national accountants to verify the debt claims eligible for the rescheduling.
The purposes of this verification procedure include the efficient auditing of
claims by an impartial expert of professional standing to resolve the discrepancies between creditor claims and debtor records (discrepancies which
invariably exist and which might otherwise seriously delay the rescheduling), and the protection of the confidentiality of the original debt agreements.

Currencies Where the debt being rescheduled is denominated in a great **16–7**
many currencies, it may be provided that the creditors must elect to convert
their debt into one or more specified currencies commonly dealt in the international financial markets. The purpose of the conversion is to facilitate the
administration of the agreement, to provide for a relatively common basis
for determining interest and to reaffirm the pro rata principle between the
bank creditors concerned.

"Most favoured debt" clause A fundamental principle of insolvency is the **16–8**
doctrine that the unsecured creditors of the same class are paid pari passu.
Since there is no bankruptcy regime to enforce this principle in the case of
states, it has to be achieved by contract. The most significant clause in this
context is the "most favoured debt" clause which provides that if any other
foreign currency debt having the same maturity as the rescheduled debt is
paid out more quickly, then the borrower must repay the rescheduled debt.
The clause will then go on to exclude certain categories of debt which can be
paid in priority, e.g. IMF debt, trade debt, foreign exchange contract
obligations, interest, public bonds and other agreed categories. One effect of
this clause (which also appears in Paris Club minutes) is to encourage all
eligible creditors to come into the rescheduling. The clauses are theoretically
difficult to monitor but in practice states have an interest in complying.

An addition provides that, if a third party guarantees or secures any of
the rescheduled debt, or any debt eligible for the rescheduling but which did
not participate, the state will procure that the guarantee or security is made
available to the rescheduled debt pro rata. The purpose of this is to disallow
preferential protection being offered by third parties, such as an international organisation, to some debt, but not the rest. Although the state
cannot procure that a third party will not give support, in practice the state
would be involved in any such scheme, and non-compliance is sanctioned by
an event of default.

Economic management Rescheduling agreements almost invariably do not **16–9**
impose direct economic controls upon the debtor state or attempt to write
an economic austerity programme. The two main techniques for securing
improved economic management are requirements as to compliance with an

IMF programme, and the "short-leash" approach to rescheduling, i.e. the banks reschedule only limited amounts at a time, such as the maturities during the current and the following year, there being the implied sanction that subsequent maturities will not be rescheduled unless satisfactory progress is made.

16–10 **Covenants** Generally there are only three significant covenants in a rescheduling agreement; these are an extensive information covenant, a negative pledge and a pari passu clause.

1. **Negative pledge** The negative pledge provides that the state will not create or permit to subsist any security interests over its assets. In a corporate context, the clause is intended to prevent subordination of the unsecured creditor and to prevent discrimination between creditors. In the case of states, the negative pledge is designed to prevent the allocation of scarce international monetary assets or exportable assets to a single creditor and is therefore a form of pari passu clause. The prohibition commonly applies to all state-controlled entities to prevent the state from evading the negative pledge by depositing precious assets capable of earning foreign currency in a separate state company which grants the security. Usually governmental negative pledges are limited to external debt. This is commonly defined as debt denominated, payable or optionally payable otherwise than in the currency of the borrower or payable to a non-resident (even if in local currency). This formulation reflects the fact that states do not generally charge their assets as security for internal domestic borrowings. This approach is sometimes followed in rescheduling agreements.

16–11   One of the main limitations of the negative pledges is that, if they are limited to a prohibition on security, they will not catch various forms of quasi-security or title finance which, although not security in legal form, may be security in substance. Typical examples are set-off accounts for revenues and royalties, swaps (e.g. swaps of gold, currency and securities swaps), factoring of commodity receivables, title retention and financial leasing.

Where a state is in financial difficulties, its attempt to raise external finance becomes increasingly asset-based and resort is often had to title finance transactions. Hence, modern negative pledges in rescheduling agreements extend to all manner of preferential arrangements in order to stop the evasive transaction. The effect may be to catch wholly innocent transactions which are in the ordinary course of business and lead to distortion of normal trade, but this is inevitable.

Typical exceptions from the negative pledge might include liens arising solely by operation of law; security granted with the prior written consent of the majority banks; security created in connection with project financings (only if the finance exhibits certain limited recourse restrictions, the project is self-generating and the security is limited to project assets); purchase money mortgages in the ordinary course of trade; and security over documents of title, insurance policies and sale contracts in relation to commercial goods in the ordinary course of business.

The negative pledge may also permit gold swaps, e.g. for bullion held by the state with the Bank for International Settlements. A difficult problem is whether the wider forms of clause catch counter-trading transactions and, if they do, whether it is appropriate to prohibit counter-trading.

Negative pledges are discussed generally elsewhere in this series.

2. **Pari passu clause** This states that the obligations of the state under the **16–12** rescheduling agreement rank pari passu with all its other unsecured external debt. In a corporate context, this clause is a statement that on a forced insolvency, debts are, by law, paid rateably. It does not mean that one debt cannot be paid before another in time.

In the state context, the meaning of the clause is uncertain because there is no hierarchy of payment which is legally enforced under a bankruptcy regime. Probably the clause means that on a de facto inability to pay external debt as it falls due, one creditor will not be preferred by virtue of an allocation of international monetary assets achieved by a method going beyond contract; and (perhaps) that there will be no discrimination between creditors of the same class in the event of insolvency.

Events of default The events of default will include usual defaults, such as **16–13** non-payment, breach of warranty, breach of other obligations in the rescheduling agreement, cross-default, creditors' processes, repudiation or moratoriums, insolvency and winding-up of state entities, material adverse change and illegality. In addition there will be special events of default applicable to the special circumstances of rescheduling agreements. In particular:

1. The treatment of other stipulated creditors in a more favourable manner. This applies to debt which was eligible to come into the rescheduling but did not, and Paris Club and other official debt.

2. Suspension of purchases under the IMF stand-by arrangement entered into in connection with the payments difficulty or failure to observe performance criteria enabling the state to use the stand-by, or failure to comply with the stand-by. Strictly an IMF stand-by arrangement is not

a legal contract (being binding in honour only) so that it would be inappropriate to use contractual language, such as characterising non-observance as a "breach" or "default".

3.   Suspension of membership of the IMF or IBRD or ineligibility to use, or a limitation on the use of, IMF or IBRD facilities.

16–14   **Pro rata sharing clause** A pro rata sharing clause provides that if any bank receives a greater proportion of its share, it must pay the excess to the agent who redistributes to the banks pro rata and the paying bank is subrogated to the claims paid. The clause is discussed elsewhere in this series.

The clause is an equality clause designed to share individual receipts, such as receipts by set-off, proceeds of litigation, individual guarantees, or direct payment by borrower and helps to fill the vacuum caused by the absence of an enforced pari passu bankruptcy code. In particular, the piecemeal seizure of the assets of an insolvent state (a seizure frozen on the insolvency of an ordinary corporation) is discouraged by the clause, thereby promoting an orderly retirement of debt and co-ordinated action by creditors. Creditors are inhibited from unilateral action because they must share the proceeds. Preferential discriminatory payments by a state to favoured creditors are inherently objectionable and, it may be argued, the clause merely carries into effect the doctrine of recapturing preferences universally adopted by municipal bankruptcy law. The sharing of set-offs against deposits is different from bankruptcy, but reflects private corporate rescheduling agreements.

Some government rescheduling agreements have excluded payments in local currency and transactions comprising debt-for-equity swaps.

16–15   **Creditor voting** The market practice as to the extent to which a majority of the participations can control the administration of the agreement varies. The number of creditors involved in a rescheduling is much greater than in a syndicate loan agreement. It may be in the interests of the bank creditors as a whole to be able to restrain divisive unilateral action by a single bank, and usually some specified majority (half or two-thirds by participations) is required to accelerate and the covenants are usually controlled by majorities. But, as in syndicate loan agreements, a specific "no-action" clause would be unusual.

Impact of state insolvency on private sector

16–16   Where a state is insolvent, the private sector will not be able to service external debt because no foreign currency is available: this is the "transfer risk" and is distinguished from the credit risk of these private obligors. The problem has been met sometimes by nationalisation (particularly of the banking sector) but more often by novation offers whereby the private sector debt can be transferred to the state or the central bank. Each private obligor pays the local currency amount of its external debt to the central bank and the foreign creditor accepts a rescheduled government note, or a note of the central bank guaranteed by the government.

Bankruptcy proceedings can be disastrous for foreign creditors if (somewhat unusually) foreign creditors are subordinated or if (almost universally) the foreign currency debts are converted into local currency at the date of the bankruptcy: this can result in a repaid diminution of the foreigner's claim if the local currency is depreciating, as it usually is.

Debt for debt swaps

Some states have attempted to replace their defaulted debt, or some of it, by the issue of the very long term bonds which may be collateralised, e.g. by US government bonds. Creditors may bid for bonds which are then sold to the highest bidders, i.e. those who are prepared to discount their defaulted debt the most. These schemes commonly require consents under "most favoured debt", pari passu, and pro rata sharing clauses, and may cause problems for lead banks which have sub-participated their loans because a payment to the original bank may spark off an obligation of the original bank to pay its sub-participant. Collateralisation would also require a waiver of the negative pledge. Mexico is an example of a country which adopted a debt for debt programme in the 1980s.   16–17

Debt for equity swaps

Under a debt/equity swap, a creditor owed a foreign currency debt by the state or its central bank agrees to cancel the foreign currency debt in return for the issue to the creditor of shares in a local company or a privatised state company. The bank creditor could sell the debt to an investor who achieves the swap.   16–18

Various mechanics are possible. One method is for the local company to agree with the creditor to assume the liability of the state to pay the creditor and to convert that foreign currency debt into local currency. The foreign creditor then pays the subscription price for the shares issued by the local company by discharge or set-off of the original debt now converted into local currency. Alternatively, and more commonly the foreign creditor and the state could agree that the state can pay the foreign currency debt in local currency on terms that the creditor uses the local currency proceeds to pay the subscription price for shares in the local company.

16–19   The main problems are:

— What is a fair rate of exchange? – since the local currency often has a low value.

— Does any pro rata sharing clause exclude recoveries in local currency so that they do not have to be shared? If it does, the swap is impossible without a waiver from the other banks, because the bank has to share the money intended for investment in equity.

— Does any sub-participation agreement bind the sub-participant to the conversion?

— Can a bank invest in unlisted equities (or in listed equities) under its regulatory regime? If so the bank must sell to an investor who is not subject to this restriction and it is the investor who converts. Banks might also have to value the debt at the price they sold.

Argentina, Chile, Mexico and the Philippines were amongst the countries which embarked on these programmes in the 1980s. They were largely unsuccessful for a variety of reasons. For example, many foreign investors were not content to take an equity investment which was subject to foreign repatriation restrictions. Another reason was that the local fears of domination by foreign investors led to the placing of restrictions on the use of the programmes which operated as a disincentive, e.g. minimum hold periods, unrealistic conversion rates, and compulsory new money. And finally, the conversions often exacerbated local inflation.

CHAPTER 17

RECOGNITION OF STATES

Generally

Questions of recognition arise when a new sovereign state claims that it has **17–1** come into existence or when a new government of an existing state assumes power by coup d'état or other unconstitutional means. Other states then have to decide whether or not they are prepared to deal with the new sovereign state or the new government as the representative of the state. Their courts may have to decide whether the state exists and who represents it.

Revolutionary changes of government without a change in the head of state do not generally give rise to recognition problems, e.g. no recognition was required when in 1967 a coup d'état in Greece deposed the Prime Minister but not the King of Greece. Nor is there a question of recognition when the change in the head of state is constitutional, e.g. the election of a new President of the United States.

The question of whether a state exists for legal purposes has implications for lenders in a number of areas, e.g. (i) which regime, in the event of competing regimes, is entitled to borrow under the loan agreement, (ii) whether a borrowing state can be sued in the courts of a country which does not recognise that state, and (iii) whether the acts of the borrowing state or its judiciary will be given effect to by non-recognising countries.

Manner of recognition

Recognition of a foreign state may be a deliberate political act of the execu- **17–2** tive of a state whereby it acknowledges the fact that either an entity satisfies the main criteria of statehood in international law (i.e. territory, population and a stable government) or that a new government is capable of maintaining effective control, with the intention that certain legal consequences will flow from that acknowledgement. Alternatively, the courts may themselves decide whether a state exists and can therefore be afforded judicial recognition as a judicial person.

The first question in recognition cases so far as municipal courts are concerned is whether the court is bound by an executive statement on recognition (or defers to executive suggestions) or whether the court can decide of its own accord whether the state exists and who is the government of that state.

In the United Kingdom the policy followed until 1980 (although not consistently) was that the government was generally prepared to certify to the court whether or not it recognised a state and the courts considered themselves bound by that statement. A certificate from the Foreign Office, stating whether or not that government has been recognised by the executive was held conclusive: *Taylor v Barclay* (1828) 2 Sim 213. The rationale was that the judiciary and executive should speak with one voice on matters of diplomacy and foreign relations and the courts should not embarrass the executive by interfering with political functions: "the court of the King should act in unison with the government of the King": *Taylor v Barclay* per Sir L Shadwell VC at 221. The US courts have similarly deferred to "suggestions" of the executive.

17–3   The policy of formal recognition has been found in both the United Kingdom and United States to be inexpedient, primarily because recognition has been interpreted as conferring a seal of approval of the government concerned. Although recognition, or its withholding, has often been used as a political weapon, in theory recognition was merely intended to determine whether the recognising state acknowledged the existence of the new state for the purposes of foreign relations. This is not necessarily the same thing as determining whether the new state actually exists.

A statement made in the House of Commons on April 25, 1980 announced a change in the British Government's policy on recognition of governments: the Government would no longer accord recognition to governments although it would recognise states in accordance with international law. See also the statement on May 23, 1980. The practical effect of this change of policy was that the Foreign Office will apparently not state formally whether or not the government recognises a regime. It seems that, if in fact the Foreign Office issues a certificate, the courts will consider themselves bound by it: *GUR Corpn v Trust Bank of Africa Ltd* [1987)] QB 599, CA. Otherwise presumably the courts will decide status for themselves.

17–4   In international law, recognition can be express (e.g. by formal announcement or by a bilateral treaty) or implied, namely, where the state does an unequivocal act which clearly implies an intention to recognise. For instance, UK recognition of the Italian Government as the de facto government of Ethiopia was effected in the 1930s by the establishment of diplomatic relations; and the Trade Agreement between the United Kingdom and the Soviet Government of Russia of 1921 is taken to be the date when de facto recognition was accorded to the Soviet Union. Recognition can also be conditional or unconditional.

In certain countries, the courts decide themselves whether a regime has sufficient authority (which seems likely to be permanent) over population and territory for a state to exist and they do not regard themselves as bound by the official attitude of the Ministry of Foreign Affairs.

> Thus in the Dutch case of *Republic Muluka Selatan v Kon Paketvaart My* (NJ 191, No 129), the Amsterdam Court of Appeal held that the insurgent non-recognised Republic of Moluccas forming part of the Republic of Indonesia had de facto authority over population and territory showing a stability and effectiveness essential for a state to exist and it therefore had legal standing, even though its authority might not in the future be maintainable against the overwhelming force of the Republic of Indonesia.

There are significant differences between the effect of recognition in international law and the effect in municipal law: we are here concerned only with municipal law .

De facto and de jure recognition

At one time the United Kingdom adopted a two tier system of recognition, de facto recognition and de jure recognition. This split has now presumably been abandoned by the UK Government as a result of the 1980 statement. The distinction was not (in theory at least) based on a view of legitimacy or a mark of approval or disapproval but rather on the degree of effectiveness of control which the new government exercised. De facto recognition was provisional and applied where the new regime had effective control but was not firmly established. A government recognised de facto had locus standi in the English courts as a plaintiff. Its laws were recognised in the English courts and its contracts were acknowledged; see *Republic of Peru v Dreyfus Bros & Co* (1888) 38 Ch D 348 where an agreement comprising certain disputes made by the de facto government was held to be valid. **17–5**

Non-recognised government as plaintiff

Prior to the UK change of policy in 1980, a non-recognised government had no locus standi in the English courts as a plaintiff, e.g. *Berne City v Bank of England* (1804) 9 Ves 347; *Jones v Garcia del Rio* (1823) Turn & R 297. If therefore a revolutionary government which had taken over all or part of the borrowing state called for a drawdown under the loan agreement then the lenders should properly have refused to lend until such time as the insurgent authority was recognised. It seems that this rule has not been changed by the UK change of policy in 1980, although an executive certificate might **17–6** not be forthcoming, in which event the decision as to status rests with the court.

The position in the United States appears to be that non-recognised governments also have no locus standi: see *Russian Socialist Federated Soviet Republic v Cibrario*, 235 NY 255 (1923) and *National Union Fire Insurance Co v Republic of China*, 254 F 2d 177 (1958).

The Supreme Court of Sweden declined to adjudicate in the case of the *The Soviet Government v Ericsson* (1919–22) 1 Ann Dig, 1919–22, Case No 30, expressly on the ground of non-recognition.

On the other hand in the Dutch case of *"Exportchleb" Ltd v Goudeket*, Ann Dig, 1935–37, Case No 36, the District Court of Amsterdam decided that if the state de facto existed then it could appear as a plaintiff in the Dutch courts, regardless of the attitude of the Netherlands government.

Non-recognised government as defendant

17–7   The question here is whether a creditor can bring an action against a state debtor in the English courts if the United Kingdom has not recognised the borrowing state. Prior to 1980 the United Kingdom courts were obliged to treat an unrecognised government as not being there for legal purposes; it followed that in principle no such action could be brought in the United Kingdom. It is considered that in principle the law will remain the same, although now the courts may themselves decide the recognition issue.

It was held before the coming into effect of the State Immunity Act 1978 that a non-recognised state as defendant could not claim immunity from the jurisdiction of the English courts: see *Fenton Textiles Association v Krassin* (1922) 38 TLR 259; *The Annette* [1919] P 105.

Legal acts of unrecognised government

17–8   Will legislation passed by an unrecognised government or the acts of officials appointed by that government, such as its judiciary or consuls, be acknowledged by the courts of countries which have not recognised the government concerned? Examples are: exchange control regulations and moratorium laws (which, if the governing law of the loan agreement is the law of the borrower's country, might be recognised); the imposition of a withholding tax; a decree amalgamating the borrowing with another corporation; the winding-up of the borrower; the introduction of a new currency; or a decree nationalising a project company or removing a concession.

In England the legislative acts of a non-recognised state have not been acknowledged as valid by the English courts unless perhaps they are a matter of everyday administration.

> In *Luther v Sagor* [1921] 1 KB 456 (reversed on further facts [1921] 3 KB 532, CA) the court held that "legislation" passed by the unrecognised Soviet Government of Russia, depriving the plaintiff of his right to the disputed property, was ineffective. In *Adams v Adams* [1971] P 188 [1970] 3 All ER 572, a divorce decree granted by a Rhodesian judge appointed by a non-recognised government was not recognised in the English courts. In *Taylor v Barclay* (1828) 2 Sim 213, contracts made by unrecognised governments were held not to be enforceable in the English courts. In *Eastern Carrying Insurance Co v National Benefit of Life and Property Insurance Co* (1919) 35 TLR 292, no judicial cognisance was given to legislation altering the legal status of companies. But in England the older rigid doctrine has been modified by case law: see *Carl Zeiss Stiftung v Rayner and Keeler Ltd (No 2)* [1967] 1 AC 853, 954, *Hesperides Hotels Ltd v Aegean Turkish Holidays Ltd* [1978] QB 205, 218, CA; *Re James* [1977] Ch 41.

> In *GUR Corpn v Trust Bank of Africa Ltd* [1987] QB 599, CA, the question arose whether the territory of Ciskei had locus standi to sue and be sued in the English courts. *Held*: Foreign Office certificates were conclusive that the Republic of Ciskei was not recognised as an independent state. However, the courts would take cognisance of the legislation of the Republic of South Africa, which had sovereign authority over Ciskei. That legislation delegated legislative power to the Republic of Ciskei. Accordingly, the latter had locus standi to sue and be sued in the English courts as being a subordinate body set up by the Republic of South Africa to act on its behalf.

The above position has been modified in the United Kingdom by the passing of the Foreign Corporations Act 1991 under which a body having corporate status under the laws of a recognised state shall be treated as if the state were recognised, i.e. legal personality conferred by those laws will be recognised in the UK courts provided that those laws are applied by a "settled court system" in that state. The Australian Foreign Corporations (Application of Laws) Act 1989 is to similar effect. By s 7 (3) (a) of the Act, any question relating to the status of a foreign corporation (including its identity as a legal person and its legal capacity and powers) is to be "determined by reference to the law applied by the people in the place in which the foreign corporation was incorporated". **17–9**

It is obvious that if, e.g. the courts fail to recognise a dissolution decree the effect would be to permit "fugitive ghosts endowed with extra-territorial immortality" to haunt the corridors of the courts: Pound CJ in *Salimoff and Co v Standard Oil Co of New York*, 262 NY 220 (1933). There are numerous English cases involving Russian banks dissolved by Soviet Russia after the Russian Revolution but leaving their branches abroad apparently still in existence.

17–10   In the US case of *Salimoff* the court, with some encouragement from the US Government, gave recognition to a Soviet decree expropriating the plaintiff's oil fields. But see, e.g. *The Maret*, 145 F 2d 431 (1944) where the court did not confer recognition on a Soviet decree nationalising a ship of Estonian registry owned by Estonian citizens after the non-recognised annexation of Estonia by Russia in 1940, and compare *Upright v Mercury Business Machines Co Inc*, 213 NYS 2d 417 (1961) where it was held that the plaintiff could sue the defendant on a bill assigned to the plaintiff by a public corporation created by the unrecognised German Democratic Republic since the government of the GDR was established de facto.

On the European Continent, if the divorce cases are anything to go by, it would seem that Belgian courts might give recognition (*Pulenciks v Augustovskis*, ILR (1951), Case No 20 – Soviet divorce legislation), that the Swiss Federal Court might do the same so long as the acts do not "offend against the canons of public policy" (*Tcherniak v Tcherniak*, Ann Dig, 1927–8, Case No 39 at p 63), but that the French courts refuse (*Chiger v Chiger*, Ann Dig, 1925–6, Case No 18 – Soviet divorce legislation). Some of the other Continental cases involved expropriations by unrecognised governments and the decisions are apparently based rather on refusal to give effect to foreign decrees on the ground that the confiscation offended public policy than that the act was one of an unrecognised state.

Dual recognition

17–11   It used to be possible in the United Kingdom for two competing governments to be recognised at the same time, one de jure and the other de facto. In the later 1930s Emperor Haile Selassie's government was recognised by the United Kingdom as the de jure government of Ethiopia (Abyssinia) but that of the King of Italy as the de facto government by virtue of its control of most of Ethiopia. The English courts dealt with this difficulty by in effect partitioning the spheres of law-making power of the two governments and localising the issue in one or other sphere of influence, i.e. the de facto government had competence over the area within its control (e.g. the capacity to amalgamate a borrower incorporated within its territory) and the de jure government had power over the remainder, e.g. the power to recover claims payable extraterritorially, including presumably the right to call for drawdown under a loan agreement.

> Thus in *Bank of Ethiopia v National Bank of Egypt and Liguori* [1973] Ch 513, the de facto Italian government's dissolution of Bank of Ethiopia was

recognised since the Italians were completely in control of Addis Ababa and other parts of Ethiopian territory in which the bank carried out its activities.

In *Haile Selassie v Cable and Wireless Ltd (No 2)* [1939] 1 Ch 182, CA, the exiled de jure sovereign could recover a debt payable in England although Ethiopia itself was controlled by the de facto Italian government. This was reversed by the Court of Appeal ([1939] 1 Ch 194) after de jure recognition was removed from Haile Selassie and granted to the Italians.

In *Banco de Bilbao v Sancha* [1938] 2 KB 176, CA, the de jure Republican Government's decree purporting to move the corporate seat of the bank outside the area of control of the de facto government was held a nullity because General Franco's de facto government controlled Bilbao where the corporate seat was located.

Retroactivity of recognition

Once recognition was given then it was treated by the English courts as **17–12** being retroactive and dating back to the commencement of the state or government's existence. This allowed the court to acknowledge legal acts which were made after the new government had come into being but which previously had not been recognised. It was held that where the date was specified in the executive certificate this was binding on the court: otherwise the court decided on the facts of each case: *Luther v Sagor* [1921] 3 KB 532, where it was held that recognition validated a nationalisation decree previously deemed to have been invalid. On the other hand retroactive validation of the acts of a de facto government did not operate to invalidate the acts of a displaced de jure government completed prior to the validation. In *Gdynia Ameryka Linie v Boguslawski* [1953] AC 11, [1952] 2 All ER 470, HL it was held that a decree made by the de jure exiled Polish Government ordering payment of gratuities to Polish seamen was not overridden by the subsequent de jure recognition of the previous de facto Lublin government newly formed in Poland. Hence actions taken under a loan agreement by the displaced de jure government would have stood. The distinction between de facto and de jure recognition has probably now disappeared in English law.

In the United States the courts appear to have adopted the retroactive principle with qualifications: see *Lehigh Valley Railroad Co v Russia*, 21 F 2d 396 (1927), and *United States v Pink*, 315 US 203 (1942).

CHAPTER 18

STATE SUCCESSION

Generally

18–1 Questions of state succession arise whenever there is a "replacement of one state by another in the responsibility for the international relations of territory" (definition from the 1978 Vienna Convention on Succession of States in Respect of Treaties). Examples are partitions, unifications and successions where there is a loss of territorial sovereignty by the borrowing state ("the predecessor state") in favour of another state ("the successor state").

Political changes of this sort must obviously affect the position of lenders. Which state is entitled to borrow? Which state is liable for the debt? What happens to any security in the transferred territory or externally? How does one decide the money of account if a currency is extinguished or split? How does one determine the governing law or forum if the legal and judicial system of the predecessor state disappears? The answers (if any) to these and similar questions are the province of the law of state succession. This review will concern itself only with succession to debt claims, not, e.g. tort or expropriation claims.

State continuity

18–2 As a preliminary matter it is necessary to distinguish between the state succession and state continuity. In the case of state continuity all that has happened is that there has been a change in the government. It is thought that municipal law in Western countries would generally hold that mere political changes in the government or form of government do not affect the state's obligations and the continuity of that state: the binding nature of a state's obligations is independent of changes of regime, constitutional or otherwise.

> In the *Tinoco Arbitration* [1923] 1 UNRIAA 369, Tinoco established himself as dictator of Costa Rica. He granted concessions to British companies and issued bank notes. After a change of government, the new government declared the concessions and bank notes invalid. *Held* by the arbitrator, Chief Justice

Taft: Tinoco had been the effective ruler of Costa Rica and therefore his acts were binding on successive governments. It was immaterial that his regime was unconstitutional under Costa Rican law or that his government was not recognised by several countries including the United Kingdom.

In *Republic of Peru v Dreyfus Bros & Co* (1888) 38 Ch D 348 it was held that, where a government was displaced by a regime which was recognised as the de facto government and where the original government was subsequently restored by revolution, the restored government is bound by international law to treat the contracts made by the de facto government as valid and is bound by the contract. See also *Republic of Peru v Peruvian Guano Co* (1887) 36 Ch D 489; *USA v McRae* (1869) LR 8 Eq 69; *Irish Free State v Guaranty Safe Deposit Co*, 222 NYS 182 (1927).

The view of state continuity has not gone unchallenged. After the 1917   **18–3** revolution Russia argued that the revolution was so violent and profound that the change of regime was state succession and not a state continuity and that therefore the new state was not bound by the debts of the Czarist and Kerensky governments.

It is often difficult to distinguish changes of government from changes of sovereignty if they are accompanied by territorial modifications. Did Austrian sovereignty survive the 1938–45 Anschluss intact as official Austrian theory would have it? When one comes to state succession one encounters a divergence of academic opinion and state practice and an absence of consistent rules of international law.

English case law on the subject is virtually non-existent and hence the attitude of the courts is a matter for surmise. While it is true that the English courts are willing to give effect to public international law in appropriate cases (see, e.g. *Trendtex Trading Corpn v Central Bank of Nigeria* [1977] QB 529, CA) the rules of international law on the subject are obscure. This review can therefore do nothing more than provide orientation and background as opposed to substantive law.

Vienna Convention of 1983

The matter is the subject of the Vienna Convention on Succession of States   **18–4** in respect of State Property, Archives and Debts, adopted in 1983 (the "Convention").

Although the Convention was the product of the views of a wide number of states, these included a preponderance of new states, so that its provisions often did not reflect the views of industrialised states or of the possible attitudes of their municipal courts. It did not by any means achieve universal acceptance.

Local, localised, national and odious debt

18–5 In the theory and practice of the matter, distinctions are often made between (a) local debt, (b) localised debt, (c) national debt, and (d) odious debt.

18–6 **Local debt** This may be defined as debt which is contracted by a territorial public authority which is inferior to a state, which possesses separate legal personality and a degree of financial autonomy, being debt for which that authority is responsible. Examples of local debt are debts contracted by provinces, cities and public enterprises.

18–7 **Localised debt** Generally, this is debt contracted by the state itself but which is linked to a particular territory, e.g. as where it is secured on assets or fiscal resources there, or is earmarked for territorial use there, because the loan proceeds were used to finance a local project.

National debt Broadly, this is the national debt of a state which is not related to any particular territory or assets and is charged to general revenue account.

18–8 **Odious debts** Odious debts include regime debts, subjugation debts and war debts and are defined by the Convention (in terms influenced perhaps by third world countries) as debts contracted by the predecessor state with a view to obtaining objectives contrary to the major interests of the successor state or not in conformity with international law.

As a general rule, local debt is not state debt and has nothing to do with the succession of states. Thus it is thought that loans to municipalities remain the responsibility of the municipal borrower regardless of changes in sovereignty. Localised debts may travel with the transferred territory if these are localised there.

Many states argue that odious debts do not become the responsibility of a successor state. A lender whose loan is used to finance a war or subjugation of the successor state takes the risk. On this basis Great Britain refused to liquidate the War Bonds of the Boer Republics. Similarly the United States refused to agree to a repatriation of Spanish national debt on the independence of Cuba in 1898 on the grounds that it had been contracted largely in the interests of Spanish colonisation.

The distinctions between the various types of debt, while analytically helpful, can be difficult in practice. We are however concerned only with national debt and localised debt.

State responsibility generally

In what circumstances must a successor state assume the liability for loans   18–9
made to a predecessor state? If devolution or partition arrangements are
entered into between successor and predecessor states, it would seem ques-
tionable whether these can bind third party creditors or whether such creditors could take the benefit of a treaty to which they are not a party. Further
there is no means whereby a predecessor state can unilaterally shift the obligation on to a successor state, nor in principle does there appear to be any
general rule whereby a successor state becomes, as a matter of international
law, responsible for the obligations of the predecessor state towards third
parties unless it so agrees with the third party.

Sometimes these matters have been resolved by agreement, express or
implied, between the creditors and the territory concerned.

A distinction should be made between partial succession and total succession. In the case of *partial succession*, a contracting entity survives except
that the loss or acquisition of territory modifies the sovereignty of the entity.
If the state loses territory, its economic ability to service its foreign debt may
be reduced. It is thought that, so long as a continuous contracting entity
survives (a matter which may be controversial), that entity remains bound,
subject perhaps, in most exceptional circumstances, to a claim that the contract is frustrated.

In the case of *total succession*, the predecessor state is totally absorbed
into a union and loses its fiscal and legal identity or the predecessor state is
totally dismembered in the course of a partition. In these cases, the original
contracting party has disappeared. Perhaps here the lenders' remedy would
be based on a quasi-contractual claim for unjust enrichment. In practice
there is generally no clear-cut case of surviving entity or total absorption.

The circumstances in which state succession comes about are inexhaust-
ible but the following is a classification adapted from the Convention. The
examples are taken (mainly) from the Convention where supporting citation
may be found.

Transfer of part of the territory of a state

Historically these circumstances have usually arisen in connection with   18–10
nineteenth century annexations. Article 37 of the Convention proposes that,
in the absence of agreement, an equitable proportion of the debt passes to
the successor state taking into account, among other things, the property,
rights and interests which pass to the successor state in relation to the state
debt.

Treaty practice has shown a readiness to assume localised debt but not national debt even though the predecessor state may be economically ruined by the loss of a major part of its resources to service the loan.

> In *West Rand Central Gold Mining Co v R* [1905] 2 KB 391, it was held that the Crown did not succeed to the contractual liabilities of the South African Republic after it had been annexed by the United Kingdom. The case was not followed by the Permanent Court of International Justice in the *German Settlers'* case [1923] PCIJ, Series B, No 6.

Decolonisation and newly independent states

18–11   The transfer of debt to independent territories on decolonisation in the mid twentieth century was politically an explosive issue in state succession because of the resentment against former colonial masters and because of the weak financial condition of many of the new states. Article 38 of the Convention reflected the predominance of anti-colonial feeling in the United Nations by providing that no state debt of a predecessor state passes to a newly independent state unless (in effect) that state so agrees.

In most cases the matter has been settled by treaty. The thirteen American colonies did not take over any United Kingdom debt on independence. Brazil agreed to make a small payment to Portugal in 1825. Mexico took over localised debt in 1836 from Spain as did Ecuador in 1840 and Venezuela in 1845. Cuba did not take over localised debt from Spain in 1898 on the theory that the debt was odious. After World War II, India remained responsible for state debt but Pakistan paid a contribution to India. Indonesia took over some localised debts in 1949 but repudiated them in 1956. Libya did not take over any Italian public debt in 1950. The Belgian Congo position was confused on independence in 1960 and ended in a compromise. Similarly in the case of Algeria which sought to use the "odious debt" exception with regard to some of the debts incurred by France and finally compromised with France in 1966. British dependent territories usually succeeded to clearly localised loans by treaty: those generally included four categories of loans, all of which were contracted by the British authority and were charges on the colonial revenues: loans under the Colonies Stock Acts; loans from the IBRD; colony welfare and development loans; and other loans raised in the London and local stock markets.

Uniting of states

18–12   Article 39 of the Convention proposes that when two or more states unite and so form a successor state, the state debt of the predecessor state passes to the successor state. The successor state may in accordance with its internal law apportion the state debt of the predecessor state amongst its component parts. No attempt is made to regulate the manner by which any apportionment is made by the successor state.

Usually the matter has been dealt with by treaty. On the unification of Belgium and the Netherlands in 1814 all debts were transferred to the general treasury of the Netherlands. Similar arrangements were arrived at on the unification of Italy in 1866 and the treaty of 1897 establishing the short-lived Republic of Central America. In 1957 the Federation of Malaysia generally took over localised debts which under the terms of the constitution had been assumed by the Federation. The documents constituting the United Arab Republic in 1958 were not very specific on the matter. The latest example is the reunification of the two Germanies.

It is however almost universally accepted that where a predecessor state loses its former fiscal autonomy and ceases to be a legal entity then the successor state is committed to the obligation, although internal allocations may be made.

Separation of part of the territory of a state

Article 40 of the Convention proposes that when part or parts of the territory of a state separate from the state and form a state (the predecessor state continuing in existence), then, unless the predecessor state and the successor state otherwise agree, an equitable proportion of the state debt of the predecessor state shall pass to the successor state, taking into account all relevant circumstances. This applies when part of the territory of a state separates from the state and unites with another state.   **18–13**

When Ireland obtained from the United Kingdom the status of a Dominion and became the Irish Free State, a Treaty of 1921 provided for an equitable apportionment of debts. However the separation of Bangladesh and Pakistan did not produce an agreed apportionment.

Dissolution of a state

Article 41 of the Convention states that when a predecessor state dissolves and ceases to exist and the parts of its territory form two or more states, then, unless the successor states otherwise agree, an equitable proportion of the state debt of the predecessor state shall pass to each successor state, taking into account all relevant circumstances.   **18–14**

Historical precedents include the dissolution of Great Columbia (1829 to 1831), the dissolution of the Union of Norway and Sweden (1905), the disappearance of the Austro-Hungarian Empire (1919), the disappearance of the Federation of Mali (1960), the dissolution of the United Arab Republic (1961) the dissolution of the Federation of Rhodesia and Nyasaland (1963), and the dissolution of the USSR, Yugoslavia and Czechoslovakia around 1990. Often there was an agreed apportionment of state debt.

CHAPTER 19

INTERNATIONAL ORGANISATIONS

Introduction

International organisations are entities created by treaty between sovereign **19–1** states. There is now a proliferation of these organisations. Some have broad political functions, such as the United Nations Organisation and the European Union; some are of a military character, such as the North Atlantic Treaty Organisation; some are financial organisations, such as the International Monetary Fund and the various development banks (the International Bank for Reconstruction and Development, the Asian Development Bank, the African Development Bank and the European Bank for Reconstruction and Development); some are commodity organisations, such as the International Cocoa Organisation; some are cultural, such as the United Nations Educational, Scientific and Cultural Organisation, or administrative, such as the Universal Postal Union; some are purely commercial enterprises owned by states, e.g. the United Arab Shipping Corporation SAG.

Although these organisations are not new (one of the earliest is perhaps the Central Commission for the Navigation of the Rhine set up under the Congress of Vienna in 1815), they pose difficult legal problems. Where the treaty establishing the international organisation has been legislated into municipal law, many of the questions will be answered by reference to the treaty itself.

Recognition

Since international organisations of the type under review are not incorpor- **19–2** ated under the laws of any particular state, they are not creatures of the law of a municipal state. An international organisation therefore has no nationality or domicile in the municipal legal sense of the word, notwithstanding that it has its head office in a particular state. Thus the United Nations is not a New York corporation merely because it has its headquarters there.

The question of recognition is therefore of fundamental importance since if the courts of one state were not prepared to recognise an international organisation created by other states, the organisation could not be sued in those courts.

19–3   The UK International Organisations Act 1968 provides for the making of Orders in Council to "confer on the organisation the legal capacities of a body corporate" where the United Kingdom is a member of the organisation (s 1(2)(a)) or where the organisation "maintains or proposes to maintain an establishment in the United Kingdom": s 4(a). Orders have been made in relation to the UN and regional development banks, for example.

Where the Act does not apply or no Order in Council has been made, e.g. where the United Kingdom is not a member of the organisation, the English courts will recognise the legal personality of an organisation created by agreement between states if the organisation enjoys legal personality under the municipal law of a state recognised by the United Kingdom: thus in *Arab Monetary Fund v Hashim (No 3)* [1991] 2 AC 114, a monetary fund created by agreement between certain Arab states was recognised as having legal personality because a domestic decree of the United Arab Emirates conferred on it legal capacity.

As regards sovereign states, the courts of the United Kingdom hold that a certificate of the executive as to the existence or otherwise of a state is conclusive and binding (see chapter 17) but apart from political organisations like UNO, most international organisations do not share the attributes of sovereignty.

19–4   The position in the United Kingdom was clarified by a publicised exchange of correspondence between the Bank of England and the Foreign and Commonwealth Office in May 1978. In replying to the Bank of England's request for guidance, the Minister of Foreign and Commonwealth Affairs stated that an organisation set up by foreign states by treaty, which had legal personality in states outside the United Kingdom

> "would enjoy legal personality and capacity in this country without any formal statement by or on behalf of Her Majesty's Government, in the same way and to the same extent as any other banking, commercial or other trading organisation established in a country other than the United Kingdom and enjoying legal personality in that country. It is considered that the legal personality and capacity in this country of such a bank or other entity would be acknowledged by the English courts, and the Foreign and Commonwealth Office would welcome such a finding by the courts."

On the question of whether the Foreign and Commonwealth Office would provide a statement regarding the attitude of the execution in relation to the question of the personality and capacity of such an entity if called to do so by a court, the Minister replied:

> "I am advised that the capacity of such a bank or legal entity to enter into a loan

or other contracts and to sue and be sued on them in this country does not depend upon the entity's being recognised by the United Kingdom Government.

It is of course conceivable that the court might take a different view of the law and require a statement of the attitude of the Executive ... In these circumstances, and on the assumption that the entity concerned enjoys, under its constitutive instrument or instruments and under the law of one or more member states or the state wherein it has its seat or permanent location, legal personality and capacity to engage in transactions of the type concerned governed by the law of a non-member state, the Foreign & Commonwealth Office, as the branch of the Executive responsible for the conduct of foreign relations would be willing officially to acknowledge that the entity concerned enjoyed such legal personality and capacity and to state this."

Consequently it appears safe to assume that in the above circumstances an international organisation having legal personality under the domestic laws of at least one recognised state will be treated as having legal personality in the English courts.

See also the European Convention on the Recognition of International Non-Governmental Organisations of 1986, in force in 1991.

Status

Status, e.g. whether an organisation is a corporation, is in some respects a   **19–5** different concept from recognition. Status is a bundle of concepts and there may be degrees of corporate personality. Attributes of status which are of interest to lenders are:

(a) whether the organisation can be sued in its own name: this is partly a matter for the lex fori which may have procedural rules governing suit against unincorporated associations of persons in the name of the association.

(b) whether the members of the organisation are personally and directly liable to the extent of personal assets or are liable only in respect of unpaid contributions to the organisation or only through the intermediary of the equivalent of a liquidator and not directly;

(c) whether the organisation owns its property beneficially or owns it only as nominee or on behalf of its members, in which event the property is that of the members.

Generally English law looks to the law applying to the formation of an association to determine its status. Outside the International Organisations Act 1968, the English courts should acknowledge the status asserted by the law of the state in which the organisation has its seat: *Arab Monetary Fund v Hashim (No 3)* [1991] 2 AC 114, HL.

19–6   A typical formulation is that the organisation has "juridical personality".
See, e.g. Art 7(2) of the Agreement establishing the IBRD; Art 9(2) of the
Arts of Agreement of the International Monetary Fund; Art (11(2) of the
Agreement of the Inter American Development Bank; Art 1 of the Agree-
ment for the Central American Bank of Economic Integration; Art 50 of the
African Development Bank Agreement.

Powers

19–7   As a general rule, as in the case of corporations created under municipal
law, the English courts have referred to the laws under which the corporation is formed to determine (i) its powers, (ii) what authorisations are
necessary to approve transactions, (iii) the liability of its members and (iv)
whether it is in liquidation or has been dissolved.

As to powers, some treaties proclaim as wide a power as possible, e.g. Art
211 of the Treaty of Rome provides that the European Community

> "shall possess the fullest legal capacity accorded to legal persons by the national
> laws; in particular it may acquire or dispose of moveable or immovable prop-
> erty and be a party to legal proceedings. For this purpose it shall be represented
> by the Commission."

The European Investment Bank Treaty provides that the Bank

> "shall enjoy the most extensive capacity accorded to legal persons under their
> laws; it may, in particular, acquire or dispose of moveable or immovable prop-
> erty and may be party to legal proceedings" (EIB Statute Art 28(1)).

Other treaties confer such powers as are necessary to the achievement of
the objectives of the organisation set out in its treaty: for example, Art 6 of
the instrument establishing the European Coal and Steel Community:

> "In its international relationships the Community shall enjoy the juridical
> capacity necessary to the exercise of its functions and the attainment of its
> ends."

19–8   There appears to be no English reported authority deciding whether the
company law doctrines of implied powers and ultra vires apply to international organisations. There seems no reason why general principles
should not apply. It appears from the reasoning in the *International Reparations for Injuries Cases* (1949) ICJ Rep 174, 182, that in public international law an organisation will have such implied powers as are necessary
for the most efficient performance of its functions:

> "Under international law, the Organisation must be deemed to have those

powers which though not expressly provided in the Charter, are conferred upon it by necessary implication as being essential to the performance of its duties."

Authorisations

The mode of authorisation for each organisation is generally set out in the   19–9
relevant treaty. Many treaties provide for a dual system of authorisation: often a plenary body (an assembly of shareholders) can give general directives whose detailed implementation will be effected by the executive body.

It is unresolved whether the English courts will, in the case of international organisations, adopt agency rules of holding out and the old English company law rule that third parties are not affected by internal irregularities if there is ostensible authority. There seems no reason for the abrogation of generally accepted principles of the law of agency as applied to corporations.

Liability of members

The treaties of many international organisations limit the liability of the   19–10
member to the amount unpaid on their shares.

Treaties of development banks modelled on the International Bank for Reconstruction and Development Agreement have in addition a separate class of callable capital to be called up only in order to meet certain borrowing and similar liabilities in order to enlarge investor confidence.

In the absence of incorporation of the treaty into municipal law, it appears that an English court would not, on the application of a creditor, enforce the contractual obligations of members between themselves to contribute towards the debts of an international organisation: there is no privity of contract. In a series of cases arising out of the collapse of the International Tin Council, the House of Lords held that a creditor could not enforce the treaty obligations of members between themselves to contribute to the International Tin Council's debts, even by means of appointing a receiver to act in the name of the ITC. A treaty between sovereign states was not justiciable in the English courts and could not be relied upon as a ground for enforcing contributions against the members. Where the organisation enjoys legal personality, the liability of its members for its debts is to be determined by the law of the place of its incorporation: *J H Rayner (Mincing Lane) Ltd v Department of Trade and Industry* [1990] 2 AC 418, [1989] 3 WLR 969, HL. For other litigation arising out of the International Tin Council, see *Maclaine Watson & Co Ltd v Department of Trade and Industry* [1988] 3 All ER 257, [1988] 3 WLR 1033, CA; *(No 2)* [1989] Ch 286, CA; *Maclaine Watson & Co, Ltd v International Tin Council (No 3)*,

The Times June, 27, 1988, CA; *Re International Tin Council* [1989] Ch 309, CA; *Shearson Lehman Brothers Inc v Maclaine Watson & Co Ltd* [1988] WLR 16, HL.

Withdrawal of members

19–11 The ability of a member to withdraw from an international organisation, and the terms on which it may do so, are of interest to creditors since withdrawal may result in the repayment of share capital or the loss of a country whose credit reputation is commercially important to the general credit of the organisation.

On the whole treaties tend to lack detail in this area. Some treaties do not contemplate withdrawal at all, e.g. the Treaty of Rome establishing the EEC and the United Nations Charter. Other treaties allow withdrawal provided certain requirements are satisfied, e.g. Art 9(1) of the Inter American Development Bank Agreement provides that not less than six months' written notice must be given. See also Art 43 of the Agreement establishing the African Development Bank.

The treaties establishing certain financial institutions contain specific provisions for the settling of credits and debits of members wishing to withdraw. This is as one would expect in the case of organisations intending to operate commercially. See the Agreements for the International Bank for Reconstruction and Development Art 6(4), International Finance Corporation Art 5(4), the International Development Association Art 7(4), and the Inter American Development Bank: Art 9(3).

Dissolution and insolvency

19–12 The treaties of many international organisations tend to lapse into vacuum when dealing with the question of the rights and liabilities of members on a dissolution.

Some treaties do not contemplate a dissolution at all, e.g. the statute of the European Investment Bank. Many treaties setting up financial agencies, however, provide for the organisation's debts to external creditors to be paid before the remaining assets are distributed among member states. See, e.g. the Statute of the Inter American Development Bank Art 10(4) and the Agreement of the African Development Bank Art 49.

It is unlikely that an organisation can be wound up under the Insolvency Act 1986, particularly in the case of an organisation set up by treaty between sovereign states: *Re International Tin Council* [1989] Ch 309.

Immunity of international organisations

Treaty provisions Many treaties distinguish between immunity from suit   19–13
and immunity from execution.

Some treaties specifically provide for immunity from suit but the treaties
of certain of the development banks exclude immunity from suit in order to
safeguard investor confidence. Some of these treaties however restrict the
courts in which action may be brought to the territories of the members
where they have an office, have appointed an agent for the purpose of
accepting service of notice of process or have issued or guaranteed securities. See, e.g. Art 7(3) of the Agreement for International Bank for Reconstruction and Development and Art 52 of the Agreement of the African
Development Bank. Some development banks have a further restriction
limiting actions to those in connection with the exercise of the bank's
powers to borrow, guarantee securities or to buy, sell or underwrite securities.

Where such provisions have not been legislated into United Kingdom
domestic law, it is doubtful that derogation provisions of this sort would be
binding on an English court.

The treaties of many organisations reserve immunity from execution, e.g.
the property or assets of the European Communities may not be "the subject of any administrative or legal measure of constraint without the authorisation of the Court of Justice": Art 1 of the Protocol on the Privileges and
Immunities of the European Communities.

Some international and regional banks expressly permit execution provided the judgement is a final one. See, e.g. Art 9(3) of the Inter American
Development Bank Agreement and Art 52(2) of the African Development
Bank Agreement. Such a provision would purport to exclude, e.g. prejudgment attachments, such as the Mareva injunction.

Recognition of the treaty provisions English courts will give effect to treaty   19–14
provisions where municipal legislation has incorporated the treaty into
English law.

The International Organisations Act 1968 (as amended by the International Organisations Act 1981) enables Orders in Council to be made in
relation, inter alia, to the immunities of international organisations of which
the United Kingdom is a member: see s 1(2). Such immunities may include
immunity from suit and legal processes: Part 1 of the First Schedule.

Orders in Council may also be made in respect of international organisations of which the United Kingdom is not a party where the organisation
"maintains or proposes to maintain an establishment in the United Kingdom": IOA, as amended, s 4. There are special rules for international commodity organisations: see the International Organisations Act 1981.

Reference must be made to the respective Order for details of the immunities of a particular organisation.

19–15   In the absence of express statute or order dealing with immunity it is thought that the provisions of the organisation's treaty conferring immunity are irrelevant. Immunity is a matter for the lex fori, not a matter of capacity. In such a case the immunity of the international organisation in the English courts depends initially on the State Immunity Act 1978. Section 4 of that Act provides for the deimmunisation in certain circumstances of "separate entities", namely, "any entity . . . which is distinct from the executive organs of the government of the state and capable of suing or being sued": para 14–20 *et seq*. It is doubtful whether an international organisation could be within the scope of this language. In *Standard Chartered Bank v International Tin Council* [1986] 3 All 257, [1987] 1 WLR 641, it was held that at common law international organisations are not accorded sovereign status and are not entitled to sovereign immunity or diplomatic immunity. Accordingly, they only enjoy immunity when immunity is granted by statute: see *J H Rayner (Mincing Lane) Ltd v Department of Trade and Industry* [1989] Ch 72, CA, affirmed [1990] 2 AC 418, HL.

In the United States, international organisations in which the US participates have immunity under the International Organisations Immunities Act of 1945. It is unclear whether the Foreign Sovereign Immunities Act of 1976 overrides this immunity in the case of creditor actions. Most of the cases have been employee-related.

OUTLINES AND PRECEDENTS

OUTLINES AND PRECEDENTS

Part I: Project Finance

1. Outline of project finance credit agreement
2. Outline of completion guarantee
3. Outline of equity subscription agreement
4. Outline of direct agreement with project contractor
5. Outline of intercreditor agreement

Part II: Subordinated Debt

6. Outline of turnover subordination agreement
7. Specific credit turnover subordination agreement for unsecured creditors
8. All moneys turnover subordination agreement for secured creditors
9. Contractual subordination agreement

Part III: State Loans

10. Special definitions for state loan agreements
11. Representations and warranties in state loan agreement
12. Covenants in state loan agreement
13. Events of default in state loan agreement
14. Waiver of immunity in state loan agreement

APPENDIX: PART I

PROJECT FINANCE

1. Outline project finance credit agreement

Note: This outline illustrates some typical provisions in a syndicated bank credit agreement to finance a project. For a discussion, see para 4–5 *et seq*. Many of the ordinary syndicated bank credit agreement clauses are discussed in another work (on international loans, bonds and securities regulation) in this series of works on international financial law.

Parties

1. Project company as borrower
2. Banks as lenders
3. Agent bank as agent for the banks

1. Loan commitments

1.1 Commitments Each bank will make loans to the borrower up to its specified commitment during the commitment period from the date of this agreement to the project completion date but ending not later than a specified date. [For an outline definition of the project completion date, see the completion guarantee in this Appendix.]

1.2 Severality The commitment of each bank is several. No bank is responsible for any other bank's commitment. Each bank's rights are divided rights.

1.3 Drawdowns Loans will be made against a borrower request in the scheduled form (setting out details of the loan, first interest period, and application of proceeds – sometimes confirmed by consultant's certificates – and confirming no default and that the warranties are true) on not less than five business days prior notice to the agent bank. Loan proceeds will be made available through the agent bank and credited to a bank account in the country of the loan currency for credit to the disbursement account at the borrower's bank.

2. Application of proceeds

2.1 Approved purposes The borrower will apply the proceeds of the loans towards:

- project capital costs (as defined) incurred prior to project completion;
- project operating costs and commissioning costs (all as defined) incurred prior to project completion;
- project taxes incurred prior to project completion;
- interest on the loans and fees and expenses under or in respect of the documentation falling due prior to project completion.

Agent bank may pay contractors direct against certificates.

2.2 No monitoring Neither the agent bank nor any bank is obliged to monitor use of proceeds.

3. Conditions precedent

3.1 Conditions to all loans The obligation of each bank to make any loan is subject to the prior receipt by the agent bank of:

- the borrower's constitutional documents;
- the borrower's authorising resolutions for this agreement and all the documents specified below to which the borrower is a party;
- the information memorandum for the project;
- the following executed financial documents:
    - security documents and trust deed conferring security over the project assets and evidence of perfection of the security;
    - equity agreement (whereby the project sponsors agree to inject equity or subordinated debt into the borrower);
    - completion guarantee (whereby the project sponsors agree to procure completion);
    - direct agreements (whereby the project contractors agree to allow the banks to step in and preserve the project contracts on a default by the borrower);
    - fee letters (whereby the borrower agrees to pay the bank fees);
- interest hedge agreement (whereby a bank agrees to provide an interest swap to the borrower, i.e. to pay amounts equal to floating interest on the loans in return for fixed interest so as to fix the interest costs);
- project account agreement (whereby the borrower's bank agrees to operate the project bank accounts);
- acceptance by the agent for service of process under the jurisdiction clause 29;

— notices and acknowledgements of assignment of:

  — the project contracts
  — the government concession
  — the project site lease
  — the insurances

— the following executed project contracts:

  — shareholders' joint venture agreement;
  — supply agreements for the supply of raw materials, fuel, etc., to the borrower;
  — purchase agreements for the purchase of the project product from the borrower (e.g. minerals, refined oil, electricity);
  — construction contract for the construction of the project and any accompanying contract bonds;
  — operating and maintenance agreement whereby the operator agrees to operate and maintain the project;
  — other relevant contracts, e.g. electricity grid connection agreements for electricity projects, pipeline construction contracts for refinery projects;

— executed lease of the project site;

— government concession for the project;

— the following licences and permits:

  — planning or zoning consents to build and operate the project;
  — official consents to operate the project, e.g. generating licence for a power station, licence to operate a bridge, tunnel or road, licence to operate a refinery;
  — all necessary wayleaves and easements;
  — environmental consents, e.g. effluent discharge into atmosphere or rivers;
  — all other licences and permits for the project;

— the following insurance documents:

  — certificate of the banks' insurance adviser that the specified insurances are in force;
  — report of the insurance adviser as to the insurances;
  — brokers and insurers undertakings (see clause 15.33);

— certificate that the conditions precedent in other project financing agreements are satisfied and the other lenders are committed;

— legal opinions in scheduled form as to:

  — the financial documents;

- the project contracts (usually limited to powers, due execution and authorisation);
- the government concession;
- the site lease.

3.2 Conditions to each loan Each individual loan is subject to following additional conditions precedent:

- the representations and warranties are true and would be true on the making of the loan;

- no event of default or pending event of default has occurred or might result from a loan;

- pro rata drawdowns under other credit agreements (if relevant);

- pro rata subscription of equity capital or subordinated debt by project sponsors (if relevant);

- no actual or projected overruns on project capital costs (unless financed in manner acceptable to the majority banks);

- cover ratios in clause 12 are met;

- no environmental liability.

The majority banks may waive any condition precedent (except certain specified entrenched conditions).

4. Interest

4.1 Interest periods The borrower may select interest periods of three or six months duration by three business days advance notice. Interest periods must end on specified semi-annual dates (to facilitate the forecasting and revenue calculations described below), on a business day and on repayment dates.

4.2 Interest rate The borrower will pay interest for each interest period at the reference banks' London interbank offered rate p.a. (ascertained in the prescribed manner) plus the specified margin payable on the last day of each interest period.

4.3 Default interest The borrower will pay default interest on overdue sums (as well after as before judgment) at 1 per cent p.a. over the higher of the current rate and LIBOR plus the margin, compounded at the end of each fixing period.

4.4 **Alternative interest rate** If market conditions prejudice normal interest fixing, the majority banks may prescribe an alternative rate or currency or both unless otherwise agreed, so long as the disruption lasts.

5. Repayment

5.1 **Minimum repayment** The outstanding loans will be reduced by repayment by the scheduled minimum amounts on the scheduled due dates.

5.2 **Dedicated percentage** The borrower will repay the loans by not less than a specified percentage of net revenues (as defined) from the project accruing during the six-month period ending 10 business days prior to each scheduled repayment date (in order to capture excess revenues and achieve an earlier pay-back if the project generates higher revenues than scheduled or if revenues vary).

5.3 **Cover ratio** The borrower will repay on the scheduled repayment dates sufficient of the loans to ensure that, after repayment, a specified loan life cover ratio is met (see clause 12 – this is usually higher than the default ratio in clause 12, e.g. 1.7:1).

6. Prepayment and cancellation

6.1 **Prepayments** The borrower may prepay a loan in rounded amounts at the end of interest periods. Prepayments will be applied towards the minimum repayment instalments in the inverse order of their maturity. Prepayments prior to project completion must be of all the loans.

6.2 **Cancellation** The borrower may cancel the commitments of the banks to lend in whole (together with a cancellation fee) but not in part unless the majority banks are satisfied that sufficient finance is available to finance the project and (if appropriate) that the commitments of other lenders are cancelled pro rata.

7. Payments

7.1 **Place and funds** The borrower will pay through the agent bank in the prescribed currency and funds at a bank in the prescribed financial centre. The agent bank will distribute payments received to the banks pro rata.

7.2 **Agent bank** The agent bank need not pay loan proceeds to the borrower, and need not pay receipts from the borrower to the banks, unless the agent is satisfied that it has received cleared funds. If the agent bank does pay, but has not received, the payee will refund plus interest.

7.3   No set-off The borrower will pay without set-off or counterclaim.

7.4   Partial payments Partial payments by the borrower will be applied as the majority banks direct.

8.   Taxes

The borrower will pay without deduction, except as required by law. The borrower will gross-up for any taxes which must be deducted, and may prepay and cancel an affected bank. The borrower will supply tax certificates of deduction.

9.   Increased costs

If any law, or regulation or official directive increases a bank's costs in relation to the loan or reduces its return, the borrower will pay the increase and may prepay and cancel the commitment of the affected bank.

10.   Illegality

If it becomes illegal for a bank to lend or maintain a loan, the borrower must prepay and cancel the commitment of that bank.

11.   Representations and warranties

11.1   Warranties The borrower represents and warrants:

— its due incorporation and valid existence;

— its powers and authority for the financial and security agreements, the concession and the project contracts (for these documents, see clause 3.1);

— the legal validity of those agreements, the concession and contracts;

— the carrying out of those documents does not conflict with any law or regulation or the borrower's constitution or any borrower contract;

— all authorisations and permits have been obtained for those documents and the project;

— there is no event of default or pending default;

— there is no material litigation or other proceedings involving the borrower or relating to the project;

— the information memorandum is materially correct and there are no material omissions; there has been no adverse change since the date of the information memorandum; the forecasts are reasonably based;

— the security is first priority, is not subject to pari passu security interests and is not liable to be set aside on insolvency;

— the borrower owns the project site free from encumbrances and restrictions;

— the prescribed insurances are in force and not liable to be set aside for non-disclosure or otherwise;

— the borrower owns all necessary intellectual property rights for the project;

— environmental compliance and no environmental liability.

11.2 Repetition The representations and warranties will remain true (subject to agreed exemptions for commercial warranties) so long as the loans are outstanding or any bank commitment is in force.

12. Forecasting and cover ratios

12.1 Forecasts Every six months the borrower will supply a forecast certificate showing:

— (prior to project completion) the *forecast maximum loan outstandings*, project costs and interest costs;

— the *total discounted forecast net revenues* from the project during the life of the loan. First calculate the total of forecast project gross revenues for each future six-month operating period, after deduction of operating costs, capital expenditure, royalties and taxes (but before deduction of interest on the loans). Discount each forecast for each six-month period back to the date of the forecast at the agreed fixed discount rate (reflecting interest rates). The discounted totals for each six-month period are then added together to produce the total discounted forecast net revenues for the life of the loan;

— the *loan life cover ratio* which is the ratio of the total discounted forecast net revenues to the (forecast) maximum loan outstandings (so as to confirm that net revenues will cover the loan peak by the agreed margin). After drawdown in full, this ratio relates to actual loan outstandings when the ratio is tested;

- the *debt service cover ratio* for the next 12-month period, being the ratio of net revenues to the total of loan repayments and loan interest and other servicing costs for that 12 months (so as to confirm that net revenues are forecast to exceed the financing costs during the next 12 months by the agreed margin).

Note: There may also be a project life cover ratio which is the ratio of the net present value of the forecast project revenues over the life of the project to the loan outstandings. It is common to disregard revenues after a certain date, e.g. when 75 per cent of the reserves of an oilfield have been depleted, so as to bring into account only the less speculative future revenues.

A debt service cover ratio looking forward over the next year may also be accompanied by a similar ratio for the preceding year.

12.2   Assumptions The assumptions for the forecasts will be determined as follows:

- capital costs, operating costs, and sale prices of the project product: by the borrower, confirmed by the banks' independent engineer or other technical consultant;

- gas, oil or mineral reserves and rates of production: borrower, confirmed by the banks' independent engineer;

- taxes, interest rates, discount rates, currency exchange rates: by the banks, sometimes on the basis of external official indices.

12.3   Disputes Disagreements will be referred to an independent external expert (or decided by the majority banks).

12.4   Computer model The forecasts will be prepared using the agreed computer model. Procedures for protection of the computer model and the safe-keeping of a non-corruptible copy.

12.5   Cover ratios The borrower will ensure that:

- the loan life cover ratio is not less than the specified ratio (such as 1.4 to 1);

- the debt service cover ratio is not less than the specified ratio.

13. Project accounts

13.1 Account bank The borrower will open the accounts specified below at the specified borrower's bank (which may only be changed if the majority banks agree, and will be changed if the majority banks so direct).

13.2 Disbursement account The borrower will open a disbursement account to receive the proceeds of the loans. The borrower may draw on this account for the approved project purposes (including interest during construction).

13.3 Proceeds account A proceeds account to receive the gross revenues from the project and from authorised investments. The borrower may draw on this account only to pay the following in the following order of priority:

- project operating costs and project taxes

- any agreed capital costs

- scheduled loan repayments and loan interest and other servicing amounts

- specified amounts to the loan reserve account (to provide a cushion for future loan payments)

- specified amounts to the maintenance reserve account (to produce moneys to maintain the project)

- any prepayments of an individual bank under the taxes, increased costs or illegality clauses

- dividends or interest to the borrower's shareholders or any other purpose but only if (1) paid during a period of 30 days after a repayment date, (2) the cover ratios are met and (3) there is no event of default or pending default

[**Note:** The priorities are in practice ineffective if payments fall due at different times.]

13.4 Compensation account The borrower will open a compensation account to receive the proceeds of:

- insurance (except as provided in the insurance covenant in clause 15.33 below);

- nationalisation, expropriation, requisition for title or use;

- any restrictions on easements, licences or rights or the grant of easements, licences or rights;

— any redetermination of an oil or gas field (if there turns out to be an overlap with another licensee's field so that compensation is payable for the development costs).

The borrower may draw (1) liability insurance proceeds from this account only to pay the liability, (2) physical loss or damage insurance proceeds for minor casualties only when reinstatement is certified to be complete and for major casualties (above a specified threshold) in prepayment of the loans (unless the majority banks otherwise agree that they be applied in reinstatement), (3) business interruption or delay in start-up insurance proceeds by payment into the proceeds account, and (4) other non-insurance compensation, to service the loans or (if the majority banks consent) by credit to the proceeds account.

13.5 Equity account The borrower will open an equity account to receive the proceeds of shareholders equity subscriptions or subordinated loans. The borrower may draw on this account only to pay the specified capital costs or to prepay the loans plus interest.

13.6 Loan reserve account The borrower will open a loan reserve account to receive a specified proportion of gross revenues from the proceeds account. The borrower may draw on this account only to prepay the loans or to credit the proceeds account after a specified period has elapsed (to ensure that the moneys are not needed) and only if the remaining balance exceeds a specified minimum amount. (This account is to provide a cushion, e.g. if there is an unexpected shut-down or force majeure).

13.7 Maintenance reserve account The borrower will open a maintenance reserve account to receive payments out of gross revenues credited to the proceeds account (so as to provide a fund to meet scheduled maintenance expenditure for the project).

13.8 No withdrawals after default The borrower may not make any withdrawals from a project account so long as an event of default or pending default has occurred and is continuing.

13.9 Account information The banks are entitled to details of and to audit the project accounts and the borrower waives confidentiality. The borrower will provide bank statements and certificates.

13.10 No other accounts The borrower will not have any other bank accounts.

14. Authorised investments

14.1 Investment of project account moneys The borrower may invest moneys in the project accounts in specified authorised investments (sometimes restricted, e.g. to OECD government securities, triple A rated, listed and freely marketable debt securities of banks and certain money market instruments, all in specified freely convertible major currencies).

14.2 Custody Authorised investments will be held in the name of the borrower's account bank which will hold the certificates, etc.

14.3 Non-eligibility The borrower will liquidate investments which subsequently cease to be authorised.

14.4 Compulsory sale The agent bank may require the account bank to sell investments if needed.

14.5 Information The borrower will supply details of authorised investments.

15. Covenants

15.1 Waivers Each of the covenants below may be waived in writing by the majority banks. [**Note:** The relaxations and exceptions to these covenants will depend upon the circumstances.]

15.2 Financial information The borrower will supply to the agent bank:

— the borrower's audited accounts within 90 days of year-end;

— its quarterly management unaudited accounts within 45 days of quarter-end.

All accounts will be prepared in accordance with the specified generally accepted accounting principles and practices consistently applied, except as disclosed.

15.3 Project information The borrower will:

— supply a quarterly report on the progress of the project and (prior to completion) of any possible delays or cost overruns in the project;

— give the agent bank and its representatives access to the project at all reasonable times;

— supply details of any change in the project scope of works;

- supply details of any default under any project contract or adverse claims against the borrower by a project contractor, the host government or any other person;

- supply details of any shut-down of the project (other than for scheduled maintenance), any force majeure event under a project contract, any suspension of deliveries to the borrower or by the borrower under a project contract, and any event which might interrupt project construction or operations;

- supply environmental reports and details of any environmental damage or liability.

15.4 General information The borrower will:

- promptly notify the agent bank of any litigation, arbitration or administration proceedings, threatened or current, which might be material or which involve more than a specified amount;

- promptly notify the agent bank of any event of default or pending default and of the steps being taken to remedy the same;

- supply certificates on request as to compliance by the borrower with the financial, security and project documents and the absence of events of default and pending defaults;

- supply such other information as to the project or the borrower as the agent bank may request.

15.5 Authorisations The borrower will obtain, maintain and comply with all authorisations, licences and permits for:

- the financial and security agreements and the project contracts;

- the construction and operation of the project.

15.6 Negative pledge The borrower will not create or permit to subsist any security interest on any of its present or future assets except:

- liens arising by operation of law and securing amounts not more than 30 days overdue;

- the security created by the security documents.

15.7 Disposals The borrower will not sell, lease, transfer or otherwise dispose of any of its assets except:

- disposals of the project product under the project sale contracts;

- minor disposals on arms-length terms of obsolete equipment or goods no longer serviceable.

15.8   Business The borrower will not carry on any business other than the construction and operation of the project and matters necessarily incidental to that business.

15.9   Pari passu ranking The borrower will (procure) that all its unsecured obligations to the banks rank at least pari passu with all its other unsecured obligations, except for the priority of taxes and employee benefits on insolvency proceedings.

15.10   Project completion The borrower will use reasonable efforts to procure that:

— the project is constructed in accordance with the construction contract and the scheduled project development plan;

— the project is completed by a specified date.

15.11   Project development plan The borrower will develop the project in accordance with the scheduled project development plan and not materially alter the plan (subject to agreed exceptions, e.g. measured by tests of time and cost).

15.12   Project contracts The borrower will:

— comply with the project contracts and the host government concession;

— not alter or agree to any waiver or termination or abandon a project contract or the concession or grant any consent thereunder which might be material (subject to agreed exceptions) and will supply details of the above;

— enforce its rights under the project contracts and the concession.

15.13   Project site The borrower will:

— comply with the lease of the project site;

— comply with all planning and zoning licences and all easements and way-leaves relative to the project site and the project;

— notify the agent bank of any adverse claims in relation to the lease or the project site or its use;

— not enter into any negotiations regarding the compulsory acquisition or user of the site without involving the agent bank in those negotiations and will not agree to any such compulsory acquisition or user.

15.14   Operations The borrower will construct and operate the project and carry on its business diligently and efficiently and in accordance with good industry practice.

15.15   Sales The borrower will sell the project product (not covered by an agreed project purchase contract) at market prices on arms-length terms for cash payable on delivery (with agreed exceptions) in approved currencies.

15.16   Environment The borrower will use its best endeavours to prevent environmental contaminants, will comply with environmental laws, regulations and good environmental standards and will remedy environmental damage.

15.17   Maintenance The borrower will:

— keep the project in good repair;

— comply with maintenance schedules appropriate to the industry or recommended by the manufacturers.

15.18   Compliance with laws The borrower will comply with all laws and regulations applicable to the borrower and the project.

15.19   Taxes The borrower will pay all its taxes and governmental levies when due, except those reasonably contested in good faith for which adequate reserves have been set aside.

15.20   Leasing The borrower will not enter into any lease, hire purchase, rental or conditional sale agreement as lessee or buyer, except for the site lease and minor operating leases of equipment in the ordinary course of business.

15.21   Investments and subsidiaries The borrower will not:

— acquire any shares, debt instruments or other investments except for the authorised investments referred to in clause 14 above;

— hold or acquire any subsidiary;

— agree to share any of its revenues or enter into any pooling agreement in respect of its production or revenues;

— enter into any joint venture, partnership or other business association.

15.22   Borrowings and guarantees The borrower will not:

— borrow any money except under the financial agreements and except for loans from its shareholders subordinated on terms acceptable to the majority banks;

— purchase any assets on credit or under a retention of title clause except for minor equipment not exceeding a total specified amount;

- enter into any acceptance credit;

- enter into any transaction having the commercial effect of raising or borrowing money except as permitted;

- give any guarantees or other assurances against financial loss, except for normal warranties of the project product;

- enter into any interest swap or hedging agreements or any futures, forwards or option agreements or other derivative agreements except for the project contracts and the agreed interest hedges.

15.23   Capital expenditure The borrower will not incur any capital expenditure, except (1) the specified capital costs of constructing the project, (2) maintenance expenditure, and (3) expenditure not exceeding a specified annual total for works useful for the project.

15.24   Loans and credit The borrower will not make any loans or give any credit except for normal employee loans.

15.25   Intellectual property The borrower will maintain its intellectual property rights.

15.26   Material contracts The borrower will not enter into any material contracts other than the financial, security and project contracts and the concession.

15.27   Management The borrower will not delegate the management of the project to any other person.

15.28   Distributions The borrower will not pay or make any dividends, distribution or interest in respect of its share capital or subordinated loans subscribed by its shareholders except as permitted by this agreement.

15.29   Share capital The borrower will not:

- purchase, cancel or redeem any of its share capital;

- issue any share or loan capital except as contemplated by the equity agreement.

15.30   Financial year-end The borrower will not change its financial year-end.

15.31   Auditors The borrower's auditors shall be selected from an approved list.

15.32   Mergers and winding-up The borrower will:

— maintain its corporate existence in good standing;

— not enter into any merger or amalgamation;

— not apply for its winding-up or dissolution or for any insolvency proceedings unless required to do so by law.

15.33   Insurances The borrower will:

— maintain construction, property, cargo transit, third party, public liability, pollution, business interruption and delay in start-up insurances with approved insurers, through approved brokers, in approved terms, for approved amounts (e.g. full replacement cost) and deductibles (to be varied as required to reflect changing values) and against the required risks, all as scheduled;

— maintain such other insurances as would be maintained by a reasonable and prudent industry operator or as required by the agent bank after consultation with the banks' insurance adviser;

— pay the premiums on the insurances when due, maintain and comply with policies, and ensure that the insurances do not become void or voidable;

— ensure that notices of assignment to the banks (or a security trustee for the banks) are endorsed on the insurances in the scheduled form including the agreement of the insurers that the proceeds are to be paid direct to the agent bank upon notice and, until then, only if above a threshold amount, except that third party insurances are paid direct to the third party against discharge and all the proceeds of business interruption insurances are to be paid to the agent bank;

— procure that the insurers agree in scheduled form that:

  — the insurers waive all rights of subrogation against the banks;
  — the banks are additional insureds;
  — the insurers waive rights of contribution against other insurances effected by the banks;
  — the banks are not liable for premiums or other policy obligations;
  — the banks are under no duty of disclosure to the insurers;
  — as against the banks, the insurers will not be avoided by reason of any non-disclosure, misrepresentation, absence of due diligence, cancellation by the borrower, or breach of any warranty or condition in the policy (so as to preserve the policies in favour of the banks in case they can be invalidated by some action or inaction of the borrower);

- the insurers will not cancel a policy, reduce the cover or change the deductibles or limits without prior written notice to the agent bank;
- procure that the insurance brokers agree in scheduled form that, so long as they are appointed:
  - the scheduled policies have been effected and notices of assignment endorsed on the policies;
  - the brokers will arrange to have notices of assignment endorsed on future policies;
  - the brokers will notify the agent bank of (1) material changes to the policies, (2) failure to receive premiums or renewal instructions in good time, (3) cancellation, (4) circumstances giving rise to potential avoidance, but only if known to the brokers, and will also notify any revocation of their appointment;
  - the brokers will hold the insurances to the order of the agent bank;
  - the brokers will pay without set-off, but subject to the brokers' lien on the policies for unpaid premiums.

15.34   Abandonment The borrower will not abandon all or any major part of the project, but may abandon the project with the consent of the majority banks if it is uneconomic, i.e. net revenues are negative for at least 18 months and, in the opinion of the majority banks, are likely to remain negative for the period of the loan.

15.35   Process agent The borrower will maintain an agent for service of process in accordance with the jurisdiction clause 29.

15.36   Security The borrower will:

- maintain the security as first priority perfected valid non-avoidable security over the assets intended to be covered;
- grant the maximum security over its assets from time to time at the request of the agent bank;
- deposit all title deeds and the like with the agent bank (or security trustee);
- co-operate with the agent bank's lawyers in any investigation of the borrower's title to its land and other assets.

15.37   Power to remedy The agent bank may (but is not obliged to) remedy any failure of the borrower to comply with its covenants as to authorisations, repair and insurances, itself or through its agents who may enter on the borrower's premises to do so, and the borrower will indemnify the agent bank against costs and liabilities in doing so.

16. Events of default

16.1 Events If any one or more of the following events occur and are continuing (whether or not through the fault of the borrower), then, on the instructions of the majority banks, the agent bank, by notice to the borrower, may declare the principal of and all accrued interest on the loans (together with all other amounts accrued or payable under this agreement) to be immediately due and payable and cancel the banks' commitments to lend. [**Note:** Some of the events would often be qualified by grace periods, thresholds, materiality tests or other relaxations.]

(a) **Non-payment** The borrower does not pay any principal of, or interest on, the loans when due as required by this agreement.

(b) **Non-compliance** The borrower, a shareholder, a guarantor or a counterparty to a project contract (an "Obligor") does not perform any of its obligations under this agreement, the security agreements, the equity agreement, a guarantee of this agreement, the completion guarantee, a direct agreement, a project contract, or the host government concession. (For these documents, see clause 3.1).

(c) **Project contracts** Any project contract prematurely ceases to be in force.

(d) **Warranties** Any representation or warranty in, or in connection with, any of the documents specified in (b) above is or becomes materially incorrect.

(e) **Nationalisation** Any government or governmental authority (actually or constructively) (1) condemns, nationalises, seizes, or expropriates all or any substantial or material part of the assets of the borrower or its share capital, or (2) assumes custody or control of such assets or of the business or operations of the borrower or of its share capital, or (3) takes any action for the dissolution or disestablishment of the borrower, or (4) takes any action that would prevent the borrower or its officers from carrying on its business or operations or a substantial or material part thereof, or (5) materially restricts the prices or terms on which the project product may be sold.

(f) **Cross-default**

(1) Any financial debt (as defined) of any Obligor or any of its subsidiaries is not paid when due; or

(2) an event of default howsoever described (or any event which with the giving of notice, lapse of time, determination of materiality or fulfilment of any other applicable condition or any combination of the foregoing would constitute such an event of default) occurs under any document relating to financial debt of any Obligor or any of its subsidiaries; or

(3) any financial debt of any Obligor or any of its subsidiaries becomes prematurely due and payable or is placed on demand as a result of an event of default (howsoever described) under the document relating to that financial debt.

(g) **Insolvency**

(1) Any Obligor or any of its subsidiaries is, or is deemed for the purposes of any law to be, unable to pay its debts as they fall due or to be insolvent, or admits inability to pay its debts as they fall due, or stops payment, or declares a moratorium on any of its debts or, by reason of financial difficulties, begins negotiations with one or more of its creditors with a view to the readjustment or rescheduling of any of its indebtedness.

(2) Any order is made or resolution passed for, or step (including petition or convening a meeting) is taken with a view to, the rehabilitation, administration, custodianship, liquidation, winding-up or dissolution of any Obligor or any of its subsidiaries or a composition with creditors or any other insolvency proceedings involving any Obligor or any of its subsidiaries.

(3) Any liquidator, trustee in bankruptcy, judicial custodian, compulsory manager, receiver, administrator or the like is appointed in respect of any Obligor or any of its subsidiaries or is requested by any Obligor or any of its subsidiaries.

(h) **Creditors' process** Any attachment, sequestration, distress or execution affects any asset of any Obligor or any of its subsidiaries and is not discharged within 14 days.

(i) **Analogous proceedings** There occurs, in relation to any Obligor or any of its subsidiaries, any event anywhere which, in the opinion of the majority banks, corresponds with any of those mentioned in (g) and (h).

(j) **Unlawfulness** It is or becomes unlawful for any Obligor to perform any of its obligations under any of the documents specified in (b) above.

(k) **Project**

(1) The project completion date does not occur on or before a specified date.

(2) There occurs any damage to the project or other event which, in the opinion of the majority banks, makes it unlikely that project completion will occur by a specified date.

(3) There occurs after project completion (i) any material damage to the project or other event which in the opinion of the majority banks will prevent the borrower from being in compliance with this

agreement or (ii) any stoppage of operations for more than a specified period in any year.

   (4) The borrower abandons or proposes to abandon all or a material part of the project.

(l) **Guarantee** Any guarantee ceases to be in full force and effect.

(m) **Concession** The concession ceases to be in full force and effect.

(n) **Insurance** Any material insurance required by this agreement ceases to be obtainable on commercial terms.

(o) **Environment** The borrower breaches any environmental laws or a material environmental liability arises.

(p) **Ownership** The shares of the borrower cease to be owned legally and beneficially by the shareholders in the agreed proportions as specified in the equity agreement.

(q) **Overruns** Prior to project completion, the cost of completing the project exceeds the availability of finance under the financial agreements and the shareholders have not financed the excess by equity or subordinated debt.

(r) **Material adverse change** Any event or series of events occurs which, in the opinion of the majority banks, might have a material and adverse effect on the project or the financial condition or operations of any Obligor.

16.2   Enforcement After a default notice:

— the security may be enforced immediately (subject to the intercreditor agreement);

— the agent bank may operate the project accounts to the exclusion of the borrower.

17.   Agent bank

17.1   Appointment Each bank appoints the agent bank to carry out the rights and powers delegated to it in this agreement and the other relevant agreements.

17.2   No fiduciary duties The agent bank is not a fiduciary and hence need not hold moneys in trust for the banks, may have any business with the borrower and other project parties, and exercise its powers and rights as a bank as if it were not the agent.

17.3 Majority bank directions The agent bank will act or refrain from acting as directed by the majority banks and has no responsibility in the absence of a direction.

17.4 Delegation The agent bank may delegate and may appoint lawyers.

17.5 Exculpation The agent bank is not responsible for:

- the documentation;

- the information memorandum;

- the documentation under the conditions precedent clause;

- monitoring the project or the credit of the borrower or other project parties;

- notifying defaults unless its agency administration department has been notified in writing of the default concerned (stating that it is a default);

- requesting any certificates or the like unless required to do so by the majority banks;

- any action or inaction in relation to its powers or duties in the absence of gross negligence or wilful misconduct.

17.6 Reliance The agent bank may rely on communications and documents believed to be genuine.

17.7 Indemnity Each bank will indemnify the agent bank against liabilities incurred in relation to the agency pro rata, but without prejudice to the borrower's liability. The borrower will reimburse each bank.

17.8 Identity of banks The agent bank may treat each bank as such (and hence entitled to payments) unless it has been notified to the contrary in good time.

17.9 Removal and resignation The majority banks may remove the agent and the agent bank may resign, subject in each case to the concurrent appointment of a successor. The benefit of this clause 17 will continue to benefit a removed or resigning agent.

18. Fees and expenses

The borrower will pay:

- the agreed front-end fee;

- a commitment fee of a specified percentage p.a. on each bank's unused commitment, payable quarterly and on whole or partial termination of a commitment;
- the agreed agency fee;
- the fees of the banks' engineers and insurance advisers;
- the fees of the agent bank's lawyers for the preparation of the documentation and for any waivers;
- the costs of each bank and the agent bank of enforcement and preserving of rights.

19.   Advisers

The majority banks may remove any bank independent engineer or insurance adviser. If any such adviser is removed or resigns, the agent bank will appoint another after consultation.

20.   Stamp duties

The borrower will pay all stamp duties and documentary taxes in relation to the documentation.

21.   Indemnities

The borrower will indemnify each bank and the agent bank against the costs (including breakage costs) incurred by reason of:

- a default or event of default or an acceleration;
- a payment otherwise than at the end of an interest period (including under the pro rata sharing clause);
- a loan not being borrowed after a request for the loan has been served;
- any order, judgment, claim or proof of debt being denominated in a currency other than the agreed currency under this agreement.

22.   Evidence and calculations

Accounts Accounts maintained by a bank are prima facie evidence.

Certificates A certificate of a bank as to the amount owing to it is conclusive in the absence of manifest error.

360-day year basis Interest and commitment fees are calculated on the basis of a 360-day year for the precise number of days elapsed.

23. Amendments and waivers

Majority bank voting Where any matter may be determined by the majority banks, the agent bank may impose a time limit for responses, and if a bank fails to respond within that time, it will be excluded in determining the majority.

Permitted variations In addition to the waivers, provided in this agreement, a higher majority of banks (e.g. 80 per cent) may amend or waive any term of this agreement (so as to be binding on all the banks), the equity agreement, the completion guarantee, a direct agreement or the security documents except:

– maturity dates
– the amount or currency of payments
– the definition of majority banks or this clause
– any increase in a bank's commitment or obligations
– any substitution of any obligor
– any term which expressly requires the consent of all the banks.

24. Assignments

Borrower The borrower may not assign all or any of its rights or obligations.

Banks Each bank may:

– change its lending office;
– assign its rights or novate its rights and obligations in accordance with prescribed procedures (but only with the consent of the borrower, not to be unreasonably withheld or delayed, except that no consent is required for an assignment or novation after a default or after project completion or to a bank's affiliate);
– sub-participate its participation.

25. Confidentiality

The agent bank and each bank will keep the affairs of the borrower confidential in accordance with the bankers' duty of confidentiality except that disclosure is permitted:

- in connection with a change of lending office, an assignment, novation or sub-participation by a bank;
- where required by law or regulation or official request or directive or to comply with securities or bank regulation or stock exchange rules;
- where the information is in the public domain;
- to professional advisers and auditors;
- to bank supervisory authorities.

26. Pro rata sharing

If any bank receives a greater proportion of an amount due to it than the others, it will pay an amount equal to the excess to the agent bank which will distribute it pro rata and the paying bank will to that extent be subrogated to the rights of banks receiving a distribution. The payments will be unwound if the original payment is recovered from the original bank as a preference or otherwise.

27. Notices

(a) **Writing** Any notice or other communication under this agreement must be in writing (including electronic communication).

(b) **Service** A notice or communication will be deemed to have been duly served when it arrives at the relevant party's specified address or at such other address as the party has designated by notice to the relevant other parties.

28. Miscellaneous

28.1 Language All documents to be furnished or communications under this agreement will be in English or, if an official document in another language, will be accompanied by a certified translation

28.2 Remedies cumulative The rights and remedies of the banks and the agent bank under this agreement are additional to and not exclusive of those provided by law.

28.3 Set-off A bank may set off any matured obligation owed by the borrower under this agreement against any obligation owed by the bank to the borrower, regardless of the place of payment or currency of either obligation. If the obligations are in different currencies, the bank may convert either obligation at a market rate of exchange in its usual course of business for the purpose of the set-off.

28.4   Counterparts This agreement may be executed in several counterparts, each of which shall be deemed an original, but all of which together shall constitute one and the same agreement.

29.   Jurisdiction

For the benefit of the agent bank and the banks, the borrower agrees that the courts of [   ] have jurisdiction to settle any disputes in connection with this agreement, submits to the jurisdiction of those courts, and, without prejudice to any other mode of service, irrevocably appoints [   ] as its agent for service of process relating to any proceedings before those courts in connection with this agreement. Nothing in this clause limits the right of the agent bank and the banks to bring proceedings against the borrower in connection with this agreement in any other court of competent jurisdiction.

30.   Governing law

This Agreement is governed by the law of [   ].

2. Outline completion guarantee

Note: This outline illustrates the typical provisions of an agreement whereby the shareholders of the project company agree to procure completion of the project by a specified date and to provide overrun funds. For a comment, see para 3–4.

Parties

1. Shareholders of the project company

2. Project company

3. Banks

4. Agent bank as agent for the banks

1. Completion

The completion of the project occurs when:

- the construction of the project has been completed in accordance with the scheduled project development plan as certified by the banks' independent engineer;

- the specified performance and commissioning tests have been carried out to the satisfaction of the banks' independent engineer;

- no event of default or pending event of default has occurred and is continuing;

- the representations and warranties in the credit agreement are true as if made on the date for completion.

2. Completion undertaking

Each shareholder agrees with the banks to ensure that project completion will take place not later than a specified date and will indemnify the banks against losses they may incur under the credit agreement if project completion does not occur by that date.

3. Completion overrun finance

Each shareholder agrees with the banks, on demand of the agent bank from time to time, to provide funds to the project company, to the extent necessary, to ensure that the project company has sufficient funds to complete the project by the specified date. [The agreement may set out detailed provisions for calculating deficiencies, stipulate a maximum liability and provide for the deficiencies to be provided by way of equity or subordinated debt along the lines of the outline equity agreement in this Appendix.]

4. Obligations unconditional

Each shareholder's obligations under the above clauses are unconditional and irrevocable and apply regardless of:

- any force majeure or other event (however fundamental) inhibiting or preventing completion by the project company;

- any default by a lender in supplying finance or by another shareholder;

- any liquidation or dissolution of the project company.

5. Obligations several

The obligations of each shareholder are several. No shareholder is liable for the obligations of any other shareholder. Non-compliance by one shareholder does not relieve the others.

6. Guarantee protections

[The agreement will contain conventional guarantee-type clauses, e.g. waiver of defences, non-competition with banks, immediate recourse by banks.]

7. Miscellaneous provisions

Payments without set-off or deduction; tax grossing-up; default interest on overdue payments; expenses; stamp duties; confidentiality; currency indemnity; notices; language; severability; counterparts; submission to jurisdiction; governing law.

3. Outline equity subscription agreement

Note: This outline illustrates the provisions of an agreement whereby the project sponsors agree to subscribe equity in the project company in order to provide finance in addition to the bank finance. Often the direct shareholders in the project company are subsidiaries of the project sponsors in which event the project sponsors may be called upon to give a guarantee to the banks of the obligations of their subsidiaries. For a brief description of sponsor support for a project, see para 3–1 *et seq*.

Parties

1. Project company

2. Shareholders in the project company

3. Banks

4. Agent bank as agent for the banks

1. Equity subscription

Each shareholder will subscribe and pay in cash at par for ordinary voting share capital of the project company in the scheduled amounts and at the scheduled times. [These may be prior to any loan draw-down, pro rata with loans, or at project completion. If the share capital is not subscribed initially, then the banks bear a credit risk on the shareholders which may become insolvent before the capital is subscribed. The banks may require a bank guarantee or bond for shareholder obligations. The total equity must be provided prematurely if an event of default occurs and the bank loans are accelerated or the project is abandoned under a permitted abandonment clause prior to completion. The equity amounts may be increased if there is an unfinanced overrun in project construction costs, subject to a maximum liability.]

2. Subordinated debt

2.1 Subscription Instead of subscriptions for share capital, the shareholders may make subordinated loans to the project company in a specified currency and on the terms of the scheduled form of subordination or intercreditor agreement.

2.2 Terms of loan The terms of the loans will be as agreed between the project company and the shareholders (but at a rate of interest not exceeding a specified rate). In the absence of agreement, the loans will be repayable on demand and bear interest at a specified rate, but subject to the subordination agreement.

3. Procedures for subscription of share capital

3.1 Authorised capital The project company will maintain sufficient authorised but unissued share capital to meet the above subscription.

3.2 Compliance The project company and the shareholders will do all things necessary for the creation, issue and allotment of shares or the constitution of subordinated loans as contemplated above.

3.3 Single class The share capital of the company will be of one class only, comprising ordinary voting shares, unless the majority banks otherwise agree.

3.4 Equity account Subscriptions for equity or subordinated loans will be paid into the equity account maintained by the project account bank, to be applied as provided in the credit agreement (usually in payment of project capital costs or in prepayment of the bank loans plus interest).

4. Inability to subscribe

If any shareholder does not subscribe for share capital or subordinated debt (by reason of the liquidation of the project company, non-acceptance of the project company of the capital, non-compliance by the project company with its obligation to issue shares or otherwise), the shareholder will on demand pay the amount concerned to the agent bank as a guarantee of the loans, to be applied by the agent bank in prepayment of the loans plus interest or as the majority banks direct (e.g. to pay project capital costs).

5. Management of project company

5.1 Compliance The shareholders will exercise their voting and other rights as shareholders of the project company to procure to the extent practicable that the project company complies with the banks' credit agreement. [The shareholders may also agree with the banks to provide technical, engineering, marketing and other assistance to the project company].

5.2 No guarantee Except as specifically stated, nothing in this clause imposes any obligation upon the shareholders personally to meet a payment obligation of the project company or to put the project company in funds to meet its payment obligations.

6. Ownership of the project company

6.1 Minimum ownership The shareholders agree with the banks that they will hold, legally and beneficially, the entire share capital of the project company in the specified proportions and in not less than the specified percentages of the total share capital, except that after project completion (1) the share capital may be held in different specified proportions and percentages, and (2) the shareholders may transfer their shares to transferees approved by the majority banks (or satisfying specified eligibility criteria) so long as the original shareholders between them continue to hold not less than the specified percentage of the total share capital.

6.2 Affiliates The shareholders may hold their shares via affiliates so long as the affiliate remains an affiliate, but each shareholder will continue to be responsible for its affiliate's obligations under this agreement and for the performance of its affiliate's obligations as shareholder. Each affiliate holding shares will execute an accession agreement in scheduled form.

6.3 Negative pledge No shareholder will create or permit to subsist any security interest over its shares in the project company or grant options over or agree to transfer those shares except as specifically permitted by this agreement.

7. Shareholders agreement

This agreement overrides any provision of the joint venture agreement between the shareholders in conflict with this agreement. Subscriptions under this agreement are performance of subscription obligations under the joint venture agreement.

8. Representations and warranties

8.1 General The shareholders and the project company warrant due incorporation, valid existence, powers and authority, legal validity, non-conflict with laws, regulations and their constitutions and contracts, all authorisations obtained, no material default, no material threatened or current litigation or proceeding, latest accounts correct.

8.2 Information memorandum Each shareholder warrants that information as to itself in the information memorandum is materially correct and omits no material information, and that there has been no adverse change as to itself since then.

8.3 Repetition The representations and warranties will remain true (subject to agreed exceptions for commercial matters, e.g. the information memorandum, no litigation).

9. Covenants of shareholders

9.1 Information Each shareholder will supply the agent bank with:

- its annual audited accounts;
- quarterly unaudited accounts for each quarter prior to project completion;
- details of its shareholdings in the project company;
- other reasonable information on request of the agent bank;
- compliance certificates.

9.2 Distributions The shareholders will not receive any dividend or other distribution, in cash or in kind, revenue or capital, or any payment or distribution in respect of subordinated debt except as permitted by the banks' credit agreement and the subordination or intercreditor agreement.

9.3 Liquidation of the company No shareholder will take any step with a view to the winding-up, dissolution, merger or amalgamation of the project company.

10. Waiver of defences and competition

10.1 Variations, etc. Each shareholder's obligations under this agreement will not be affected by:

- waivers or amendments in respect to the financial and security documents or compositions with the project company;
- release of rights or security in respect of these documents or a shareholder's obligations;

- any invalidity of the obligations of the project company or another shareholder;

- any other circumstances which might prejudice those obligations.

10.2   Non-competition No shareholder may compete with the banks in claiming payment from another shareholder or the project company by virtue of having made a payment under this agreement.

11.   Payments

Payments by the shareholder to the banks will be made in the prescribed currency and funds and without any set-off or deduction. The shareholders will gross up for taxes which must be deducted from a payment.

12.   Severality

Each shareholder's obligations under this agreement are several. No shareholder is liable for the obligations of another shareholder. Non-compliance by one shareholder does not relieve the others.

13.   Miscellaneous

Default interest on overdue payments; reimbursement of expenses; payment of documentary taxes; currency indemnity; non-assignment by shareholders; transfers by banks; bank right of set-off; confidentiality; notices; language; severability; counterparts; submission to jurisdiction; governing law.

4. Outline direct agreement

Note: These agreements allow the banks to preserve essential contracts with the project company on a default by the project company: see para 5–6. The contracts may include the construction contract, the supply contracts, contracts for the sale of the project product, operating and maintenance contracts, a lease of the project site, and the government concession. Without rights of preservation, the project contractors would be able to strip the project company of the essential contracts on a default by the project company – the very time that the banks need the contracts to remain in place.

The ideal result from the banks' point of view is that it should be possible to preserve the contract initially, e.g. by a bank guarantee, and then to hive down the contracts to a bank-controlled vehicle company (or to transfer to a bank-controlled company initially) and then to sell the new company to a purchaser willing to continue the project.

The rights are inhibited if the jurisdiction of the project company does not permit universal security over all the project assets since it would then be difficult to transfer them all, together with the project contracts, so as to keep the project as a single unit. This is not a problem in English-based countries permitting the universal fixed and floating charge over all the assets of a company. In other cases golden shares should be considered (para 5–2) but transfers of the project assets not subject to security may be caught by bulk sales or other rules avoiding preferential transfers by an insolvent. Transferring project assets may require other consents or attract stamp duties and taxes.

In practice, direct agreements might be difficult to implement since banks are generally unwilling to assume commercial contracts, which may involve lender liability, even if the banks are shielded by a bank-controlled company. The time taken to reach syndicate decisions may be much longer than the usual periods during which step-in rights are exercisable (because of problems of agreement by the syndicate as to what to do and because of uncertainties as to whether the project will be viable in the future). The risks of abandonment costs and environmental liabilities are relevant. Some direct agreements give the banks rights to step-in initially for a "look-round" period without assuming existing liabilities. Nevertheless direct agreements are better than nothing.

The agreement also usually deals with the formalities associated with the initial security assignment of the project contract to the banks.

The precise terms of a direct agreement will depend upon the circumstances and in particular the type of contract which is covered by the direct agreement and this outline merely illustrates points worth considering.

Parties

1. Project company

2. Project contractor

3. Banks

4. Agent bank

1. Assignment

The project contractor acknowledges notice of the assignment of the project company's rights under the contract to the banks (or the security trustee) by way of security and,

— consents to the assignment and to any further assignment on enforcement of the security;

— confirms that it has not received notice of any other assignment of the contract;

— will not set off any sum due to it by the project company against sums due by it under the contract unless both cross-claims arise under the contract;

— agrees that all sums payable by the project contract or to the project company under the contract will continue to be so paid until the agent bank gives notice to the contrary, when such sums will be paid to the agent bank [The agent bank is permitted by the security assignment to give this notice on an event of default.]

— agrees that the banks have no liability under the contract by virtue of the assignment:

2. Notice of default

The project contractor will promptly notify the agent bank of defaults or pending defaults by the project company under the contract.

3. Notice of termination

3.1 Notice The project contractor will not terminate the contract, or suspend performance under the contract (otherwise than for express force majeure) without first giving the agent bank at least 20 business days prior written notice with full details of:

— the circumstances giving rise to the right of termination or suspension;

— existing unperformed liabilities of the project company under the contract (in a certificate).

3.2 Suspension The project contractor's right to terminate or to suspend performance will be suspended during the period of notice (the "suspension period").

4. Step-in

4.1 Notice During the suspension period, the agent bank may notify the project company that an eligible person will step-in and will (so as to take effect during the suspension period):

— assume the contract in place of the project company; or

— guarantee the obligations of the project company under the contract.

The eligible person which steps in is a "substitute obligor".

4.2 Eligible person An eligible person is:

— the agent bank, or one or more of the banks, or any of their affiliates; or

— a receiver appointed by the banks in respect of the security (suitable only if universal security enforceable by possessory management is available); or

— another entity acceptable to the project contractor, such acceptance not to be unreasonably withheld; or

— a company directly or indirectly wholly-owned by one or more of the above eligible persons so long as it is wholly-owned by them.

4.3 Effect From the step-in date the substitute obligor will:

— assume the rights and liabilities of the project company under the contract including the existing liabilities (but only up to the amount initially certified by the project contractor as stated above); or

— be liable as guarantor of the obligations of the project company under the contract on the terms set out in the schedule (normal contract guarantee terms).

Thereafter the project contractor may not exercise any right of termination or suspension of performance arising prior to the step-in date, and may not exercise a right of termination or suspension of performance for breaches by the project company covered by the substitute obligor guarantee so long as the guarantee is performed. The substitute obligor will have an additional 20 business days from step-in to cure any outstanding default under the contract. In the absence of a step-in, the project contractor may terminate or suspend performance at the end of the suspension period. The project company remains a co-obligor. A step-in right may be exercised once only.

5.   Acceleration step-in

If the loans are accelerated on an event of default, or if the contract is prematurely terminated or a premature termination is threatened, the agent bank may, within 10 business days, serve a step-in notice on the project contractor with the same result as described above, to be effective within sixty days of the acceleration or other event. [The contract may be terminated by the insolvency representative of the project company if insolvency proceedings are instituted – in such a case the banks have an additional step-in right.]

6.   Step-out

6.1   Notice After a step-in, the agent bank or the substitute obligor may give the project contractor not less than 30 days prior written notice of a step-out.

6.2   Effect On the expiry of the notice, the liability of the substitute obligor under the contract will cease except for liabilities arising during the step-in period and the substitute obligor will have no further liability for any subsequent matters. The contract will revert to the project company.

7.   New substitute obligors

The agent bank may change the substitute obligor during a step-in period or change the step-in from a guarantee to an assumption of the entire contract, subject to 30 days prior written notice to the project contractor. Each new substitute obligor must be an eligible person. This right may be exercised more than once. [This enables the banks first to step-in themselves via a receiver, then to cause the contract to be transferred to a bank-owned vehicle which can then be sold, provided the ultimate owner is eligible as a person acceptable to the project contractor, such acceptance not to be unreasonably withheld.]

8. Warranties

The project contractor warrants: status, powers, authorities, legal validity, official consents, non-conflict with laws or its constitution or contracts.

9. Assignment by project contractor

The project contractor may not assign any of its rights or obligations under the contract except to a person approved by the majority banks in their discretion and on terms that the assignee enters into an agreement corresponding to this agreement.

10. Miscellaneous

Indemnity by the project company for any guarantee given by the substitute obligor and for existing liabilities accrued on step-in and paid by the substitute obligor; notices; assignments by banks; change of agent bank; expenses; stamp duties; confidentiality; remedies cumulative; language; severability; counterparts; submission to jurisdiction; governing law.

5.   Outline intercreditor agreement

Note: This outline illustrates a range of provisions which may be found in an intercreditor agreement if there are several classes of lender or guarantor. There are no standard provisions for intercreditor agreements and their terms depend upon the circumstances and the negotiations, and one could not expect to find all of the provisions of this outline in a particular agreement. If part of the finance is provided by a finance lease of equipment or plant for the project – often guaranteed by a syndicate of banks – the provisions of the intercreditor agreement are more complicated, but the principles remain the same. A single global agent may be appointed by the senior creditors to pay over loan proceeds, to receive payments from the obligors and to distribute them and to act as a conduit for notices. There may also be a monitoring committee of banks to monitor the project. In addition to common security, there may be a common bank for the holding of project revenues and retention moneys.

Parties

1.   Project company as borrower

2.   Project sponsors

3.   International commercial banks

4.   Local commercial banks

5.   Export credit agency ("ECA") lenders

6.   ECA guarantors guaranteeing part of the loans of the commercial banks

7.   Hedging bank providing an interest swap to the project company

8.   Agent bank of international commercial banks

9.   Agent bank of local commercial banks

10. Agent bank of ECA lenders

11. Security trustee holding the security granted by the borrower for all the creditors, including the project sponsors as junior creditors and including the hedging bank

---

1. Senior creditors

The "senior creditors" are the international commercial banks, the local commercial banks, the ECA lenders and the hedging bank [i.e. all the creditors except the project sponsors which are junior creditors. The ECA guarantors become senior creditors when they pay the guarantees which they have given to the commercial banks and hence take over the loans of those banks by subrogation].

2. Restrictions on enforcement

2.1   No action Unless the majority senior creditors so decide, no senior creditor or its agent will:

— accelerate its loans or cancel its loan commitment or, in the case of the hedging bank, terminate its interest swap, on an event of default;

— make a demand under the equity agreement or the completion guarantee (as to these, see above in this Appendix);

— sue for any amounts owing to it under its credit agreement or the equity agreement or completion guarantee;

— enforce any obligation of the borrower or a project sponsor by execution, attachment or the like for these amounts;

— institute any prejudgment attachment or injunction for those amounts;

— enforce any security for those amounts;

— take any steps to wind up or dissolve the borrower or a project sponsor;

— institute or vote in favour of any insolvency or reorganisation proceeding involving the borrower or a project sponsor;

— apply for any injunction or order for specific performance against the borrower or a project sponsor;

— exercise any step-in rights under the direct agreements.

2.2   Permitted action Notwithstanding the above, a senior creditor,

— may accelerate a loan guaranteed by an ECA guarantor so as to be able to call the ECA guarantee;

— may set off against the borrower or a project sponsor.

3. Security interests

3.1 Pari passu The security interests granted by the borrower to the senior creditors or the security trustee rank pari passu.

3.2 Enforcement The security trustee must act or refrain from acting in accordance with the directions of the majority senior creditors in connection with the enforcement of those security interests. In the absence of directions, the security trustee will not enforce, or, if enforcement has commenced, may conduct the enforcement as it sees fit without any responsibility to the creditors.

3.3 Application of proceeds The proceeds of the enforcement of those security interests will be applied in the following order:

— the costs and fees of the security trustee

— the costs and fees of the agents pro rata

— the enforcement costs of the senior creditors

— principal, interest and fees due to the senior creditors pro rata

— subordinated debt of the project sponsors

— any surplus to the borrower.

3.4 Separate security If any creditor has separate security not granted to the security trustee it will administer, enforce and apply the security consistently with the provisions of this agreement relating to security granted to the security trustee.

4. Step-in rights

A decision of the majority senior creditors as to the exercise of step-in or step-out rights and other rights under any direct agreement (see above in this Appendix) will be binding on all the senior creditors, provided that any new liability undertaken by a bank or its affiliate will require its prior consent.

5. Drawdowns

[**Note:** These provisions would usually appear separately in each credit agreement.]

5.1   Conditions precedent The borrower may not borrow a loan from any senior lender until all the initial conditions precedent in all the credit agreements have been fulfilled.

5.2   Pro rata drawdowns The borrower will draw down loans under the senior credit agreements pro rata except:

— where the drawdown is to pay a cost not permitted to be paid by the other lender (e.g. local currency costs);

— where the drawdown is under an ECA guaranteed credit to pay the price of national goods and services for which that credit is available.

5.3   Suspension of drawings If any senior creditor suspends drawdowns under its credit agreement, all the other senior creditors may suspend drawdowns under their credit agreements.

6.   Prepayments and cancellations

6.1   Prepayments If the borrower voluntarily prepays a senior creditor's loan, it must prepay the loans of all the senior creditors pro rata (subject to specified exceptions).

6.2   Cancellations If the borrower voluntarily cancels the loan commitment of a senior creditor, it must cancel the loan commitments of all the senior creditors pro rata.

6.3   Other prepayments and cancellations Notwithstanding the above, the borrower may prepay the loan of, and cancel the commitment of, a particular senior creditor otherwise than pro rata if the prepayment or cancellation is under clauses relating to the following:

— alternative interest rate basis on market disorder

— tax grossing-up

— increased costs imposed on a lender

— illegality of lender's obligations.

7.   Insurances

7.1   Proceeds All insurance proceeds received by a senior creditor (other than political risk insurance) will be paid to the security trustee to be applied in accordance with the security deed (e.g. reinstatement, prepayment of loans, discharge of third party liability). [There may be a similar provision for requisition and nationalisation proceeds. See generally clause 13.4 of the outline project finance credit agreement in this appendix.]

7.2   Reinstatement No creditor may require insurance proceeds above a specified threshold to be applied in reinstatement unless the majority senior creditors so direct or unless required to be applied in reinstatement by the security deed.

8.   Information

8.1   Disclosure Each creditor may disclose information about the borrower and other project obligors to any other creditor involved in the financing.

8.2   Notice Each agent will supply copies to each other agent of material notices received under its credit agreement.

8.3   Defaults Each senior creditor will notify its agent of events of default or potential defaults actually known to its department responsible for administering the credit. Each agent will notify the other agents of the events of default or potential defaults in its agreement which are actually known to its agency department concerned with the loan in its capacity as such. No creditor or agent has a duty to monitor or investigate defaults or compliance by the obligors.

8.4   Amount of debts Each creditor will on request of an agent or the security trustee notify it of the amounts owing to the creditor by the borrower.

9.   Amendments and waivers under finance documents

9.1   Majority control No senior creditor may amend the following provisions of its credit or other agreement or grant consents thereunder without the approval of the majority senior creditors except where the amendment must be made or the consent cannot be refused, e.g. because it is not to be unreasonably withheld:

– the due dates, amounts and currency of payments

– any security for its credits

– any guarantee.

Each creditor (or group of creditors) may in other respects amend its agreement or give consents thereunder except as prohibited by this agreement.

9.2 Common terms [If the senior creditors have agreed common terms for their several credit agreements which are set out in a common terms agreement, then the intercreditor agreement may specify the majority required to amend it or to grant waivers or consents and stipulate that a majority decision agreed by the borrower or other relevant obligor is binding on all the senior creditors. A common terms agreement will often include common conditions precedent, representations and warranties, covenants, events of default, set-off, currency indemnity, notices, stamp duties, boiler-plate, jurisdiction and governing law, so that each separate loan agreement deals only with the financial terms applicable to that lender, plus any special provisions. Certain common terms will usually be entrenched and require unanimity for amendments, e.g. release of security, changes in the amounts, due dates or currency of payments, release of security, changes to voting majorities, changes to the priority of payments and changes to a pro rata sharing clause, etc.]

9.3 Security The security trustee may agree amendments to the security deed if considered not to be prejudicial to the senior creditors or if considered to be technical or minor. Those amendments will be binding on all the creditors.

10. Subordination of project sponsor debt

[Insert provisions subordinating the debt of the project sponsors along the lines of those in the relevant form of subordination agreement in this Appendix.]

11. Voting

11.1 Agency voting Voting will be ascertained by each agent of a group of creditors. The security agent or an agent may call for voting on any issue. If a creditor or an agent does not notify a vote within 10 business days of a request, the creditor (or the agent's creditors) will be excluded in calculating a majority.

11.2 Calculation of votes Votes are by amount of participations. Participations in currencies other than US dollars shall be converted into US dollars at the prevailing spot rate in the London foreign exchange market.

11.3   Majority A majority is more than 50 per cent [or $66\frac{2}{3}$ per cent].

12.   Protection of agents and security trustee

12.1   Agents [Insert provisions on the lines of the agency clauses in clause 17 of the first form in this Appendix.]

12.2   Security trustee The security trustee holds the security on trust for the creditors in accordance with the security deed and this agreement.

12.3   New security agreements The security trustee may negotiate the terms of, and as trustee for the creditors, enter into, security agreements whereby the borrower confers additional security.

12.4   Perfection of security The security trustee is not liable for failure to perfect the security (by filing, registration or otherwise).

12.5   Title The security trustee is not bound to investigate the title of the borrower to the security assets.

12.6   Documents The security trustee need not hold any title deeds or documents in respect of the security assets, but will reasonably take care of deeds and documents in its possession (without obligation to insure).

12.7   Investment The security trustee may invest moneys received by it in authorised investments.

12.8   Payments The security trustee may properly pay amounts for the benefit of a creditor to the agent of that creditor against that agent's certificate of the amount due to that creditor.

13.   Application of receipts

13.1   Order The proceeds of the enforcement of the security granted by the borrower will be applied in the order stated in clause 3.3 above. All receipts by a senior creditor or its agent under the completion guarantee or the equity agreement will be applied to the debt of the relevant senior creditors pro rata. All receipts by a senior creditor from the borrower or otherwise after an acceleration agreed by the majority senior creditors as stated above shall be applied to the debt of all the senior creditors pro rata. Pro rata payment does not apply to:

– receipts by a senior creditor under an ECA guarantee [or under any political risk insurance];

– receipts by an ECA from the host government or one of its agencies by virtue of a payment by the ECA to a senior creditor under its ECA guarantee;

– any interest subsidy payments received by a senior creditor under an ECA interest make-up agreement.

13.2   Security trustee and agents The costs and fees of the security trustee and then the agents are to be paid before any pro rata distribution.

13.3   Currencies For the purposes of determining pro rata payment, debts in currencies other than US dollars will be converted into US dollars at the security trustee's prevailing spot rate in the London foreign exchange market.

14.   Pro rata sharing

If any senior creditor receives an amount (including a receipt by set-off) which it is not entitled to receive by virtue of this agreement or receives a greater proportionate payment than the other senior creditors, it will pay a sum equal to that amount to the security trustee which will distribute the sum pro rata or in the other order specified in this agreement. The paying creditor will be subrogated to the rights of those which are paid out of the redistribution. The redistribution and subrogation will be unwound if the paying creditor's original receipt is avoided as a preference or otherwise.

15.   Amendments to this agreement

The majority senior creditors may, with the agreement of the borrower and project sponsors where their rights are affected, amend or waive any provisions of this agreement, except that the following require unanimity of creditors [specify, e.g. restrictions on enforcement, order of application, governing law, majorities required.]

16.   Warranties

Each party warrants powers, authorisations, validity, and non-conflict with laws and its constitutional documents and contracts.

17. Transfers

Borrower The borrower may not assign its rights or obligations under this agreement.

Senior creditors If any senior creditor assigns its rights or novates its rights and obligations under its credit or other agreement, it will procure that the transferee executes a deed of accession to this agreement in the scheduled form.

18. Conflict

This agreement prevails over the senior credit agreements, the hedging agreement and the ECA guarantees.

19. No fiduciary relationship

Nothing in this agreement creates any partnership between creditors or imposes fiduciary duties on creditors except as specifically and expressly stated.

20. Competition law

If any provision of this agreement requires notification under applicable restrictive practices or anti-trust legislation, it will not take effect until that notification.

21. Miscellaneous

Default interest on overdue payments; expenses; stamp duties; confidentiality; notices; language; severability; counterparts; submission to jurisdiction; governing law.

APPENDIX: PART II

SUBORDINATED DEBT

6. Outline of turnover subordination agreement

This outline lists a menu of possible clauses whose inclusion will depend on the circumstances. The agreements are discussed in chapters 6 to 11.

Initial checks

Corporate powers and authorisations, contractual restrictions in junior creditor's loan agreements (negative pledge, no disposals). Turnover, or contractual subordination to all creditors? Priority of turnover proceeds. Efficacy of contractual subordination on debtor's insolvency. Efficacy on junior creditor's insolvency (transaction at an undervalue, insolvency preference, transfer of future proceeds). Turnover subordination as security interest requiring registration or filing? Taxation and stamp duty. Desubordination without consent of senior creditors. Capital adequacy requirements.

1. **Senior debt**

    - all present and future debt, or specific debt, or class of debt?
    - are the following included in senior debt: senior debt acquired by purchase; refinancings or variations of specific senior debt; increases in specific senior debt (up to a limit?); debt springing up on return of preferential payment of senior debt; non-provable senior debt e.g. post-insolvency interest; damages on rescission of senior debt

2. **Junior debt**

    - all present and future debt owed to junior creditor, or specific debt or class of debt? Does this cover: damages on rescission of junior debt; debt acquired by purchase?
    - turnover to apply to recoveries from all sources (not just from the junior creditor), e.g. third party guarantees or security?

3. **Permitted payments on junior debt**

    - scheduled interest and principal? – exclude voluntary and compulsory prepayments and accelerations (default acceleration, illegality clause, substitute basis clause, poison pills, change of control, etc.)
    - fees, costs, commissions, tax grossing-up, increased costs, breakage costs, indemnities, stamp duties, salaries and fringe benefits, supplier debt, rent?
    - suspension of permitted junior payments if senior debt unpaid;

senior pending event of default; actual event of default or acceleration (limited freeze period in mezzanine finance); junior pending event of default; actual event of default or acceleration (cross-default this in senior loan); solvency ratio not met?

4. **Common debtor's undertakings**

    – non-payment of junior debt except permitted payments. Cover purchase of debt by debtor and its subsidiaries, indirect payment by compensation deals, payments by affiliates, and distributions in kind
    – no set-off against junior debt unless permitted payment
    – no security for junior debt?
    – no amendment of junior debt
    – no corporate mergers
    – no impairment of subordination
    – (in junior bond issues) all other subordinated debt to be equally subordinated (to avoid complex stacking and investor confusion)
    – representations and warranties

5. **Junior creditor's undertakings**

    – no receipt of junior debt except permitted payments
    – no set-off discharging junior debt unless permitted payment
    – pay senior creditor amounts equal to set-offs received
    – no security or guarantees for junior debt?
    – refer to subordination on junior negotiable instruments
    – no conversion of junior debt into equity? Conversion is often permitted since in practice the junior creditor is likely to convert only if the debtor's business prospers. The conversion option may reduce the interest rate on the junior debt and hence the financial load on the debtor. Whether equity can be repaid (and hence defeat a tighter debt subordination) is a matter for local corporate law.
    – no transfer of or security over junior debt unless transferee agrees to be bound
    – no subordination of junior debt to another creditor (priorities and dilution of turnover)
    – turn over to senior creditor non-permitted recoveries on junior debt and all recoveries on insolvency of common debtor
    – conversion of turnovers received in kind or in foreign currency
    – pay senior creditor amounts equal to recoveries if turnover or trust obligation is invalid, e.g. because not registered as a charge
    – no acceleration of junior debt – unless senior debt also accelerated or debtor's insolvency instituted
    – no enforcement of junior debt by execution

- no initiation of insolvency proceedings against common debtor (limited freeze period?)
- prove for junior debt in timely manner on insolvency of common debtor
- vote junior debt as directed by senior creditor
- notify senior creditor of details of junior debt and of junior events of default
- no variation of junior debt? – especially definition of junior debt, subordination, amount, time and currency of payments, covenants, events of default and acceleration rights
- no waiver or release of junior debt (to preserve turnover)
- ability of senior creditor to override covenants and events of default in junior credit agreement. Any entrenched junior covenants (information, dividends, financial ratios, negative pledge, disposals)? Tolerances and thresholds? Should junior creditor be allowed covenants?
- representations and warranties

In insider subordinations where the senior creditor is relying on the turnover of distributions on the junior debt, there might be warranties by the junior creditor in favour of the senior creditor that the amount of the junior debt is as disclosed; the junior creditor is the sole owner of the junior debt; the junior debt is unsecured except as disclosed and any security for the junior debt is valid and enjoys the contemplated priority; the junior debt has not been subordinated in favour of any other creditor; the junior debt is not subject to any set-off or defence by the debtor.

6. **Protective clauses**

Many of these would not be necessary in a "contingent debt" subordination to all other creditors:

- subrogation to senior debt by junior creditor but only after senior debt is paid in full
- suspense account for turnover proceeds
- waiver of defences, e.g. waivers or compositions affecting senior debt; variations of senior debt; releases or non-perfection of security or guarantees for senior debt
- exclusion of contribution between junior creditors
- termination of subordination as regards future debt owing to junior creditor
- no exhaustion of recourse by senior creditor
- turnover to cover non-provable senior debt, e.g. post-insolvency interest?

     – free appropriation of payments by senior creditor?

7. **General**

     – breakage costs if turnover received by senior creditor during a funding period
     – limited cross-acceleration clause in junior credit agreement?
     – events of default in senior credit agreement – non-compliance or breach of warranty under subordination agreement; inefficacy of subordination; default under junior debt instrument; acceleration of junior debt?
     – assignments by senior creditor; novations by senior creditor. There must be mechanism whereby the contracts of the common debtor and junior creditor are extended to the incoming senior creditors. Trustee necessary if the senior debt is secured; deeds of accession for new debtors, junior creditors and senior creditors; expenses, powers of attorney (for voting, recovery of proceeds etc.); stamp duty indemnity; currency indemnity; default interest; waivers; remedies cumulative; severability; counterparts; notices; governing law and jurisdiction.
     – perpetuity period

8. **Secured debt**

     – subordinate the junior debt as well as the junior security
     – is variation of mandatory statutory priorities possible? Consider order of registration, notification to debtors, notification to insurers
     – trustee to hold security for senior and junior creditors?
     – can senior creditor add new money to senior security?
     – restrictions on enforcement rights of junior creditor, e.g. sale, foreclosure, possession, receiver – unless senior creditor has enforced
     – order of application of realisation proceeds
     – junior creditor to co-operate in private sale
     – senior creditor's responsibilities to junior creditor? e.g. protection of senior security, no releases, deposit of title deeds, maximisation of enforcement proceeds?
     – application of insurance proceeds and exclusion of junior creditor's right to insist on reinstatement
     – senior creditor's right to consolidate securities

7. Specific credit turnover subordination agreement for unsecured creditors

Note on the form

The senior and junior creditors are unsecured.

The junior creditor subordinates debts owed to it under a specific credit agreement to those owed to the senior creditor under a specific credit agreement.

This document is in shorter form; for more detailed provisions, see the next form.

THIS SUBORDINATION AGREEMENT is dated [   ] and made

BETWEEN:

1. [BORROWER] (the "Borrower");

2. [SENIOR CREDITOR] (the "Senior Creditor" which term includes its successors and assigns);

3. [JUNIOR CREDITOR] (the "Junior Creditor" which term includes its successors and assigns).

1. Definitions

In this Agreement:

"**Junior Debt**" means all present and future liabilities of the Borrower to the Junior Creditor under or in connection with or on rescission of the Junior Credit Agreement.

"**Junior Credit Agreement**" means the Credit Agreement dated [   ] between the Borrower and the Junior Creditor and all variations thereof.

"**Permitted Payments**" means payments and receipts (directly or by set-off) of scheduled interest, commissions and costs payable under the Junior Credit Agreement but only so long as no Senior Debt is due and unpaid and no event of default (or event which with giving of notice, lapse of time or other condition might be an event of default) has occurred and is continuing under the Senior Credit Agreement.

"**Senior Debt**" means all present and future liabilities of the Borrower to the Senior Creditor under or in connection with, or on rescission of, the Senior Credit Agreement.

"Senior Credit Agreement" means the Credit Agreement dated [ ] between the Borrower and the Senior Creditor and all variations thereof.

2. Borrower's undertakings

So long as any Senior Debt is or may become outstanding, the Borrower will not (except as the Senior Creditor has previously consented in writing):

(a) (subject to Clause 5) pay or repay, or make any distribution in respect of, or purchase or acquire, any of the Junior Debt in cash or in property or securities except for Permitted Payments;

(b) permit any of its subsidiaries to purchase or acquire any of the Junior Debt;

(c) discharge any of the Junior Debt by set-off except for a Permitted Payment;

(d) create or permit or subsist security over any of its assets for any of the Junior Debt;

(e) vary the Junior Credit Agreement;

(f) take or omit any action whereby the subordination achieved by this Agreement may be impaired.

3. Junior Creditor's undertakings

So long as any Senior Debt is or may become outstanding, except as the Senior Creditor has previously consented in writing, the Junior Creditor will:

(a) (subject to Clause 5) not demand or receive payment of, or any distribution in respect or on account of, any of the Junior Debt from the Borrower or any other source or apply any money or assets in discharge of any Junior Debt, except for Permitted Payments;

(b) not discharge the Junior Debt by set-off except for Permitted Payments;

(c) not permit to subsist or receive any security for any of the Junior Debt;

(d) not permit to subsist or receive any guarantee or other assurance against loss in respect of any of the Junior Debt;

(e) promptly notify the Senior Creditor of any default or event of default in respect of the Junior Debt;

(f) unless Clause 5 applies, not:

(i)   accelerate any of the Junior Debt;

(ii) enforce the Junior Debt by execution or otherwise

(iii) initiate or support or take any steps with a view to any insolvency, reorganisation or dissolution proceedings in respect of the Borrower; or

(iv) otherwise exercise any remedy for the recovery of the Junior Debt;

(g) not

(i)   assign or dispose of, or create or permit to subsist any security over, any of the Junior Debt or its proceeds or any interest in the Junior Debt or its proceeds to or in favour of any person, or

(ii) subordinate any of the Junior Debt or its proceeds to any sums owing by the Borrower to any person other than the Senior Creditor, or

(iii) transfer by novation or otherwise any of its rights or obligations under the Junior Credit Document or in respect of any Junior Debt to any person,

unless in each case that person agrees with the Senior Creditor that he is bound by all the terms of this Agreement as a Junior Creditor in a manner satisfactory to the Senior Creditor.

4. Turnover of non-permitted recoveries

4.1 Non-permitted payment If:

(a) the Junior Creditor receives a payment or distribution in respect of any of the Junior Debt (other than a Permitted Payment) from the Borrower or any other source,

(b) the Junior Creditor receives the proceeds of any enforcement of any security or any guarantee for any Junior Debt, or

(c) the Borrower or any of its subsidiaries makes any payment or distribution on account of the purchase or other acquisition of any of the Junior Debt,

the Junior Creditor will hold the same in trust for and pay and distribute it to the Senior Creditor for application towards the Senior Debt until the Senior Debt is irrevocably paid in full.

4.2 Non-permitted set-offs If any of the Junior Debt is discharged by set-off (except a Permitted Payment), the Junior Creditor will immediately pay an amount equal to the discharge to the Senior Creditor for application towards the Senior Debt until the Senior Debt is irrevocably paid in full.

4.3 Failure of trust If for any reason, a trust in favour of, or a holding of property for, the Senior Creditor under this Agreement is invalid or unenforceable, the Junior Creditor will pay and deliver to the Senior Creditor an amount equal to the payment, receipt or recovery in cash or in kind (or its value, if in kind) which the Junior Creditor would otherwise have been bound to hold on trust for or as property of the Senior Creditor.

5. Subordination on insolvency

If the Borrower becomes subject to any insolvency, bankruptcy, reorganisation, administration, assignment or arrangement with creditors, liquidation, dissolution or other similar proceeding or distribution of its assets, whether or not involving insolvency:

(a) the Senior Creditor may, and is irrevocably authorised on behalf of the Junior Creditor to, (i) claim, enforce and prove for the Junior Debt, (ii) file claims and proofs, give receipts and take all such proceedings and do all such things as the Senior Creditor sees fit to recover the Junior Debt and (iii) receive all distributions on the Junior Debt for application towards the Senior Debt;

(b) if and to the extent that the Senior Creditor is not entitled to do any of the foregoing, the Junior Creditor will do so in good time as directed by the Senior Creditor;

(c) the Junior Creditor will hold all distributions in cash or in kind received or receivable by the Junior Creditor in respect of the Junior Debt from the Borrower or its estate or from any other source in trust for the Senior Creditor and will (at the Junior Creditor's expense) pay and transfer the same to the Senior Creditor for application towards the Senior Debt until the Senior Debt is irrevocably paid in full;

(d) the trustee in bankruptcy, liquidator, assignee or other person distributing the assets of the Borrower or their proceeds is directed to pay distributions on the Junior Debt direct to the Senior Creditor until the Senior Debt is irrevocably paid in full. The Junior Creditor will give all such notices and do all such things as the Senior Creditor may direct to give effect to this provision.

6. Voting

So long as the Senior Debt is or may become outstanding:

(a) the Senior Creditor may (and is hereby irrevocably authorised to) exercise all powers of convening meetings, voting and representation in respect of the Junior Debt and the Junior Creditor will provide all forms of proxy and of representation needful to that end, and

(b) if and to the extent that the Senior Creditor is not entitled to exercise a power conferred by the above the Junior Creditor (i) will exercise the power as the Senior Creditor directs, and (ii) will not exercise it so as to impair this subordination.

7. Consents

7.1 New transactions The Junior Creditor will have no remedy against the Borrower or the Senior Creditor by reason of any transaction entered into between the Senior Creditor and the Borrower which violates the Junior Credit Agreement and the Junior Creditor may not object to any such transaction by reason of any provisions of the Junior Credit Agreement.

7.2 Waivers Any waiver or consent granted by the Senior Creditor will also be deemed to have been given by the Junior Creditor if any transaction or circumstances would, in the absence of such waiver or consent by the Junior Creditor, violate the Junior Credit Agreement.

8. Subrogation by Junior Creditor

If the Senior Debt is wholly or partially paid out of any proceeds received in respect of or on account of the Junior Debt, the Junior Creditor will to that extent be subrogated to the Senior Debt so paid (and all securities and guarantees for that Senior Debt) but not before all the Senior Debt is paid in full.

9. Protection of subordination

9.1 Continuing subordination The subordination provisions in this Agreement constitute a continuing subordination and benefit the ultimate balance of the Senior Debt.

9.2 Waiver of defences The subordination in this Agreement and the obligations of the Junior Agent will not be affected by any act, omission, matter or thing which, but for this provision, would reduce, release or prejudice the subordination or any of those obligations in whole or in part, including without limitation:

(a) any waiver granted to, or composition with, the Borrower or other person;

(b) the taking, variation, compromise, exchange, renewal or release of, or refusal or neglect to perfect, take up or enforce, any rights against, or security over assets of, the Borrower or other person in respect of the Senior Debt or otherwise or any failure to realise the full value of any security;

(c) any unenforceability, illegality or invalidity of any obligation of the Borrower or security in respect of the Senior Debt or any other document or security.

9.3   Immediate recourse The Junior Creditor waives any right it may have of first requiring the Senior Creditor (or any trustee or agent on its behalf) to proceed against or enforce any other rights or security or claim payment from any person before claiming the benefit of this Agreement. The Senior Creditor (or any trustee or agent on its behalf) may refrain from applying or enforcing any money, rights or security.

9.4   Appropriations Until the Senior Debt has been irrevocably paid in full, the Senior Creditor (or any trustee or agent on its behalf) may:

(a) apply any moneys or property received under this Agreement or from the Borrower or from any other person against the Senior Debt in such order as it sees fit;

(b) (if it so decides) apply any moneys or property received from the Borrower or from any other person (other than money or property received for the Junior Creditor under this Agreement) against any liability other than the Senior Debt owed to it;

(c) hold in suspense any moneys or distributions received from the Junior Creditor under Clauses 4 and 5 or on account of the liability of the Junior Creditor under this Agreement.

9.5   Non-competition Until the Senior Debt has been irrevocably paid in full, the Junior Creditor will not by virtue of any payment or performance by it under this Agreement or by virtue of the operation of Clauses 4 or 5:

(a) be subrogated to any rights, security or moneys held, received or receivable by the Senior Creditor (or any trustee or agent on its behalf) or be entitled to any right of contribution or indemnity;

(b) claim, rank, prove or vote as a creditor of the Borrower or other person in competition with the Senior Creditor (or any trustee or agent on its behalf); or

(c) receive, claim or have the benefit of any payment, distribution or security from or on account of the Borrower or other person.

10. Preservation of junior debt

The Junior Debt shall, solely as between the Borrower and the Junior Creditor, remain owing or due and payable in accordance with the terms of the Junior Credit Agreement, and interest and default interest will accrue on missed payments accordingly.

11. Miscellaneous

11.1 Perpetuity The perpetuity period for the trusts in this Agreement is 80 years.

11.2 Power of attorney By way of security for the obligations of the Junior Creditor under this Agreement, the Junior Creditor irrevocably appoints the Senior Creditor as its attorney to do anything which the Junior Creditor (a) has authorised the Senior Creditor to do under this Agreement and (b) is required to do by this Agreement but has failed to do. The Senior Creditor may delegate this power.

11.3 Expenses The Borrower will forthwith on demand pay the Senior Creditor the amount of all costs, expenses and stamp duties incurred by it in connection with this Agreement and its enforcement.

11.4 Notices All notices under, or in connection with, this Agreement shall be given in writing or by telex or fax to the following addresses (or such other addresses as may be notified from time to time):

[Addresses]

11.5 Jurisdiction For the benefit of the Senior Creditor, each of the Borrower and the Junior Creditor agrees that the courts of England are to have jurisdiction to settle any disputes in connection with this Agreement and appoints [   ] as its agent for service of process relating to any proceedings before the English courts in connection with this Agreement. Nothing in this Clause limits the right of the Senior Creditor to bring proceedings against another party hereto in connection with this Agreement in any other court of competent jurisdiction.

11.6 Governing law This Agreement is governed by English law.

This Agreement has been entered into on the date stated at the head of this Agreement.

[BORROWER]

By: . . . .

[SENIOR CREDITOR]

By: . . . .

[JUNIOR CREDITOR]

By: . . . .

8. All moneys turnover subordination agreement for secured creditors

Note on the form

The senior and junior creditors are secured on the same assets of the borrower but under separate security documents. Alternatively the security could be granted to a trustee for both creditors. In the latter case, the borrower should also covenant with the trustee to pay the junior and senior debt, i.e. grant to the trustee a covenant parallel to the covenants given by the borrower to the creditors directly in order to support the security granted to the trustee.

The covenant would state:

> "The Borrower agrees with the Trustee to pay the Senior Debt and the Junior Debt to the Trustee when due under the terms of the Senior Finance Documents and the Junior Finance Documents to such bank account as the Trustee may direct, except that until an Event of Default occurs under the Senior Finance Documents and the Senior Creditor notifies the Trustee, the Borrower and the Junior Creditor thereof in writing, the Borrower may (subject to the terms of this Intercreditor Agreement) pay the Senior Debt and the Junior Debt directly to the Senior Creditor and the Junior Creditor respectively and each such payment will be a pro tanto discharge of the above agreement to pay in favour of the Trustee."

The trust deed should contain:

— usual clauses protecting the trustee from liability

— usual powers in favour of the trustee

— provisions requiring the trustee to enforce the security as directed by the senior creditor.

The form covers all moneys, i.e. the junior creditor subordinates all present and future liabilities owed to him by the borrower to all present and future liabilities owed by the borrower to the senior creditor.

THIS INTERCREDITOR AGREEMENT is dated [ ] and made BETWEEN:

1. [BORROWER] (the "Borrower");

2. [SENIOR CREDITOR] (the "Senior Creditor");

3. [JUNIOR CREDITOR] (the "Junior Creditor").

1. Definitions

1.1 Terms defined In this Agreement:

"Event of Default" means any event of default or other event entitling the creditor concerned to accelerate the due date of any liability.

"Junior Debt" means all present and future liabilities of the Borrower to the Junior Creditor, absolute, contingent or otherwise, whether or not matured, whether or not liquidated, and whether or not owed solely or jointly by the Borrower or to the Junior Creditor solely or jointly, including without limitation (a) liabilities which the Junior Creditor acquires by purchase, security assignment or otherwise, (b) interest, (c) damages, (d) claims for restitution and (e) costs.

"Junior Finance Documents" means the Junior Security Documents and all other present and future documents and agreements relating to the Junior Debt.

"Junior Security Documents" means:
- (a) the security documents specified in Schedule 1 to this Agreement,
- (b) any existing and future guarantees or the like of, and any document conferring or evidencing security for, any of the Junior Debt, and
- (c) any variations, replacements and novations of, and supplements to the foregoing but without prejudice to any restrictions on the same.

"Pending Event of Default" means any event which with giving notice, lapse of time, determination of materiality or fulfilment of any other condition (or any combination of the foregoing) would be an Event of Default.

"Permitted Payments" means the payments and receipts permitted by Clause 4 so long as they are so permitted.

"Senior Debt" means all present and future liabilities of the Borrower to the Senior Creditor, absolute, contingent or otherwise, whether or not matured, whether or not liquidated, and whether or not owed solely or jointly by the Borrower or to the Senior Creditor solely or jointly, including without limitation (a) liabilities which the Senior Creditor acquires by purchase, security assignment or otherwise, (b) interest, (c) damages, (d) claims for restitution and (e) costs.

"Senior Finance Documents" means the Senior Security Documents and all present and future documents and agreements relating to the Senior Debt.

"Senior Security Documents" means:

(a) the security documents specified in Schedule 2 to this Agreement,

(b) any existing or future guarantees or the like of, and any existing or future document conferring or evidencing security for, any of the Senior Debt, and

(c) any variations, replacements, and novations of and supplements to the foregoing.

"Subsidiary" means an entity from time to time:

(a) of which another entity has direct or indirect control or another entity owns directly or indirectly more than 50 per cent of the share capital; or

(b) which is a subsidiary of another under the laws of the jurisdiction of its incorporation.

1.2   Assigns Without prejudice to any restrictions on assignments or other dispositions, references to the Borrower, the Senior Creditor and the Junior Creditor include their respective successors and assigns.

1.3   Headings Headings are to be ignored in construing this Agreement.

2.   Borrower's undertakings

So long as any Senior Debt is or may become outstanding, the Borrower will not (except as the Senior Creditor has previously consented in writing):

(a) (subject to Clause 6) pay or repay, or make any distribution in respect of, or purchase or acquire, any of the Junior Debt in cash or in kind except for Permitted Payments;

(b) permit any of its Subsidiaries to purchase or acquire any of the Junior Debt;

(c) set off against the Junior Debt except for Permitted Payments;

(d) create or permit to subsist security over any of its assets for any of the Junior Debt except for security under the existing Junior Security Documents;

(e) merge or consolidate into or with any other company;

(f) take or omit any action whereby the subordination achieved by this Agreement may be impaired.

3. Junior Creditor's undertakings

So long as any Senior Debt is or may become outstanding, except as the Senior Creditor has previously consented in writing, the Junior Creditor will not:

(a) (subject to Clause 6) demand or receive payment of, or any distribution in respect or on account of, any of the Junior Debt in cash or kind from the Borrower or any other source or apply any money or assets in discharge of any Junior Debt, except in each case for Permitted Payments and except for the proceeds of security received and applied in the order permitted by Clause 10;

(b) set off any of the Junior Debt except for Permitted Payments;

(c) permit to subsist or receive any security for any of the Junior Debt except for security under the existing Junior Security Documents;

(d) permit to subsist or receive any guarantee or other assurance against loss in respect of any of the Junior Debt except for guarantees and security under the existing Junior Security Documents;

(e) permit the Junior Debt to be evidenced by a negotiable instrument unless the instrument is legended with this subordination or is deposited with the Senior Creditor;

[(f) convert any of the Junior Debt into shares of the Borrower.]

4. Permitted payments

4.1   Subject to Clause 6, so long as no Senior Debt is overdue and unpaid and no Event of Default or Pending Event of Default has occurred under any Senior Finance Document, the Borrower may pay and the Junior Creditor may receive and retain payment of, the following:

(a) scheduled payments of interest on the Junior Debt under the Junior Credit Agreement not earlier than the date the same are scheduled to be due in accordance with the original terms of the documents evidencing the same and not exceeding interest at a commercial rate of return;

(b) [Specify other permitted payments].

4.2   A payment or receipt includes a payment or receipt by set-off.

5. Turnover of non-permitted recoveries

5.1   Non-permitted payment If:

(a) the Junior Creditor receives a payment or distribution in cash or kind in respect of or on account of any of the Junior Debt from the Borrower or any other source except for a Permitted Payment;

(b) the Junior Creditor receives the proceeds of any enforcement of any security conferred by the Junior Security Documents otherwise than in the order set out in Clause 10 or payment under any guarantee for any Junior Debt; or

(c) the Borrower or any of its Subsidiaries makes any payment or distribution, in cash or kind on account of the purchase or other acquisition of any of the Junior Debt;

the Junior Creditor will hold the same in trust for and pay and distribute it to the Senior Creditor for application towards the Senior Debt until the Senior Debt is irrevocably paid in full.

5.2   Non-permitted set-offs If any of the Junior Debt is discharged by set-off (except for a Permitted Payment), the Junior Creditor will immediately pay an amount equal to the discharge to the Senior Creditor for application towards the Senior Debt until the Senior Debt is irrevocably paid in full.

6.   Subordination on insolvency

If:

(i)   any resolution is passed or order made for the winding-up, liquidation, dissolution, administration or reorganisation of the Borrower; or

(ii) the Borrower becomes subject to any insolvency, bankruptcy, reorganisation, receivership, liquidation, dissolution or other similar proceeding, voluntary or involuntary and whether or not involving insolvency; or

(iii) the Borrower assigns its assets for the benefit of its creditors or enters into any arrangement with its creditors generally; or

(iv) the Borrower becomes subject to any distribution of its assets; or

(v)   any analogous event occurs anywhere,

then:

(a)   the Senior Creditor may, and is irrevocably authorised on behalf of the Junior Creditor to, (i) claim, enforce and prove for the Junior Debt, (ii) file claims and proofs, give receipts and take all such proceedings and do all such things as the Senior Creditor sees fit to recover the Junior Debt, and (iii) receive all distributions on the Junior Debt for application towards the Senior Debt;

(b) if and to the extent that the Senior Creditor is not entitled to do any of the things mentioned in (b) the Junior Creditor will do so in good time as directed by the Senior Creditor;

(c) the Junior Creditor will hold all distributions in cash or in kind received or receivable by the Junior Creditor in respect of the Junior Debt from the Borrower or its estate or any other source in trust for the Senior Creditor and will pay and transfer the same to the Senior Creditor for application towards the Senior Debt until the Senior Debt is irrevocably paid in full;

(d) the trustee in bankruptcy, liquidator, assignee or other person distributing the assets of the Borrower or their proceeds is directed to pay distributions on the Junior Debt direct to the Senior Creditor until the Senior Debt is irrevocably paid in full. The Junior Creditor will give all such notices and do all such things as the Senior Creditor may direct to give effect to this provision.

7. Treatment of distributions

7.1 Realisation If the Senior Creditor receives any distribution otherwise than in cash in respect of the Junior Debt from the Borrower or any other source, the Senior Creditor may realise the distribution as it sees fit and the Senior Debt shall not be deemed reduced by the distribution until and except to the extent that the realisation proceeds are applied towards the Senior Debt.

7.2 Transfer of distributions The Junior Creditor will at its own expense do all such things as the Senior Creditor may require as being necessary or desirable to transfer to the Senior Creditor all payments and distributions which must be turned over or held in trust for the Senior Creditor, including endorsements and execution of formal transfers, and will pay all costs and stamp duties in connection therewith.

7.3 Currencies If the Senior Creditor receives any payment required to be paid by the Junior Creditor under this Agreement or paid in respect of the Junior Debt in a currency other than the currency of the Senior Debt, the Senior Creditor may convert the currency received into the currency of the Senior Debt at a prevailing market rate of exchange and the Senior Debt shall not be deemed reduced by the payment until and except to the extent that the proceeds of conversion are applied towards the Senior Debt.

7.4 Failure of trust If for any reason, a trust in favour of, or a holding of property for, the Senior Creditor under this Agreement is invalid or unenforceable, the Junior Creditor will pay and deliver to the Senior Creditor an amount equal to the payment, receipt or recovery in cash or in kind (or its value, if in kind) which it would otherwise have been bound to hold on trust for or as property of the Senior Creditor.

8.   Priority of security

8.1   Ranking Existing and future security conferred by the Senior Security Documents will:

(a) rank in all respects prior to existing and future security conferred by the Junior Security Documents, regardless of order of registration, notice, execution or otherwise;

(b) secure all the Senior Debt in priority to the Junior Debt, regardless of the date upon which the Senior Debt arises, regardless of whether or not the Senior Creditor is obliged to advance moneys included in Senior Debt, and regardless of any intermediate discharge of the Senior Debt in whole or in part.

8.2   Registration and notice The Junior Creditor will co-operate with the Senior Creditor with a view to reflecting the priority of the security conferred by the Senior Security Documents in any register or with any filing or registration authority and in giving notice to insurers, debtors liable for receivables covered by the security conferred by the Senior Security Documents and other persons.

8.3   Custody of documents So long as the Senior Security Documents are in force, the Senior Creditor will be entitled to the deposit of any title deeds, share certificates or other title documents, certificates or paper in respect of any assets subject to the security conferred by the Senior Security Documents in priority to the entitlement of the Junior Creditor. The Senior Creditor has no responsibility to the Junior Creditor to require or maintain such deposit.

8.4   Consolidation The Senior Creditor may consolidate security against the Junior Creditor.

9.   Enforcement of security

9.1   Restrictions on enforcement by Junior Creditor So long as any of the Senior Debt is or may become outstanding, unless Clause 6 applies or unless the Senior Creditor has previously consented in writing, the Junior Creditor will not:

(a) accelerate any of the Junior Debt or otherwise declare any of the Junior Debt prematurely payable on an Event of Default or otherwise;

(b) enforce the Junior Debt by execution or otherwise;

(c) enforce any security conferred by the Junior Security Documents or any other security for the Junior Debt by sale, possession, appointment of a receiver or otherwise;

(d) initiate or support or take any steps with a view to any insolvency, liquidation, reorganisation, administration or dissolution proceedings or any voluntary arrangement or assignment for the benefit of creditors or any similar proceedings involving the Borrower, whether by petition, convening a meeting, voting for a resolution or otherwise; or

(e) otherwise exercise any remedy for the recovery of any of the Junior Debt.

9.2   Enforcement by Senior Creditor If the Senior Creditor enforces any security conferred by the Senior Security Documents:

(a) the Junior Creditor will not be entitled to take or have possession of any such assets or maintain a receiver in possession in respect of such assets;

(b) the Senior Creditor will have the entire conduct of any sale of assets covered by any security created by a Senior Security Document;

(c) if pursuant to an enforcement the Senior Creditor sells any asset over which any Junior Creditor (or any trustee or agent on its behalf) has security for the Junior Debt, or if the Borrower sells such asset at the request of the Senior Creditor after an Event of Default under the Senior Credit Agreement, the Junior Creditor will on such sale release its security over that asset if [the sale is at a fair value and if] the proceeds are to be applied towards the Senior Debt.

9.3   No foreclosure The Junior Creditor shall not be entitled to the remedy of foreclosure in respect of any assets subject to the Junior Security Documents.

9.4   Waiver of marshalling The Junior Creditor waives any existing or future right it may have to marshalling in respect of any security held by a Senior Creditor or by a trustee or agent on its behalf.

9.5   No right to require reinstatement The Junior Creditor waives any right it may have of requiring that insurance proceeds by applied in reinstatement of any asset subject to security under the Senior Security Documents.

9.6 No enforcement The Senior Creditor may refrain from enforcing the security conferred by the Senior Security Documents as long as it sees fit.

9.7 Manner of enforcement If the Senior Creditor does enforce the security conferred by the Senior Security Documents, it may do so in such manner as it sees fit, shall not be responsible to the Junior Creditor for any failure to enforce or to maximise the proceeds of any enforcement, and may cease any such enforcement.

10. Proceeds of enforcement of security

Subject to the rights of any prior or preferential encumbrancers or creditors, the net proceeds of enforcement of the security conferred by the Senior Security Documents and the Junior Security Documents shall be paid to the Senior Creditor and applied in the following order:

First in payment of all costs and expenses incurred by or on behalf of the Senior Creditor in connection with such enforcement.

Second in payment to the Senior Creditor for application towards the balance of the Senior Debt in such order as the Senior Creditor may decide.

Third in payment to the Junior Creditor for application towards the Junior Debt in such order as the Junior Creditor may decide.

Fourth in payment of the surplus (if any) to the Borrower or other person entitled thereto.

11. Voting

So long as the Senior Debt is or may become outstanding:

(a) the Senior Creditor may (and is hereby irrevocably authorised to) exercise all powers of convening meetings, voting and representation in respect of the Junior Debt and the Junior Creditor will provide all forms of proxy and of representation needful to that end;

(b) if and to the extent that the Senior Creditor is not entitled to exercise a power conferred by the above the Junior Creditor (i) will exercise the power as the Senior Creditor directs, and (ii) will not exercise it so as to impair this subordination.

12. Consents

12.1 New transactions The Junior Creditor will have no remedy against the Borrower or the Senior Creditor by reason of any transaction entered into between the Senior Creditor and the Borrower which violates or is an Event of Default or Pending Event of Default under any Junior Finance Document and the Junior Creditor may not object to any such transaction by reason of any provisions of the Junior Finance Documents.

12.2 Waivers Any waiver or consent granted by the Senior Creditor will also be deemed to have been given by the Junior Creditor if any transaction or circumstances would, in the absence of such waiver or consent by the Junior Creditor, violate any Junior Finance Document or constitute an Event of Default or Pending Event of Default under any Junior Finance Document.

13. Representations and warranties of the Borrower

The Borrower represents and warrants to the Senior Creditor:

(a) **Status** The Borrower is a limited liability company, duly incorporated and validly existing under the laws of [   ].

(b) **Powers and authority** The Borrower has the power to enter into and perform, and has taken all necessary action to authorise the entry into, performance and delivery of, the existing Junior Finance Documents and this Agreement and the transactions contemplated by those Junior Finance Documents and this Agreement.

(c) **Legal validity** The existing Junior Finance Documents and this Agreement constitute its legal, valid and binding obligations enforceable in accordance with their terms.

(d) **Non-conflict** The entry into and performance by the Borrower of, and the transactions contemplated by, the Junior Finance Documents and this Agreement do not and will not:

  (i) conflict with any law or regulation; or

  (ii) conflict with the constitutional documents of the Borrower or of any of its Subsidiaries; or

(iii)   conflict with any document which is binding on the Borrower or on any of its Subsidiaries or any asset of the Borrower or of any of its Subsidiaries.

(e) **Authorisation** All authorisations, consents, registrations, filings, notarisations and the like required or desirable in connection with the entry into and performance by it, the validity and enforceability of, and of the transactions contemplated by, the Junior Finance Documents and this Agreement have been obtained or effected (as appropriate) and are in full force and effect.

(f) **Security** The Junior Security Documents confer the security expressed to be conferred thereby which is valid and enforceable on the insolvency of the Borrower and which is not subject to any prior or pari passu security other than that conferred by the Senior Security Documents.

14.   Representations and warranties of Junior Creditor

The Junior Creditor represents and warrants to the Senior Creditor:

(a) **Legal validity** This Agreement is within its powers, has been duly authorised by it, constitutes its legal, valid and binding obligations enforceable in accordance with their terms and does not conflict with any law or regulation or its constitutional documents or any document binding on it and that it has obtained all necessary consents for the performance by it of this Agreement.

(b) **Disclosure** There has been provided to the Senior Creditor true and complete copies of the existing Junior Finance Documents containing all terms relating to the Junior Debt.

(c) **Ownership** The Junior Creditor is the sole beneficial owner of the Junior Debt and of the benefit of the Junior Finance Documents free of encumbrances, options and subordinations in favour of any person other than the Senior Creditor.

[(d) **Set-off** The Junior Debt is not subject to any set-off, counterclaim or other defence.]

15.   Repetition of representations and warranties

The representations and warranties in Clauses 14 and 15 are deemed to be repeated by each of the Borrower and the Junior Creditor respectively on each date so long as any Senior Debt is outstanding with reference to the facts and circumstances then existing.

16. Information by Junior Creditor

16.1 Defaults The Junior Creditor will promptly notify the Senior Creditor of the occurrence of any Event of Default or Pending Event of Default under any Junior Finance Document.

16.2 Amount of Junior Debt The Junior Creditor will on written request by the Senior Creditor from time to time notify the Senior Creditor in writing of details of the amount of the Junior Debt and give the Senior Creditor copies of all Junior Finance Documents as soon as entered into.

17. Subrogation by Junior Creditor

If any of the Senior Debt is wholly or partially paid out of any proceeds received in respect of or on account of the Junior Debt, the Junior Creditor will to that extent be subrogated to the Senior Debt so paid (and all securities and guarantees for that Senior Debt) but not before all the Senior Debt is paid in full.

18. Protection of subordination

18.1 Continuing subordination The subordination provisions in this Agreement constitute a continuing subordination and benefit the ultimate balance of the Senior Debt regardless of any intermediate payment or discharge of the Senior Debt in whole or in part.

18.2 Waiver of defences The subordination in this Agreement and the obligations of the Junior Creditor under this Agreement will not be affected by any act, omission, matter or thing which, but for this provision, would reduce, release or prejudice the subordination or any of those obligations in whole or in part, including without limitation:

(a) any time or waiver granted to, or composition with, the Borrower or other person;

(b) the taking, variation, compromise, exchange, renewal or release of, or refusal or neglect to perfect, take up or enforce, any rights against, or security over assets of, the Borrower or other person under the Senior Finance Documents, in respect of the Senior Debt or otherwise or any non-presentment or non-observance of any formality or other requirement in respect of any instruments or any failure to realise the full value of any security;

(c) any unenforceability, illegality or invalidity of any obligation of the Borrower or security under the Senior Finance Documents, in respect of the Senior Debt or any other document or security.

18.3   Immediate recourse The Junior Creditor waives any right it may have of first requiring the Senior Creditor (or any trustee or agent on its behalf) to proceed against or enforce any other rights or security or claim payment from any person before claiming the benefit of this Agreement. The Senior Creditor (or any trustee or agent on its behalf) may refrain from applying or enforcing any money, rights or security.

18.4   Appropriations Until the Senior Debt has been irrevocably paid in full, the Senior Creditor (or any trustee or agent on its behalf) may:

(a) apply any moneys or property received under this Agreement or from the Borrower or from any other person against the Senior Debt in such order as it sees fit;

(b) (if it so decides) apply any moneys or property received from the Borrower or from any other person (other than money or property received from the Junior Creditor under this Agreement) against any liability other than the Senior Debt owed to it;

[**Note:** The above para (b) will be relevant only if the Senior Debt does not include all debt owed by the Borrower to the Senior Creditor.]

(c) hold in suspense any moneys or distributions received from the Junior Creditor under Clauses 5, 6, 7 and 10 or on account of the liability of the Junior Creditor under this Agreement.

18.5   Non-competition Until the Senior Debt has been irrevocably paid in full, the Junior Creditor will not by virtue of any payment or performance by it under this Agreement or by virtue of the operation of Clauses 5, 6, 7 or 10

(a) be subrogated to any rights, security or moneys held, received or receivable by the Senior Creditor (or any trustee or agent on its behalf) or be entitled to any right of contribution or indemnity;

(b) claim, rank, prove or vote as a creditor of the Borrower or any other person or their respective estates in competition with the Senior Creditor (or any trustee or agent on its behalf); or

(c) receive, claim or have the benefit of any payment, distribution or security from or on account of the Borrower or other person.

19. Preservation of junior debt

Notwithstanding any term of this Agreement postponing, subordinating or preventing the payment of any of the Junior Debt, the Junior Debt concerned shall, solely as between the Borrower and the Junior Creditor, remain owing or due and payable in accordance with the terms of the Junior Finance Documents, and interest and default interest will accrue on missed payments accordingly.

20. Termination of subordination

By not less than 30 days prior written notice to the Senior Creditor, the Junior Creditor may terminate this subordination agreement. However the termination will not apply to Junior Debt which is incurred prior to such expiry or which arises as a result of any transaction or under or in connection with any agreement entered into prior to such expiry.

21. Responsibility of Senior Creditor

The Senior Creditor will not be liable to the Junior Creditor

(a) for the manner of exercise or for any non-exercise of its powers under this Agreement; or

(b) for failure to collect or preserve the Junior Debt, any security or guarantees for the Junior Debt, or any assets subject to any security for the Junior Debt.

22. Expenses

22.1 Initial costs The Borrower will forthwith on demand pay the Senior Creditor the amount of all costs and expenses incurred by it in connection with the negotiation, preparation, execution and performance of this Agreement and all waivers in relation to and variations of this Agreement.

22.2 Enforcement costs Each of the Borrower and the Junior Creditor shall, forthwith on demand, pay to the Senior Creditor the amount of all costs and expenses incurred by it in connection with the enforcement against the Borrower or Junior Creditor (as the case may be) of the Senior Creditor's rights against it under this Agreement.

22.3 Legal expenses and taxes The costs and expenses referred to above include, without limitation, the fees and expenses of legal advisers and any value added tax or similar tax, and are payable in the currency in which they are incurred.

23.   Changes to the parties

23.1   Successors and assigns This Agreement is binding on the successors and assigns of the parties hereto.

23.2   Borrower The Borrower may not assign or transfer any of its rights or obligations under this Agreement.

23.3   Junior Creditor So long as any Senior Debt is or may become outstanding, the Junior Creditor will not:

(a) assign or dispose of, or create or permit to subsist any security (fixed or floating) over, any of the Junior Debt or its proceeds or any interest in the Junior Debt or its proceeds, or any security therefor, to or in favour of any person; or

(b) subordinate any of the Junior Debt or its proceeds to any sums owing by the Borrower to any person other than the Senior Creditor;

(c) transfer by novation or otherwise any of its rights or obligations under any Junior Finance Document or in respect of any Junior Debt to any person;

unless in each case that person agrees with the Senior Creditor that he is bound by all the terms of this Agreement as a Junior Creditor in a manner satisfactory to the Senior Creditor.

23.4   Senior Creditor The Senior Creditor may assign or otherwise dispose of all or any of its rights under this Agreement.

23.5   Memorandum on documents The Junior Creditor will endorse a memorandum of this Agreement on the Junior Finance Documents.

24.   General

24.1   Perpetuity period The perpetuity period for the trusts in this Agreement is 80 years.

24.2   Power of attorney By way of security for the obligations of the Junior Creditor under this Agreement, the Junior Creditor irrevocably appoints the

Senior Creditor as its attorney to do anything which the Junior Creditor (a) has authorised the Senior Creditor to do under this Agreement and (b) is required to do by this Agreement but has failed to do. The Senior Creditor may delegate this power.

24.3 Stamp duties The Borrower shall pay and forthwith on demand indemnify the Senior Creditor [and the Junior Creditor] against any liability it incurs in respect of any stamp, registration and similar tax which is or becomes payable in connection with the entry into, performance or enforcement of this Agreement.

24.4 Currency indemnity The Junior Creditor will indemnify the Senior Creditor against losses suffered by the Senior Creditor if any claim by the Senior Creditor (or any agent of trustee on its behalf) against the Junior Creditor under this Agreement is converted into a claim, proof, judgment or order in a currency other than the currency in which the amount is contractually payable under this Agreement.

24.5 Waivers, remedies cumulative The rights of the Senior Creditor under this Agreement:

(a) are cumulative and not exclusive of its rights under the general law; and

(b) may be waived only in writing and specifically.

Delay in exercising or non-exercise of any such right is not a waiver of that right.

24.6 Set-off The Senior Creditor may set off any matured obligation owed by the Junior Creditor under this Agreement (to the extent beneficially owned by the Senior Creditor) against any obligation (whether or not matured) owed by the Senior Creditor to the Junior Creditor, regardless of the place of payment, booking branch or currency of either obligation. If the obligations are in different currencies, the Senior Creditor may convert either obligation at a market rate of exchange in its usual course of business for the purpose of the set-off.

24.7 Default interest If the Junior Creditor fails to pay any amount payable by it under this Agreement to the Senior Creditor, it shall, on demand by the Senior Creditor from time to time, pay interest on the overdue amount from the due date up to the date of actual payment, as well after as before judgment, at the rate of [   ] [calculated on a 360 day year basis for the precise number of days elapsed.]

24.8 Severability If a provision of this Agreement is or becomes illegal, invalid or unenforceable in any jurisdiction, that shall not affect:

(a) the validity or enforceability in that jurisdiction of any other provision of this Agreement; or

(b) the validity or enforceability in other jurisdictions of that or any other provision of this Agreement.

24.9   Counterparts This Agreement may be executed in any number of counterparts, and this has the same effect as if the signatures on the counterparts were on a single copy of this Agreement.

25.   Notices

25.1   Service of notices All notices under, or in connection with, this Agreement shall be given in writing or by telex or fax. If correctly addressed, any such notice is deemed to be given at the following times:

(a) if in writing, when delivered;

(b) if by telex, when correctly despatched; and

(c) if by fax, when received.

However, a notice given in accordance with the above but received on a non-working day or after business hours in the place of receipt is deemed to be given on the next working day in that place.

25.2   Addresses for notices The address, telex number and fax number of each party hereto for all notices under, or in connection with, this Agreement, are:

[   ]

A party may change the above by prior written notice to the other parties.

26.   Jurisdiction

26.1   Submission For the benefit of the Senior Creditor, each of the Borrower and the Junior Creditor agrees that the courts of England are to have jurisdiction to settle any disputes in connection with this Agreement, submits to the jurisdiction of the English courts in connection with this Agreement, appoints [   ] as its agent for service of process relating to any proceedings before the English courts in connection with this Agreement and agrees to maintain a process agent in England notified to the Senior Creditor.

26.2   Non-exclusivity Nothing in this Clause limits the right of the Senior Creditor to bring proceedings against another party hereto in connection with this Agreement.

(a) in any other court of competent jurisdiction; or

(b) concurrently in more than one jurisdiction.

27. Governing law

This Agreement is governed by English law.

IN WITNESS whereof this Agreement has been entered into on the date stated at the head of this Agreement.

SCHEDULE 1

EXISTING JUNIOR SECURITY DOCUMENTS

SCHEDULE 2

EXISTING SENIOR SECURITY DOCUMENTS

[BORROWER]

By: . . . .

[SENIOR CREDITOR]

By: . . . .

[JUNIOR CREDITOR]

By: . . . .

9. Contractual subordination agreement

Note on the form

The subordination agreement is solely between the debtor and the junior creditor. The senior creditor is not a party.

The junior creditor subordinates claims arising under a specific credit agreement to all other liabilities of the debtor.

The subordination on the insolvency of the common debtor is achieved by rendering the junior debt conditional on the payment of the senior debt. This form is not appropriate if the junior debt or the senior debt is secured.

THIS SUBORDINATION AGREEMENT is dated [   ] and made

BETWEEN:

1.   [BORROWER] (the "Borrower");

2.   [JUNIOR CREDITOR] (the "Junior Creditor").

1.   Interpretation

1.1   Definitions In this Agreement:

"**Junior Credit Agreement**" means the credit agreement dated [   ] between the Borrower and the Junior Creditor for a credit of $[   ] and includes all variations, replacements, novations of and supplements to the credit agreement but without prejudice to any restrictions on the same.

"**Junior Debt**" means all present and future liabilities of the Borrower under or in connection with (or on rescission of) the Junior Credit Agreement.

"**Permitted Payments**" means the payments permitted by Clause 4 so long as the same are so permitted.

"**Senior Creditor**" means each holder of any Senior Debt.

"**Senior Debt**" means all present and future liabilities payable or owing by the Borrower (whether actual or contingent, jointly or severally or otherwise howsoever), other than subordinated liabilities.

1.2 Headings Headings are to be ignored in construing this Agreement.

2. Borrower's undertakings

So long as any Senior Debt is outstanding, the Borrower will not:

(a) pay or repay, or make any distribution in respect of, or purchase or acquire, any of the Junior Debt in cash or kind except for Permitted Payments;

(b) permit any of its Subsidiaries to purchase or acquire any of the Junior Debt;

(c) set off against the Junior Debt except for Permitted Payments;

(d) create or permit or subsist security over any of its assets for any of the Junior Debt;

(e) vary the Junior Credit Agreement.

3. Junior creditor's undertakings

So long as any Senior Debt is outstanding, the Junior Creditor will not:

(a) demand or receive payment of, or any distribution in respect or on account of, any of the Junior Debt in cash or kind, or apply any money or assets in discharge of any Junior Debt, except for Permitted Payments;

(b) set off any of the Junior Debt except for Permitted Payments.

4. Permitted payments

Subject to Clause 6, whether by actual payment or by set-off, the Borrower may pay and the Junior Creditor may receive and retain payment of (i) scheduled payments of principal and interest on the Junior Debt not earlier than the scheduled due dates in accordance with the original terms of the Junior Credit Agreement (for which purpose a mandatory or voluntary acceleration or prepayment is not a scheduled payment); (ii)[specify other permitted payments].

Notwithstanding the above:

(a) The Borrower may not make any payments otherwise permitted by this Clause if and so long as any of the Senior Debt is overdue and unpaid;

(b) The Borrower may not make any payments of principal otherwise permitted by this Clause unless the auditors of the Borrower have reported to the Borrower not less than 14 days before the payment that the Borrower would be solvent both at the time of and immediately after the payment. For this purpose the Borrower shall be considered to be solvent if it is able to pay all Senior Debt as it falls due and if the value of its assets is more than the amount of its liabilities, taking into account its contingent and prospective liabilities.

5. Subordination on insolvency

If an order has been made or effective resolution has been passed for the liquidation, winding up, bankruptcy, administration, rehabilitation, reorganisation or dissolution of the Borrower or any analogous event has occurred, the rights of the Junior Creditor in respect of the Junior Debt will be subordinated to the Senior Debt. Accordingly any payment in respect of the Junior Debt is conditional upon the Borrower being solvent both at the time of and immediately after the payment and shall not be made unless this condition is satisfied. For this purpose, the Borrower shall be considered to be solvent only if the Borrower is able to pay all the Senior Debt in full.

[**Note:** The Agreement may state that "No remedy against the Borrower, other than the institution of proceedings for the winding up of the Borrower, shall be available to the Junior Creditor for recovery of any of the Junior Debt".]

6. Return of non-permitted recoveries

6.1 Non-permitted payment If:

(a) the Junior Creditor receives a payment or distribution in cash, in property, securities or otherwise of in respect of or on account of any of the Junior Debt (other than a Permitted Payment); or

(b) the Junior Creditor receives the proceeds of any enforcement of any security for any Junior Debt; or

(c) the Borrower or any of its subsidiaries makes any payment or distribution, in cash or kind, on account of the purchase or other acquisition of any of the Junior Debt;

the Junior Creditor will hold the same upon trust and immediately return the same to the Borrower or its estate. Thereupon the relevant payment or distribution or receipt will be deemed not to have been made or received.

6.2 Non-permitted set-offs If any of the Junior Debt is discharged by set-off (except for a Permitted Payment), the Junior Creditor will immediately

pay an amount equal to the discharge to the Borrower or its estate. Thereupon the discharge will be deemed not to have taken place.

7. Reliance by senior creditors

The Borrower and the Junior Creditor declare in favour of each Senior Creditor that the terms of this Agreement are an inducement and consideration to each Senior Creditor to give or continue credit to the Borrower or to acquire Senior Debt. Each Senior Creditor may accept the benefit of this Agreement by giving or continuing credit to the Borrower or acquiring Senior Debt. Each of the Borrower and the Junior Creditor waives reliance and notice of acceptance. For the purpose of such inducement, each of the Borrower and the Junior Creditor agrees not to vary the terms of this Agreement nor to take or omit any action whereby the subordination achieved by this Agreement may be impaired.

[**Note:** This clause attempts to create an estoppel in favour of Senior Creditors who rely on the Agreement. Another method would be for the Borrower and the Junior Creditor each to declare a trust in favour of the Senior Creditor of the benefit of the undertaking given to it by the other.]

8. Junior credit agreement

This Agreement overrides anything in the Junior Credit Agreement to the contrary.

9. Successors and assigns

9.1 Successors and assigns This Agreement is binding on the successors and assigns of the parties hereto.

9.2 Junior Creditor So long as any Senior Debt is outstanding, the Junior Creditor will not:

(a) assign or dispose of, or create or permit to subsist any security (fixed or floating) over, any of the Junior Debt or its proceeds or any interest in the Junior Debt or its proceeds to or in favour of any person; or

(b) transfer by novation or otherwise any of its rights or obligations in respect of any Junior Debt to any person unless in each case that person agrees with the Borrower that he is bound by all the terms of this Agreement as a Junior Creditor.

10. Perpetuity period

The perpetuity period for the trusts in this Agreement is 80 years.

11. Jurisdiction

11.1 Submission Each of the Borrower and the Junior Creditor agrees that the courts of England are to have jurisdiction to settle any disputes in connection with this Agreement, submits to the jurisdiction of the English courts in connection with this Agreement, appoints [   ] as its agent for service of process relating to any proceedings before the English courts in connection with this Agreement and agrees to maintain a process agent in England notified to the other.

11.2 Non-exclusivity Nothing in this Clause limits the right of either party to bring proceedings against the other party in connection with this Agreement:

(a) in any other court of competent jurisdiction; or

(b) concurrently in more than one jurisdiction.

12. Governing law

This Agreement is governed by English law.

This Agreement has been entered into on the date stated at the head of this Agreement.

[BORROWER]

By: . . . .

[JUNIOR CREDITOR]

By: . . . .

APPENDIX: PART III

STATE LOANS

10. Special definitions for state loan agreements

Note: These definitions are used in subsequent forms in this section on state loans.

"Borrowings" means:

(a) moneys borrowed or raised and interest thereon;

(b) any liability under any debenture, note or other security or under acceptance credit facility;

(c) any liability in respect of the acquisition cost of assets or services to the extent payable after the time of acquisition or possession thereof by the party liable; and

(d) any guarantee or other assurance against financial loss in respect of such moneys borrowed or raised, interest or liability.

"Security Interest" means any mortgage, pledge, lien, charge, assignment, hypothecation, or other security interest.

"External Indebtedness" means any obligation contingent or otherwise (i) which is, or is capable at the option of any party thereto of being, payable in or calculated by reference to, any currency other than the currency for the time being of the Republic or (ii) which is owed to a non-resident of the Republic.

"Public Entity" means:

(a) any agency, department or instrumentality of the Republic;

(b) the central bank of the Republic and any entity holding all or a substantial part of the foreign reserves or investments of the Republic;

(c) any province, state or other political subdivision of the Republic other than municipalities; and

(d) any public corporation and any entity directly or indirectly controlled by the Republic.

11. Representations and warranties in state loan agreement

Note: For definitions, see form 10 in this Appendix.

1. The Borrower represents and warrants to each of the Agent, the Managers and the Banks that:

    (a) **Powers and authority** The Borrower has the power to enter into and perform this Agreement and the transactions contemplated hereby and has taken all necessary action to authorise the entry into and performance of this Agreement and the transactions contemplated hereby.

    (b) **Legal validity** This Agreement constitutes a legal, valid and binding obligation of the Borrower enforceable in accordance with its terms and would be so treated in the courts of England and of the Borrower's jurisdiction; this Agreement is in proper form for its enforcement in all such courts.

    (c) **Non-conflict with laws** The entry into and performance of this Agreement and the transactions contemplated hereby do not and will not conflict with (i) any law or regulation or any official or judicial order, or (ii) the constitution of the Republic or (iii) any agreement or document to which the Borrower or any Public Entity is a party or which is binding upon any of them or any of their respective assets, nor result in the creation or imposition of any Security Interest on any of their respective assets pursuant to the provisions of any such agreement or document.

    (d) **No default** No event has occurred which constitutes a default under or in respect of any agreement or document to which the Borrower or any Public Entity is a party or by which the Borrower or any Public Entity may be bound and no event has occurred which, with the giving of notice, lapse of time, determination of materiality or other condition might constitute a default under or in respect of any such agreement or document.

    (e) **Consents** All authorisations, approvals, consents, licences, exemptions, filings, registrations, notarisations and other matters, official or otherwise, required or advisable in connection with the entry into, performance, validity and enforceability of this Agreement and the transactions contemplated hereby have been obtained or effected and are in full force and effect.

    (f) **Litigation** No litigation, arbitration or administrative proceedings are current or pending or, to the knowledge of the Borrower, threatened which may call into question the validity or performance of the Borrower's obligations hereunder.

(g) **Information Memorandum** The information contained in the Information Memorandum was true in all material respects as at its date and did not at that date omit anything material; no adverse change has occurred since such date which renders such information materially misleading.

(h) **Pari passu ranking** The obligations of the Borrower hereunder rank at least pari passu with all its other unsecured obligations.

(i) **No immunity**

    (i) The Borrower is subject to civil and commercial law with respect to its obligations under this Agreement;

    (ii) the entry into and performance of this Agreement by the Borrower constitute private and commercial acts;

    (iii) neither the Borrower nor any of its assets enjoys any right of immunity from set-off, suit or execution in respect of its obligations under this Agreement.

(j) **Taxes on payments** All amounts payable by the Borrower under this Agreement may be made free and clear of and without deduction for or on account of any taxes imposed by, or in the territory of, the Republic.

(k) **Stamp duties** No stamp or registration duty or similar taxes or charges are payable in the Republic in respect of this Agreement.

2. The representations and warranties set out in the foregoing Clause (other than those in (d), (f) and (g)) shall be deemed to be repeated on each date so long as any amount is or may be outstanding hereunder or any Commitment is in force, with reference to the facts and circumstances then subsisting, as if made at each such time.

12. Covenants in state loan agreement

Note: For definitions, see form 10 in this Appendix.

1. **Duration**

   The undertakings, in this Clause shall remain in force from and after the date hereof and so long as any amount is or may be outstanding hereunder or any Commitment is in force.

2. **Information**

   The Borrower will promptly furnish to the Agent, in sufficient copies for each of the Banks, such information regarding the financial and economic condition of the Borrower or any Public Entity, as the Agent or any Bank may request;

3. **Notification of defaults**

   The Borrower will notify the Agent in writing of any Event of Default (or event which with giving of notice, lapse of time, determination of materiality or other condition may constitute such an Event of Default) forthwith upon the occurrence thereof.

4. **Compliance certificates**

   The Borrower will within 30 days of the end of each calendar year and also promptly at the request of the Agent or any Bank from time to time furnish the Agent with a certificate signed by two appropriate officials of the Borrower certifying that no Event of Default (or any event which with lapse of time, notice, determination of materiality or other condition may constitute such an Event of Default) has occurred and is continuing or, if the same has occurred, specifying the Event of Default or event and the steps being taken to remedy the same.

5. **Consents**

   The Borrower will obtain and promptly renew from time to time, and will promptly furnish certified copies to the Agent of, all such authorisations, approvals, consents, licences and exemptions as may be required under any applicable law or regulation to enable it to perform its obligations under this Agreement or required for the validity or enforceability of this Agreement and the Borrower shall comply with the terms of the same.

6. **Pari passu ranking**

   The Borrower undertakes that its obligations hereunder do and will rank at least pari passu with all other present and future unsecured External Indebtedness of the Borrower.

7. Negative pledge

The Borrower will not, and will procure that no Public Entity will, create or permit to subsist any Security Interest on the whole or any part of the respective present or future assets of the Borrower or any such Public Entity for any External Indebtedness except for the following:

(a) Security Interests created with the prior written consent of the Majority Banks;

(b) liens arising by operation of law and securing obligations not more than 30 days overdue;

(c) any Security Interest on any asset but only if simultaneously with the creation of such Security Interest the obligations of the Borrower hereunder are equally and rateably secured by a comparable Security Interest on other assets acceptable to the Agent and the Majority Banks, all in form and substance satisfactory to the Agent and the Majority Banks.

If the Borrower creates or permits to subsist any Security Interest contrary to the above, all the obligations of the Borrower hereunder shall automatically and immediately be secured upon the same assets equally and rateably with the other obligations secured thereon.

8. Transactions similar to security

Except with the prior written consent of the Majority Banks, the Borrower will not, and will procure that no Public Entity will, sell, lease or otherwise dispose of any of its assets on terms whereby such asset is or may be leased to or re-acquired or acquired by the Borrower or any Public Entity or enter into any financial lease as lessee, if such transaction is in commercial substance a raising of finance or grant of security.

13.   Events of default in state loan agreement

Note: For definitions, see form 10 in this Appendix.

1.   **Events of default**

Each of the events set out below is an Event of Default (whether or not caused by any reason whatsoever outside the control of the Borrower or of any other person):

(a) the Borrower does not pay on the due date any amount payable by it under this Agreement at the place and in the currency expressed to be payable; or

(b) the Borrower does not comply with any other provision of this Agreement; or

(c) any representation, warranty or statement made or repeated in, or in connection with, this Agreement or in any certificate, statement or opinion or in the Information Memorandum delivered by or on behalf of the Borrower under this Agreement or in connection with this Agreement is incorrect when made or deemed to be repeated; or

(d) (i) any other External Indebtedness for a Borrowing of the Borrower or any Public Entity becomes prematurely due and payable as a result of a default thereunder, or

(ii) any event of default (or event which with giving of notice, lapse of time, determination of materiality or other condition may constitute such an event of default) occurs under any contract or document relating to any such External Indebtedness, or

(iii) any such External Indebtedness or any sum payable in respect thereof is not paid when due, or

(iv) any Security Interest over any assets of the Borrower or any Public Entity to secure any External Indebtedness becomes enforceable, or

(v) the Borrower or any Public Entity proposes any rescheduling, reorganisation or conversion of all or part of its External Indebtedness by reason of financial or economic difficulties or enters into any such rescheduling, reorganisation or conversion or declares a moratorium on any of its External Indebtedness; or

(e) [any order is made or resolution passed or other action taken for the suspension of payments or dissolution, termination of existence, liquidation, winding-up or bankruptcy of any Public Entity; or]

(f) [a moratorium in respect of all or any debts of any Public Entity, or a composition or an arrangement with creditors of any Public Entity or any similar proceeding or arrangement by which the assets of any Public Entity are submitted to the control of its creditors is applied for, ordered or declared; or]

(g) [a liquidator, trustee, administrator, receiver, manager or similar officer is appointed in respect of any Public Entity or in respect of all or any part of its assets; or]

(h) [any Public Entity becomes or is declared insolvent or is unable, or admits in writing its inability to, pay its debts as they fall due or becomes insolvent within the terms of any applicable law; or]

(i) any distress, execution, attachment or other process affects any asset of the Borrower or any Public Entity; or

(j) anything analogous to or having a substantially similar effect to any of the events specified in paragraphs [(e) to (i)] above occurs under the laws of any applicable jurisdiction; or

(k) any authorisation, approval, consent, licence, exemption, filing, registration or notarisation or other requirement necessary to enable the Borrower to comply with any of its obligations hereunder is modified, revoked or withheld or does not remain in full force and effect; or

(l) at any time it is unlawful for the Borrower to perform any of its obligations under this Agreement; or

(m) the Borrower ceases to be a member in good standing of the International Monetary Fund or fully eligible to use the resources thereof in accordance with the Articles of Agreement of the International Monetary Fund; or

(n) any circumstances occur which in the opinion of the Majority Banks may affect the ability or willingness of the Borrower to comply with all or any of its obligations under this Agreement.

2. Acceleration

If any event in Clause 1 occurs and is continuing, the Agent may, and shall if so directed by the Majority Banks, by written notice to the Borrower:

(a) declare that the obligations of the Agent and the Banks under this Agreement shall be cancelled forthwith whereupon the same shall be so cancelled forthwith; and/or

(b) declare all the Loans immediately due and payable whereupon the same shall become immediately due and payable together with all interest accrued thereon and all other amounts payable under this Agreement.

14. Waiver of immunity in state loan agreement

Note: For waivers of immunity, see para 13–37 *et seq.*

The Borrower irrevocably and unconditionally waives all immunity, in respect of itself or its assets, from legal proceedings in relation to this Agreement, including, without limitation, immunity from suit, judgment or other order, from attachment, arrest or injunction prior to judgment, and from execution and enforcement against its assets.

SELECT BIBLIOGRAPHY

Articles from the journals are not listed. The main English journals on international finance include *International Financial Law Review* (Euromoney), *Journal of International Banking Law* (ESC Publishing Ltd/Sweet & Maxwell), and *Butterworths Journal of International Banking and Financial Law*. Bibliographies referring to the article literature may be found in many of the works on the domestic law of a jurisdiction and this list is obviously not intended to be a comprehensive bibliography.

1. Project finance

Peter K Nevitt	*Project Financing* (5th ed) Euromoney
Graham D Vinter	*Project Finance: A Legal Guide* (1995) Sweet & Maxwell

2. Subordination

Philip Wood	*The Law of Subordinated Debt* (1990) Sweet & Maxwell. This work contains a bibliography.

3. State loans

Kalderen, Siddiqui, Chronnell, Watson (eds)	*Sovereign Borrowers: Guidelines on Legal Negotiations with Commercial Lenders* (1984) Butterworths
Padazis Karamanolis	*The Legal Implications of Sovereign Syndicated Lending* (1992) Oceana

The standard works on public international law contain treatments of sovereign immunity, state succession, state recognition and international organisations see especially Ian Brownlie, *Principles of International Law* (4th ed 1990) Oxford. See also Charles Lewis, *State and Diplomatic Immunity* (3rd ed 1990) Lloyds of London Press; Schreuer, *State Immunity: Some Recent Developments* (1988).

For state insolvency, see Borchard & Wynne, *State Insolvency & Foreign Bondholders* 2 Vols, Yale 1951; Feis, *Europe: The World's Banker* (1870–1914) Yale 1930, reprinted AM Kelley, Clifton, 1974. The article literature on state insolvency is immense.

LIST OF RESEARCH TOPICS

This list contains topics which could be considered for a research thesis or a shorter article. The topics relate to the areas covered by this book. Research topics in relation to the areas covered by other books in this series on international financial law will be found in the volume concerned.

The selection is based on relative originality and usefulness. Topics which have already been extensively covered by the legal literature are not included. In many cases there is an existing literature on the listed topics, but further work is considered worthwhile to develop what has already been achieved or to explore a new approach. If the chosen titles do not appeal, it is hoped that they will be suggestive of those which do. Some of the titles are no more than pointers which would have to be developed into a proper topic.

The author would be very glad to receive a copy of any essays which may be written and which are derived from this list. See the address after the Preface.

Project finance

- History of the law of project finance from Roman times
- Host government agreements in project finance
- History of the insolvency of single-project companies
- Restructuring of defaulted projects: comparative law aspects
- Project contracts: construction, supply, off-take and operating agreements
- Models for contract "due diligence" in project finance
- Political risk and project finance
- Special projects
    - energy (oil and gas)
    - electricity power station
    - telecommunications
    - transportation (rail, roads, etc.)
    - mines

- industrial plant
- Project insurance
- Project joint venture agreements
- Project host government concessions and BOT projects
- Project take-or-pay contracts
- Forecasting in project finance documentation and financial modelling
- Intercreditor agreements in project finance
- The role of security in project finance

Subordinated debt

- Subordinated debt on insolvency
- Director responsibilities in relation to subordinated debt
- Shares compared to subordinated debt: international survey
- Subordinated bond issues
- Subordinated debt and insolvency set-off: comparative survey

State loans

- History of state insolvency
- State insolvency: 1979–1995
- Comparison of corporate and state insolvency law and practice
- Bankruptcy of state corporations
- Bankruptcy of international organisations
- State succession and financial contracts
- World survey of state immunity in respect of financial contracts
- History of the documentation of state loans
- International loans to municipalities
- History of sovereign secured loans

INDEX

All references are to paragraph number